D1296845

SEQUEL

A HANDBOOK *for*

the CRITICAL ANALYSIS

of LITERATURE

Preview Copy

www.thpeekpublisher.com

Not for Resale or Reproduction.

SEQUEL

A HANDBOOK *for*

the CRITICAL ANALYSIS

of LITERATURE

Fifth Edition

ELIZABETH SCHMUHL
& RICHARD C. GUCHES

T. H. PEEK, PUBLISHER

T. H. PEEK, PUBLISHER
P. O. Box 7406
Ann Arbor, MI 48107

www.thpeekpublisher.com

Executive Editor: Jill Peek
Contributing Editor: Meredith Mayberry
Book Design: Steven Seighman
Publishing Consultant: Colin O'Brien

SEQUEL: A HANDBOOK FOR THE CRITICAL ANALYSIS OF LITERATURE
Copyright © 2012 Elizabeth Schmuhl and Richard C. Guches

All rights reserved. No part of this publication may be reproduced or transmitted in any form or by any means, electronic or mechanical, including photocopy, recording, or any information and storage retrieval system, without written permission from the publisher.

ISBN 978-1-935770-01-5

17   16   15   14   13   12

Back Cover: Holbein, Hans the Younger (1497–1543). Jean de Dinteville and Georges de Selve ('The Ambassadors'), 1533. Dinteville, a French nobleman posted to London as ambassador (l.) together with his bishop friend de Selve (r.), exemplifying, respectively, the active and contemplative life. Oil on oak, 207 x 209.5 cm. Bought, 1890 (NG1314). National Gallery, London Great Britain
© National Gallery, London / Art Resource, NY

SUSTAINABLE FORESTRY INITIATIVE
Label applies to the text stock
Certified Sourcing
www.sfiprogram.org
SFI-00341

Manufactured in the United States of America

Contents

PREFACE TO THE 5TH EDITION

Like a painting, this edition of *Sequel: A Handbook for the Critical Analysis of Literature*, was not created in a single sitting, but through many different versions and revisions. I was fortunate to have a wonderful editor, Jill Peek, who brought her incisive and constructive criticism of my revisions to the text; her commitment, patience, and willingness to try new things are refreshing and make *Sequel* invaluable. Likewise, I am indebted to contributing editor Meredith Mayberry, whose keen eye made this text a truly comprehensive guidebook to analysis.

One of the challenges of the book was adding to the existing text. Richard Guches, the sole author of the previous editions, had a very distinctive approach to analysis; my job was to add to the existing text in order to bring *Sequel* into the present day. I feel that this edition honors Dr. Guches's original text while creating a new, user-friendly handbook that will aid students as they begin to look at texts critically.

This edition of *Sequel* will help students hone their analytical skills before going outside of the book to analyze different texts. It is my hope that this book encourages students to become worldly thinkers and to take what they learn from analyzing literature and apply it to their daily lives.

"Art is not what you see, but what you make others see."
—*Edgar Degas*

Elizabeth Schmuhl, May 2012

INTRODUCTION

The critical analysis of literature is about more than writing essays to earn grades. What you learn from *Sequel* will help you to better appreciate what you read, better understand the world around you, and, as a result, enjoy both all the more. The goal of *Sequel* is to introduce you to the building blocks of literature and the different methods readers use to figure out what authors are trying to convey. *Sequel* provides a wide variety of texts and analytical techniques, giving you the skills necessary to begin your own studies of literature.

Part One: Poetry, Fiction, and Drama

Poetry employs far fewer words than fiction or drama, but offers an immediate emotional impact. Its conciseness is achieved, in part, through literary techniques such as imagery, connotation, metaphor, simile, tone, and allusion. Knowledge of these devices is essential not only in gaining an understanding of poetry, but of fiction and drama as well.

Both short stories and novels are built around plots consisting of exposition, complication, climax, and resolution, while characters, settings, and points of view share equal roles of importance. *Sequel* focuses on the short story as a compact representation of fiction. The skills learned from studying short stories are easily applied to analyzing the larger context of a novel.

Drama is often a melding of poetry and fiction. By familiarizing yourself with different types of drama, such as classical tragedy, dramatic poetry, and the modern play, you will be better able to see how a playwright creates a work that can engage a single reader as well as an audience. As with poetry and fiction, to reach a fuller understanding of drama a reader must be aware of a text's literary devices and techniques; in drama, these are found in dialogue and stage direction.

Part Two: Literary Analysis

Whether you're presented with a poem, a short story, or a dramatic work, there is no single, perfect way to interpret a work of literature. Viewing a piece from a different perspective can change not only what you're able to observe, but also how you analyze what you have perceived.

"The Ambassadors" (see back cover), painted by Hans Holbein the Younger in 1533, illustrates the possibility for multiple interpretations under different perspectives. As you can see, in the bottom center of the composition, there is an elongated shape stretched across the canvas; when viewed straight on, a nondescript shape is all it appears to be. However, by approaching and viewing the painting from the side, the elongated shape becomes an accurate portrayal of a human skull. By changing perspectives, the viewer sees and interprets this painting in new and different ways.

Approaching literature from various perspectives similarly allows readers to see different meanings in a work. *Sequel* presents a variety of analytical lenses through which literature may be viewed; some focus on historical and societal influences, which are paramount in contextual and feminist analysis, while others focus on scientific movements, as in psychological analysis. The perspective of archetypal analysis, the collective unconscious as it is reflected in a literary work, is yet another method of analysis. Formalism looks at a text as a stand-alone work of art, with no external considerations. Each approach is different, and each will lead to a different culminating analysis.

The analytical perspectives presented in this text are established and important literary theories in their own right, as well as springboards for other related theories that include considerations such as linguistics, socio-historical perspectives, and gender analyses. Understanding the different perspectives from which you can view literature will allow you to better enjoy and appreciate all that literature has to offer.

Part Three: Writing a Literary Analysis

One of the richest ways to explore any type of literary work is through a written analysis. Writing an analysis helps you to understand a poem, short story, or dramatic work in a comprehensive and perhaps new way. Writing an analysis begins with critical reading and thinking—skills necessary for both academic and professional development. Through this critical reading you are apt to discover literary devices and techniques, which help reveal an author's intended meaning. By analyzing how these devices work in the piece, you can begin theorizing, outlining, and ultimately writing your literary analysis.

Your analysis, with its commentary on a work's meaning and implications, becomes part of a larger discourse of thoughts and ideas about a work postulated by many people over time. To write an analysis is to contribute to this conversation and to enrich your intellectual pursuits.

PART ONE

Literary Genres: Poetry, Fiction, and Drama

UNIT ONE

Analyzing Poetry

The Greek poet Simonides said, "Painting is silent poetry, and poetry is painting that speaks." Poetry is often compared to painting because both art forms rely on imagery to create an emotional effect. Just as painters use different methods to create a visual image, poets use the literary techniques of rhythm, rhyme, appearance, and the meaning of words in their works. Studying these literary techniques reveals important things about a poem's meaning and helps to foster an enjoyment and appreciation of the art form.

A close study of poetry is also an excellent starting point in learning to analyze other literature, for literary techniques are easily illustrated and quickly understood in short poetic selections; literary devices that would need long passages of prose to demonstrate may be illustrated with but a few lines in poetry. Observation and identification of these will lead you to an understanding of poetry as an art form, as well as provide a foundation for reading fiction and drama.

Objectives:

AFTER COMPLETING THIS UNIT, YOU WILL BE ABLE TO:

1. Find meaning in poetry;

2. Identify forms of poetry;

3. Understand the use of imagery;

4. Understand a poem's tone and how it's created;

5. Explain the difference between denotation and connotation;

6. Assess the contribution of figurative language;

7. Find allusions and identify referents.

Lesson One: **Finding Meaning**

Poetry differs from both prose and drama in its arrangement of words and its expression of experiences, ideas, and emotions. Historically, poetry is defined as a rhythmical composition, occasionally rhymed, presented in a style that is often highly concentrated, very imaginative, and considered more powerful than ordinary prose. It is traditionally believed that poetry was intended to be heard, either orally or in the "mind's ear." However, the arrangement of words on the page increases poetry's meaning by providing visual aids. Poet E. E. Cummings has such a distinctive visual style that his work is instantly recognizable. For example:

```
the sky
the
     sky
          was
can   dy  lu
minous
          edible
spry
       pinks shy
lemons
greens    coo    l choc
olate
s.
un   der,
a    lo
co
mo
     tive      s   pout
                     ing
                   vi
                   o
                   lets
```

—*e.e. cummings (1894–1962)*

Here, E. E. Cummings's poem illustrates how lines, whether interrupted mid-sentence or mid-word, can control a poem's **cadence**, the rhythmic sound of its language. We are forced to read the poem and see it in the way Cummings intended for the simple reason that our eyes must follow the sporadic rhythm of his work.

Beyond the obviousness of visual style, there exists a more subtle intention in poetry. Poetry, like prose and drama, involves a sensory, and often emotional, experience. Poetry differs from prose in that it concentrates the experience and enhances the effect of writing on our senses. With very few words, the compressed feeling is imparted from the poem to the reader.

To understand this concept, you must become aware of the experiential idea underlying any poem that you wish to analyze. Most poems have an event or idea from which the poet derives inspiration. Often, this inspiration comes from life experiences. These may be as universal as birth, love, or death, but they need not be so profound. As you've seen in E. E. Cummings's playful work, watching the sky is sometimes all the inspiration a poet needs.

Looking at a specific poem should help you begin to see how poetic visions may be derived from different sources of inspiration. Li-Young Lee is a Chinese American poet who often reflects upon his upbringing and heritage as inspiration for his writing. His poem "The Gift," recalls an early childhood experience: his father removing a splinter from his finger. In this poem, Lee not only shares his feelings about what the experience was like for him, but further reflects on the relationship between father and son, or more broadly, on giving and receiving.

The Gift

To pull the metal splinter from my palm
my father recited a story in a low voice.
I watched his lovely face and not the blade.
Before the story ended, he'd removed
the iron sliver I thought I'd die from.

I can't remember the tale,
but hear his voice still, a well
of dark water, a prayer.
And I recall his hands,
two measures of tenderness
he laid against my face,
the flames of discipline
he raised above my head.

Had you entered that afternoon
you would have thought you saw a man
planting something in a boy's palm,
a silver tear, a tiny flame.
Had you followed that boy
you would have arrived here,
where I bend over my wife's right hand.

Look how I shave her thumbnail down
so carefully she feels no pain.
Watch as I lift the splinter out.
I was seven when my father
took my hand like this,
and I did not hold that shard
between my fingers and think,
Metal that will bury me,
christen it Little Assassin,
Ore Going Deep for My Heart.
And I did not lift up my wound and cry,
Death visited here!
I did what a child does
when he's given something to keep.
I kissed my father.

—*Li-Young Lee (b. 1957)*

The depth of Lee's feelings—the emotional connection he draws from his father to himself—comes through in his words, yet the poem itself is not long. In prose, the author would have written much more, perhaps dialogue and more descriptive passages, to convey the same ideas. You can see, then, the compression that has taken place by using the poetic style. The importance of compression cannot be taken lightly. In fact, it illustrates one of the main characteristics and most important virtues of poetry: The fewer words used, the more precise the word choice must be. It is this exactness that allows poetry to effect an emotional response so quickly, whereas prose may take pages or chapters to elicit the same response.

Exercise 1.1   Write a one-paragraph summary of each of the following poems, noting its narrative plot—the sequence of its actions—along with the images you perceive. What is the poem's overarching effect?

ON FLUNKING A NICE BOY OUT OF SCHOOL

I wish I could teach you how ugly
decency and humility can be when they are not
the election of a contained mind but only
the defenses of an incompetent. Were you taught
meekness as a weapon? Or did you discover,
by chance maybe, that it worked on mother
and was generally a good thing—
at least when all else failed—to get you over
the worst of what was coming. Is that why you bring
these sheepfaces to Tuesday?

They won't do.
It's three months work I want, and I'd sooner have it
from the brassiest lumpkin in pimpledom, but have it,
than all these martyred repentances from you.

—*John Ciardi (1916–1986)*

The Chimney Sweeper

When my mother died I was very young,
And my father sold me while yet my tongue
Could scarcely cry "'weep! 'weep! 'weep! 'weep!"
So your chimneys I sweep and in soot I sleep.

There's little Tom Dacre, who cried when his head,
That curl'd like a lamb's back, was shaved; so I said,
"Hush, Tom! never mind it, for, when your head's bare,
You know that the soot cannot spoil your white hair."

And so he was quiet, and that very night,
As Tom was a-sleeping, he had such a sight!
That thousands of sweepers, Dick, Joe, Ned, and Jack,
Were all of them locked up in coffins of black.

And by came an Angel who had a bright key,
and he opened the coffins and set them all free;
Then down a green plain leaping, laughing, they run,
And wash in a river, and shine in the sun.

Then naked and white, all their bags left behind,
They rise upon clouds and sport in the wind;
And the Angel told Tom, if he'd been a good boy,
He'd have God for his father, and never want joy.

And so Tom awoke; and we rose in the dark,
And got with our bags and our brushes to work.
Though the morning was cold, Tom was happy and warm;
So if all do their duty they need not fear harm.

—*William Blake (1757–1827)*

Lesson Two: **Poetic Forms**

All poetry forms have particular standards by which they are judged. Before you can analyze any work, you first need to carefully determine into which category it might best be placed. Poetry has a plethora of forms: *epic, ballad, sonnet, free verse,* and *haiku* are but a few. Sometimes distinctions are difficult to make; some forms can be quite similar, however, there are always differences to be found. It's important to accurately establish a selection's form in order to know the standards by which it is to be analyzed—what makes a good ballad is not what makes a good sonnet.

Poetic Elements

Each poetry form has its adherents and each attempts to communicate according to a particular, predetermined structure, or lack thereof. Rhyme, meter, and arrangement of lines are all elements which vary from one poetic form to another.

Rhyme is simply a common vowel sound occurring at the end of a line of poetry, for instance "day" and "May." However, a specific arrangement of rhyming lines often indicates a poem's form, such as in a sonnet. **Meter**, the pattern of stressed and unstressed syllables, is the basis of rhythm in poetry; it's this beat that lends musicality to both reading and speaking poetry.

Poems, especially those with repeating rhyme and meter patterns, are most often arranged into divisions, or stanzas. The number of lines in a stanza, and even syllable count per line, is of great importance in some forms and not at all important in others.

Both the addition and elimination of punctuation in a poem aid the reader in understanding the poem's meaning. Often, the punctuation acts as an important cue to the reader as to how a line, stanza, or entire poem should be read. Two common examples are the comma, which is used for a brief pause, and the period, which suggests a longer silence. This is often what creates the rhythm of the poem. Some poets use no punctuation, which forces the reader find the natural pauses, silences, and rhythm in the poem. Either way, the use or elimination or punctuation allows the poem to be read as the poet intended.

Epic Poems

The oldest and one of the most easily identifiable forms of poetry is the epic poem. **Epic poems** are narrative in style—they tell a story—and are long in length. They are a notable exception to the compressed language that is associated with poetry. In the epic poem, the poet's narrative often covers a long period of time, which calls for a lengthier text. For example, "The Iliad," a poem that tells of the Trojan War, is hundreds of pages long when printed. Another characteristic that epic poems share is their importance to a culture or society. Epic poems often include heroic characters who interact with divine forces; many of these interactions reflect something important about the beliefs and culture of a society.

Though not a form used frequently by today's poets, the epic poem has been created and enjoyed for centuries. Originally, as is the case with many poetic forms, epic poems were not written and read, but memorized and recited. In ancient Greece, the epic poem "The Odyssey" was performed by traveling bards, or oral poets, in amphitheaters; crowds would listen and watch the performer in much the same way people now frequent the movies. Because of its universal themes, such as homecoming and temptation, "The Odyssey" continues to influence literary and other artistic endeavors.

Popular Epic Poems:

> Epic of Gilgamesh (Mesopotamia, 2500 BCE)
> The Iliad and The Odyssey (Greek, 800 BCE)
> Aeneid (Roman, 29–19 BCE)
> Beowulf (Old English, 800 AD)

The Ballad

Lyrical, or song-like, in nature, the **ballad** is a poem whose written verses are sung or have been or set to music and performed for audiences. The ballad has Germanic roots, but was popular in England and Scotland from the late Middle Ages to the early nineteenth century. Robin Hood was a popular subject of fifteenth-century English ballads; his continued presence in literary and popular culture is owed to these ballads. Many ballads are of anonymous origin, as they developed as they were sung by many people. While modern ballad singers are typically accompanied by a musical instrument, the ballad was traditionally sung unaccompanied.

The ballad form consists of four-line stanzas, or **quatrains**. Most often, the second and fourth lines rhyme, though some ballads differ in structure. The rhyme and meter add to the ballad's lyric quality and musical application. Ballads most often tell a story; however, the narrative of a ballad is much more concise than that of the epic poem.

Sir Walter Scott (1771–1832), a Scottish historian, was responsible for the preservation of many ballads. In the late eighteenth century, he published a volume of German ballads entitled "Translations and Imitations from German Ballads" in hopes of preserving the poetry form for future generations. The overall form of the ballad, coupled with music, helped spread the popularity of this poetic form, which still holds a presence in contemporary music.

Popular Ballads:

"The Rime of the Ancient Mariner" Samuel Taylor Coleridge (1772–1834)
"We Are Seven" William Wordsworth (1770–1850)

Exercise 1.2 The following poem has been transcribed by many scholars with variations of title and spelling. It is still performed and recorded to this day. Analyze the selection by emphasizing its form characteristics.

LORD RANDALL

"Oh where have you been, Lord Randall, my son?
Oh where have you been, my handsome young man?"
"Oh, I've been to the wildwood; mother, make my bed soon,
I'm weary of hunting and fain would lie down."

"And whom did you meet there, Lord Randall, my son?
And whom did you meet there, my handsome young man?"
"Oh, I met with my true-love; mother, make my bed soon,
I'm weary of hunting and fain would lie down."

"What got you for supper, Lord Randall, my son?
What got you for supper, my handsome young man?"
"I got eels boiled in broth; mother, make my bed soon,
I'm weary of hunting and fain would lie down."

"And who got your leavings, Lord Randall, my son?
And who got your leavings, my handsome young man?"
I gave them to my dogs; mother, make my bed soon,
I'm weary of hunting and fain would lie down."

"And what did you dogs do, Lord Randall, my son?
And what did you dogs do, my handsome young man?"
"Oh, they stretched out and died; mother make my bed soon,
I'm weary of hunting and fain would lie down."

"Oh, I fear you are poisoned, Lord Randall, my son.
Oh, I fear you are poisoned, my handsome young man."
"Oh, yes, I am poisoned; mother, make my bed soon,
I'm weary of hunting and fain would lie down."

"What will you leave your mother, Lord Randall, my son?
What will you leave your mother, my handsome young man."
"My house and my lands; mother, make my bed soon,
I'm weary of hunting and fain would lie down."

"What will you leave your sister, Lord Randall, my son?
What will you leave your sister, my handsome young man?"
"My gold and my silver; mother, make my bed soon,
I'm weary of hunting and fain would lie down."

"What will you leave your brother, Lord Randall, my son?
What will you leave your brother, my handsome young man?"
"My horse and my saddle; mother, make my bed soon,
I'm weary of hunting and fain would lie down."

"What will you leave your true-love, Lord Randall, my son?
What will you leave your true-love, my handsome young man?"
"A halter to hang her; mother, make my bed soon,
For I'm sick at my heart and I want to lie down."

—*Anonymous*

The Sonnet

The **sonnet** originated in Europe in the thirteenth century and means "little song" in Old French. It is a fourteen-line poem that has had a variety of subjects. Traditionally, it was written in **iambic pentameter**, a meter in which a stressed syllable is followed by an unstressed syllable, repeating five times per line. When spoken, the rhythm of the poem is often compared to a heartbeat, producing a bah-DUM sound in which the second sound, or in the poem's case, syllable, is stressed. When marking a poem's syllables, specific symbols indicate stresses. The first symbol, ˘, notes an unstressed syllable. The second symbol, /, marks a stressed syllable.

˘ / ˘ / ˘ / ˘ / ˘ /
Shall I compare thee to a summer's day?

William Shakespeare wrote 154 sonnets in a particular form that has become known as a **Shakespearean sonnet**. These sonnets consist of fourteen lines and are written in a particular rhyme scheme (a-b-a-b-c-d-c-d-e-f-e-f-g-g). The last two lines of a Shakespearean sonnet are known as a **turn**. The turn signals a shift in emotion relayed by the poem. The last two lines are often an overall comment on the previous twelve lines. All Shakespearean sonnets consist of the same overarching topic: love. In modern times, however, there have been many variations of both structure and topic.

Exercise 1.3 Label the rhyme scheme of the Shakespearean sonnet below. Also, identify the turn: What changes at this point of the poem? Write your response in several sentences.

SONNET 18

Shall I compare thee to a summer's day?
Thou art more lovely and more temperate:
Rough winds do shake the darling buds of May,
And summer's lease hath all too short a date:
Sometime too hot the eye of heaven shines,
And often is his gold complexion dimm'd;
And every fair from fair sometime declines,
By chance or nature's changing course untrimm'd;
But thy eternal summer shall not fade
Nor lose possession of that fair thou owest;
Nor shall Death brag thou wander'st in his shade,
When in eternal lines to time thou growest:
So long as men can breathe or eyes can see,
So long lives this and this gives life to thee.

—*William Shakespeare (1564–1616)*

Modern Poetry

Because poetry is always evolving, the variety of forms in which it is written evolve as well. The opportunities for expression seem unlimited in poetry, due to ever-increasing poetic forms available to the writer. Today, two forms of poetry that populate literary journals and anthologies are **free verse poetry** and **prose poetry**. These forms are useful in illustrating how modern poets express meaning with fewer or no restrictions of rhyme, meter, or line arrangement.

Free Verse Poetry

The free verse poem was popularized by Walt Whitman in the nineteenth century, but it can be traced back to the King James Bible. In **free verse poetry**, elements such as rhyme scheme, syllable count, line number, and line arrangements adhere to no specific rules. The poet, rather, has complete stylistic autonomy to decide the order and use of poetic elements. One example of this is **enjambment**, in which a line of verse runs over into another, causing closely related words to fall on different lines.

In Whitman's "City of Ships," the poet exercises the stylistic autonomy of the free verse form through his seemingly random syllable counts and frequent exclamations points.

CITY OF SHIPS

City of ships!
(O the black ships! O the fierce ships!
O the beautiful, sharp-bow'd steam-ships and sail-ships!)
City of the world! (for all races are here;
All the lands of the earth make contributions here;)
City of the sea! city of hurried and glittering tides!
City whose gleeful tides continually rush or recede, whirling in and out, with
    eddies and foam!
City of wharves and stores! city of tall façades of marble and iron!
Proud and passionate city! mettlesome, mad, extravagant city!
Spring up, O city! not for peace alone, but be indeed yourself, warlike!
Fear not! submit to no models but your own, O city!
Behold me! incarnate me, as I have incarnated you!
I have rejected nothing you offer'd me—whom you adopted, I have adopted;
Good or bad, I never question you—I love all—I do not condemn anything;
I chant and celebrate all that is yours—yet peace no more;
In peace I chanted peace, but now the drum of war is mine;
War, red war, is my song through your streets, O city!

—*Walt Whitman (1819–1892)*

Other writers have taken to free verse, including T. S. Eliot (see page 240), Ezra Pound (see page 126), William Carlos Williams, and Carl Sandburg. Sandburg's poem "Fog" has varied stanzas and line lengths.

FOG

The fog comes
on little cat feet.

It sits looking

over harbor and city
on silent haunches
and then moves on.

—*Carl Sandburg (1878–1967)*

Exercise 1.4 Compare and contrast the following two poems for elements such as line arrangement, rhyme scheme, syllabic count, and subject matter. Identify the form of each. What effect does the form create in each poem?

TWO DAYS

The last walk to Lookout Louise, climbing
through ridges forced up by ice, then the view
across to Canada, Thunder Bay
hazy from north shore fires and a small burn
here, over on Minong Ridge, sizzling
dried lichen, grasses, a few dead spruce.
And back down toward water . . . a bull moose,
not twenty yards from the trail. I shrink
beside him, in the shade and weight of rock.

Next morning, the island shrinks, lost like a dream
in mist, as our ship pulls back toward Houghton
and the other dream, our dailiness,
a reality, I suppose, as hard
as island rock, separated
only by one night, a fitful sleep.

—*Keith Taylor (b. 1952)*

THE MATRIX

Goaded and harassed in the factory
That tears our life up into bits of days
Ticked off upon a clock which never stays,
Shredding our portion of Eternity,
We break away at last, and steal the key
Which hides a world empty of hours; ways
Of space unroll, and Heaven overlays
The leafy, sun-lit earth of Fantasy.
Beyond the ilex shadow glares the sun,
Scorching against the blue flame of the sky.
Brown lily-pads lie heavy and supine
Within a granite basin, under one
The bronze-gold glimmer of a carp; and I
Reach out my hand and pluck a nectarine.

—*Amy Lowell (1874–1925)*

Prose Poetry

Prose is often defined as any genre of writing that is not poetry. **Prose poetry**, however, borrows one thing from prose: its form. Prose poetry is always written in paragraph form. Traditionally, the prose poem is several paragraphs in length, but it can be as few as one. Instead of using such elements as stanzas, enjambment, and line breaks, the prose poem uses paragraphs to create highly distilled passages. As with other poetic forms, this distillation encourages, and sometimes demands, rereading.

Language is often thought of as a living thing because it changes throughout time, and the prose poem is no exception. The prose poem has influenced prose authors by showing them the merit in condensing their work into fewer words. This often turns into **micro fiction**, or flash fiction, which is fiction of extreme brevity.

Exercise 1.5 Identify the elements of the prose poem below. What effect does each element create for the reader?

Salvador, Late or Early

Salvador with eyes the color of caterpillar, Salvador of the crooked hair and crooked teeth, Salvador whose name the teacher cannot remember, is a boy who is no one's friend, runs along somewhere in that vague direction where homes are the color of bad weather, lives behind a raw wood doorway, shakes the sleepy brothers awake, ties their shoes, combs their hair with water, feeds them milk and cornflakes from a tin cup in the dim dark of the morning.

Salvador, late or early, sooner or later arrives with the string of younger brothers ready. Helps his mama, who is busy with the business of the baby. Tugs the arms of Cecilio, Arturito, makes them hurry, because today, like yesterday, Arturito has dropped the cigar box of crayons, has let go the hundred little fingers of red, green, yellow, blue, and nub of black sticks that tumble and spill over and beyond the asphalt puddles until the crossing-guard lady holds back the blur of traffic for Salvador to collect them again.

Salvador inside that wrinkled shirt, inside the throat that must clear itself and apologize each time it speaks, inside that forty-pound body of boy with its geography of scars, its history of hurt, limbs stuffed with feathers and rags, in what part of the eyes, in what part of the heart, in that cage of the chest where something throbs with both fists and knows only what Salvador knows, inside that body too small to contain the hundred balloons of happiness, the single guitar of grief, is a boy like any other disappearing out the door, beside the schoolyard gate, where he has told his brothers they must wait. Collects the hands of Cecilio and Arturito, scuttles off dodging the many schoolyard colors, the elbows and wrists crisscrossing, the several shoes running. Grows small and smaller to the eye, dissolves into the bright horizon, flutters in the air before disappearing like a memory of kites.

—*Sandra Cisneros (b. 1954)*

Even as new poetic forms emerge, poets continue to reinvent traditional styles of poetry. Traditional forms offer poets some requisites that new forms do not; older forms are most often based on a set of exacting rules, which may include elements such as meter, rhyme scheme, line arrangement, and syllable count. These confines challenge poets by asking them to fit their ideas, images, and experiences into a prescribed space. Today, however, poets readily break these confines if it serves their, and the poem's, purpose.

Tanka and Haiku

Known for their brevity and their focus on images from nature, *Tanka* and *Haiku* are traditional forms of poetry still used today but often slightly changed. Originally written in Japanese, tanka and haiku are now written in a variety of languages. The flexibility with which poets use these forms and others allows for a reinvention of form while also allowing for a rediscovery of poetry's historical importance and permanence.

Tanka

Dating back to the eighth century, **tanka** is a Japanese poetry form consisting of five lines: three in a five-seven-five syllable pattern, and the final two lines seven syllables each. Traditionally, the subject of the tanka is one's inner thoughts, which often pertain to nature. Throughout time, poets have used the tanka to express a variety of emotions and experiences.

Exercise 1.6 Identify the images of nature found in the three tanka poems that follow. What emotions do they convey?

hazy autumn moon
the sound of chestnuts dropping
from an empty sky
I gather your belongings
into boxes for the poor.

—*Margaret Chula (b. 1947)*

19

Fragrant snowball puffs
the breeze of summer traveling
off Lake Michigan
I pick five white peaceful orbs
as a present for your grave.

—*Elizabeth Schmuhl (b. 1984)*

Enough
This twig of wild plum—
Temporary
Our parting
and brief

—*Tanka #24 from Tangled Hair by Akiko Yosano (1878–1942)*

[Because this tanka has been translated from Japanese to English, the line and syllable count is different.]

Haiku

Haiku is another seemingly simple poetic form. It first appeared in Japan between 800 and 1100 AD. Traditional Japanese haiku are unrhymed poems in seventeen syllables, usually arranged in three lines, often in a pattern of five syllables-seven syllables-five syllables. In English, the haiku may be either rhymed or unrhymed. Moreover, it need not adhere to the Japanese haiku's rigidity in form.

After weeks of watching the roof leak
        I fixed it tonight
by moving a single board

—*from The Back Country by Gary Snyder (b. 1930)*

. . . .

Stray white mare
        neck rope dangling
forty miles from farms

—*from The Back Country by Gary Snyder (b. 1930)*

A sleek sailing sloop
quiet as the dawn
slips past the green island

— *Richard Guches (b. 1938)*

Exercise I.7 Compose three tanka or haiku of your own.

Although most literary works are readily classifiable by genre, occasionally categories may overlap. For example, T. S. Eliot's poem "The Lovesong of J. Alfred Prufrock" (page 240) employs both narrative poetic elements and dramatic monologue:

Let us go then, you and I,
When the evening is spread out against the sky
Like a patient etherized upon a table;
Let us go, through certain half-deserted streets…

Some long prose poems, such as Sandra Cisneros's "Salvador, Late or Early" (page 18), have the characteristics of both fiction and poetry. You should be aware that you will encounter such merging of genres from time to time in your reading.

Lesson Three: **Imagery**

When writers wish to share an experience with readers, when they want readers to fully understand what something is like, they appeal to readers' senses: sight, sound, smell, touch, and taste. The term used for this technique is **imagery**, which seems to suggest that the words form a mental picture. While often a visual image, imagery is an appeal to any of the senses. Robert Frost's poetry, for example, engages many of the senses. In "Out, Out—", Frost employs sound with the snarling buzz saw that "rattled in the yard," smell with the mention of "sweet scented stuff," and sight with the image of a hand "gone already." By creating a picture that involves the senses, the poet allows readers to enter the experience of the poem.

Exercise 1.8 Look for words or phrases that appeal to your senses in the following poem.

THE FISH

I caught a tremendous fish
and held him beside the boat
half out of water, with my hook
fast in a corner of his mouth.
He didn't fight.
He hadn't fought at all.
He hung a grunting weight,
battered and venerable
and homely. Here and there
his brown skin hung in strips
like ancient wallpaper,
and its pattern of darker brown
was like wallpaper:
shapes like full-blown roses
stained and lost through age.
He was speckled with barnacles,
fine rosettes of lime,
and infested
with tiny white sea-lice,
and underneath two or three
rags of green weed hung down.
Whiles his gills were breathing in
the terrible oxygen
—the frightening gills,
fresh and crisp with blood,
that can cut so badly—
I thought of the coarse white flesh
packed in like feathers,
the big bones and the little bones,
the dramatic reds and blacks
of his shiny entrails,
and the pink swim-bladder
like a big peony.
I looked into his eyes
which were far larger than mine
but shallower, and yellowed,
the irises backed and packed
with tarnished tinfoil
seen through the lenses
of old scratched isinglass.

They shifted a little, but not
to return my stare.
—It was more like the tipping
of an object toward the light.
I admired his sullen face,
the mechanism of his jaw,
and then I saw
that from his lower lip
—if you could call it a lip—
grim, wet and weapon-like,
hung five old pieces of fish-line,
or four and a wire leader
with the swivel still attached,
with all their five big hooks
grown firmly in his mouth.
A green line, frayed at the end
where he broke it, two heavier lines,
and a fine black thread
still crimped from the strain and snap
when it broke and he got away.
Like medals with their ribbons
frayed and wavering,
a five-haired beard of wisdom
trailing from his aching jaw.
I stared and stared
and victory filled up
the little rented boat,
from the pool of bilge
where oil had spread a rainbow
around the rusted engine
to the bailer rusted orange,
the sun-cracked thwarts,
the oarlocks on their strings,
the gunnels—until everything
was rainbow, rainbow, rainbow!
And I let the fish go.

—*Elizabeth Bishop (1911–1979)*

In Bishop's poem, the reader can almost see the fish—its struggle and its pain. Bishop's imagery is so detailed that not even the fish's gills or the fishing line go unnoticed.

Exercise 1.9 For each line of the following poem, name the sense to which the poet is appealing.

MEETING AT NIGHT

1. _____   The grey sea and the long black land;
2. _____   And the yellow half-moon large and low;
3. _____   And the startled little waves that leap
4. _____   In fiery ringlets from their sleep,
5. _____   As I gain the cove with pushing prow,
6. _____   And quench its speed i' the slushy sand.

7. _____   Then a mile of warm sea-scented beach;
8. _____   Three fields to cross till a farm appears;
9. _____   A tap at the pane, the quick sharp scratch
10. _____   And blue spurt of a lighted match,
11. _____   And a voice less loud, thro' its joys and fears,
12. _____   Than the two hearts beating each to each!

—*Robert Browning (1812–1889)*

Exercise 1.10 Circle each sensory image used in the following poem.

sight   sound   touch   smell   taste

SPRING

Nothing is so beautiful as spring—
When weeds, in wheels, shoot long and lovely and lush;
thrush's eggs look little low heavens, and thrush
Through the echoing timber does so rinse and wring
The ear, it strikes like lightnings to hear him sing;
The glassy peartree leaves and blooms, they brush
The descending blue; that blue is all in a rush
With richness; the racing lambs too have fair their fling.
What is all this juice and all this joy?
A strain of the earth's sweet being in the beginning
In Eden garden.—Have, get, before it cloy,
Before it cloud, Christ, lord, and sour with sinning,
Innocent mind and Mayday in girl and boy,
Most, O maid's child, thy choice and worthy the winning.

—*Gerard Manley Hopkins (1844–1889)*

Lesson Four: **Tone**

P oets use tone to show readers their or the poem's speaker's attitude to-ward the subject or audience. In speech we are able to use our voices to indicate a wide range of tone, including sincerity, irony, humor, or sadness; in poetry, tone is created through both word choice, or **diction**, and word order, or **syntax**.

Diction

The impact of poetry is, in part, created by the exactness of the poem's words. Word choice depends upon what effect the author desires to achieve. For example:

LOVE

There's the wonderful love of a beautiful maid,
And the love of a staunch true man,
And the love of a baby that's unafraid—
All have existed since time began.

But the most wonderful love, the Love of all loves,
Even greater than the love for Mother,
Is the infinite, tenderest, passionate love
Of one dead drunk for another.

—*Anonymous*

(untitled)

i fear your freedom
thus, i must fear my own
you are a changing woman
i recognize you
and am trying to free you
of me

it is your freedom
that i love
i have not yet
learned to love
without holding on

—*Saul Williams (b. 1972)*

In the first example, an anonymous poem titled "Love," the author has chosen words normally associated with love, such as "wonderful," "tenderest," and "passionate." The tone created by the poem is one of playfulness and obviousness. Many of the words have been used time and time again to describe love. The tone, however, changes in the last line to **satiric**, where humor and ridicule are used to criticize human vices. The author has used the words "dead drunk" in order to describe the "most wonderful love": an ironic comparison.

In the second, untitled poem, by Saul Williams, a different tone is created. Williams speaks of "fear" and "changing" emotions; when viewed in terms of love, these words are not considered positive. This creates a melancholic tone, one in which the speaker of the poem seems to be experiencing loss. In the final stanza, the words "i have not yet/ learned to love/ without holding on" create the speaker's sorrowful tone: one of regret and longing for change. By choices in diction, these poems are able to create entirely different tones.

Syntax

The order in which words appear in a section of writing is called syntax. In poetry, syntax is looked at by line or by stanza. The syntax of a piece of writing is an essential part of the art of writing; different patterns produce different effects that can alter the tone, mood, and meter of a piece—such as Robert Louis Stevenson's "The Careful Angler."

THE CAREFUL ANGLER

The careful angler chose his nook
At morning by the lilied brook,
And all the noon his rod he plied
By that romantic riverside.
Soon as the evening hours decline
Tranquilly he'll return to dine.
And, breathing forth a pious wish,
Will cram his belly full of fish.

—*Robert Louis Stevenson (1850–1894)*

Stevenson has created line-breaks that arrange his poem into rhyming clauses. The resulting tempo, combined with his imagery, creates a light-hearted tone.

Exercise 1.11 Read the following excerpt from Emily Brontë's "Silent Is the House." What is the poem's tone? What diction or syntactical choices helped the poet achieve this tone?

> Come, the wind may never again
> Blow as now it blows for us;
> And the stars may never again shine as now they shine;
> Long before October returns,
> Seas of blood will have parted us;
> And you must crush the love in your heart, and I the love in mine!

Lesson Five: **Denotation and Connotation**

Denotation is what a word means according to the dictionary. While a word's formal definition is important for linguistic understanding, a word often means more than what the dictionary indicates. The meaning of a word beyond its dictionary definition is called **connotation**; this meaning points to emotional implications associated with the word. The meanings of words are important to poets, for they want readers to share images and feelings that may be evoked through the emotional value of certain words.

To better understand a word's connotative values, consider how some words cause certain emotional responses, while other words that mean nearly the same thing leave you unaffected. For example, in a romantic ballad, you won't hear of a knight leaping upon his *horse* to rescue his princess. Instead, the word *steed* is employed; it has a more romantic connotation. Certainly, a steed is a horse, but it is the kind of high-spirited horse suitable for a ballad hero. The emotional meaning links readers to the romantic era, and so "steed" is a more appropriate word choice to achieve the poet's intended meaning

Think, for a moment, about how connotation is used in our daily lives to reflect our intended meaning. When we are stopped for speeding, the person who stopped us is a *cop*; when we want to pursue that occupation ourselves, we wish to become *police officers*. The term "police officer" lends a distinguished meaning to the word that the term "cop" lacks. Therefore, the term "police officer" has more of a positive connotation associated with its meaning than the term "cop."

Exercise 1.12 For each group of words, circle the word or phrase with the most favorable connotation.

1. female parent, mother, the old lady

2. spy, secret agent, spook

3. average, ordinary, middling

4. lawyer, attorney, mouthpiece

5. dwelling, residence, home

6. physician, sawbones, doctor

7. elected official, politician, statesman

8. pupil, scholar, student

Exercise 1.13 Read the following excerpt from Christina Rossetti's "Goblin Market." The word "soil" denotes earth, a neutral term. What are its connotations and how do they affect the passage?

"We must not look at goblin men,
We must not buy their fruits:
Who knows upon what *soil* they fed
Their hungry thirsty roots?"

Exercise 1.14 After reading the poem below, complete the exercises that follow.

THERE IS NO FRIGATE LIKE A BOOK

There is no frigate like a book
To take us lands away,
Nor any coursers like a page
Of prancing poetry:
This traverse may the poorest take
Without oppress of toll;
How frugal is the chariot
That bears the human soul!

—*Emily Dickinson (1830–1886)*

For each of the following words from the poem, write a sentence or two explaining the word's connotation.

1. frigate

2. coursers

3. chariot

In line 2, why does the poet use the word "lands" rather than "miles"?

Because language changes in time, both a word's denotation and connotation evolve. Since connotations are tied to the emotional meaning associated with the word, they can vary vastly from one culture to another, even within the same historic period. Poets are sensitive to words' connotative meanings because they are trying to reach their audience in a particular way. If poets use words that have no emotional value for the reader, it is unlikely that the reader will understand the poet's intended meaning.

Exercise 1.15 Read the following poem. In a paragraph, explain the poet's use of connotation to create meaning and convey emotion.

FORMAL APPLICATION

"The poets apparently want to rejoin the human race." TIME

I shall begin by learning to throw
the knife, first at trees, until it sticks
in the trunk and quivers every time;

next from a chair, using only wrist
and fingers, at a thing on the ground,
a fresh ant hill or a fallen leaf,

then at a moving object, perhaps
a pine cone swinging on twine, until
I pot it at least twice in three tries.

Meanwhile, I shall be teaching the birds
that the skinny fellow in sneakers
is a source of suet and bread crumbs,

first putting them on a shingle nailed
to a pine tree, next scattering them
on the needles, closer and closer

to my seat, until the proper bird,
a towhee, I think, in black and rust
and gray, takes tossed crumbs six feet away.

Finally, I shall coordinate
conditioned reflex and functional
form and qualify as Modern Man.

You see the splash of blood and feathers
and the blade pinning it to the tree?
It's called an "Audubon Crucifix."

The phrase has pleasing (even pious)
connotations, like *Arbeit Macht Frei*,
"Molotov Cocktail," and *Enola Gay*.

—*Donald W. Baker (1923–2002)*

Lesson Six: **Figurative Language**

iccaF igurative language is the use of words to express something other than their literal meanings. With similes, metaphors, and symbols, poets are able to distill and compress their writing. Whereas connotations are employed to evoke emotional associations with single words or short phrases, figurative language creates meaning through explicit and implied comparisons. Identifying and understanding figurative language gives readers insight into a poet's intention.

Simile and Metaphor

Similes and metaphors are forms of comparison; they indicate some relationship between essentially different things. Simply defined, a **simile** makes a comparison using the words "like" and "as."

For example:

> My love is *like* a red, red rose.

A **metaphor** makes a direct comparison by omitting the words "like" or "as."

For example:

> My love *is* a red, red rose.

In actual use, however, the difference is much more complex. Though both metaphor and simile must reveal a significant relationship between two things (for example, roses and love), metaphors tend to be more extensive than similes. The foundation of much poetry is this metaphoric relationship, whether it is explicit or implied.

In both metaphor and simile, poets are in danger of producing a cliché. A cliché is a common word or phrase that has been used repeatedly by many people throughout history. Clichés like "sharp as a tack" or "clean as a whistle" have been repeated so often that the comparisons have lost their poignancy.

In order to avoid clichés, poets strive to employ fresh images: two things that are not often compared. This asks the reader to think about the comparison and analyze its accuracy. With the example of "My love is like a red, red rose," the careful reader considers the similarities between love and a rose.

In the following poem, the author uses simile to compare the eagle with humans.

THE EAGLE

He clasps the crag with crooked hands;
Close to the sun in lonely lands,
Ringed with the azure world, he stands.
The wrinkled sea beneath him crawls;
He watches from his mountain walls,

Simile: And like a thunderbolt he falls.

—*Alfred, Lord Tennyson (1809–1892)*

The simile in the last line compares the dive of an eagle with the speed of a thunderbolt. This allows the reader to compare the movements of the bird with the speed of lightening; the reader identifies with the bird, can almost see its dive toward earth, and experiences the rush of the drop. Because both similes and metaphors use imagery, they create comparisons that engage the reader's senses, thus making the experience even stronger.

Metaphors often require more thoughtful contemplation than most similes, both because the reader is not alerted to the comparison by the words "like" and "as," and because the comparison itself may be subtle. Read Sylvia Plath's poem, "Metaphors," and try to identify what her metaphoric comparison, in fact, is. It's not an obvious comparison and part of the enjoyment of this poem is figuring out the speaker's subject.

METAPHORS

Metaphors: I'm a riddle in nine syllables,
An elephant, a ponderous house,
A melon strolling on two tendrils.
O red fruit, ivory, fine timbers!
This loaf's big with its yeasty rising.
Money's new-minted in this fat purse.
I'm a means, a stage, a cow in calf.
I've eaten a bag of green apples,
Boarded the train there's no getting off.

—*Sylvia Plath (1932–1963)*

The figures of speech in "Metaphors" make several comparisons. Plath has compared an expectant mother with a riddle, an elephant, a house, a melon, a fruit, a loaf, a purse, a means, a stage, and a cow; yet in her humorous metaphors, the poet recognizes a resigned finality in the condition of pregnancy: Having "boarded the train," she writes, "there's no getting off." Through this series of metaphors, we can both see the physical awkwardness and share the feeling of resignation. In this example, the author achieves an intensified statement by representing each of the poem's images through metaphor.

Referents

A metaphoric comparison of two things often strives toward a closer definition of some human emotion. The poet accomplishes this by transferring the meaning of a known thing or experience, called a **referent**, to something else, often thought of as the object or idea. For example:

```
1(a

1(a

le
af
fa

ll

s)
one
l

iness
```

—e. e. cummings (1894–1962)

In Cummings's poem above, "a leaf falls" is the referent, while the emotion of loneliness is the idea. The poet expresses loneliness as a falling leaf, while conveying both the emotion and the image in the poem's shape. Conveying the meaning of a poem through the poem's shape is known as **concrete poetry**. Cummings's poem is considered an effective compressed metaphor because it not only uses figurative language by comparing a leaf falling to loneliness, but it also shows this comparison visually.

Exercise 1.16 Does the following poem use metaphor or simile? Circle one. What is suggested about Mistress Susanna Southwell through this figurative language?

Metaphor   Simile

Upon Mistress Susanna Southwell, Her Feet

Her pretty feet
Like snails did creep
A little out, and then,
As if they played at bo-peep,
Did soon draw in again.

—Robert Herrick (1591–1674)

Exercise 1.17 List each metaphoric comparison contained in the following stanza from William Blake's "Auguries of Innocence." What does each suggest about its referent?

> To see a world in a grain of sand,
> And a heaven in a wild flower,
> Hold infinity in the palm of your hand,
> And eternity in an hour.

Symbols

Images, metaphors, and symbols often overlap and are sometimes difficult to distinguish. Sometimes, an image means nothing more than what it is and only acts as a descriptive tool for a literal image. A metaphor, however, always means something other than what it states, such as in this excerpt from Emily Dickinson's metaphoric poem, "'Hope' is the thing with feathers."

> "Hope" is the thing with feathers –
> That perches in the soul –
> And sings the tune without the words –
> And never stops – at all –
>
> —*Emily Dickinson (1830–1886)*

A symbol acts as both a literal description and a metaphoric comparison; in other words, it means both what something is literally and also what it implies. In fact, symbols often have multiple meanings. Many of these meanings are both historical and cultural. For an example, look at the excerpt from Blake's poem, "The Tyger."

> Tyger! Tyger! burning bright
> In the forests of the night,
> What immortal hand or eye
> Could frame thy fearful symmetry?
>
> —*William Blake (1757–1827)*

In this stanza from Blake's poem, we can see the image of a tiger while, at the same time, we are able to equate the image with ferocity. An image does not stop being an image simply because it is used as a metaphor or a symbol. All symbols are subject to various interpretations, but many remain consistent in their meaning for many people. An example of this is the Christian cross; its meaning has remained constant throughout time. Other symbols, however, can change over time.

In literary use, symbols depend upon their context for meaning. Some symbols are widely used and, therefore, depend little on the context to give them meaning. Some examples are water as life, sleep as death, winter as old, dove as peace, sunrise as birth; sunset as death.

Sometimes a poet employs personal symbols, and these depend entirely upon their context for interpretation. Contextual use, emphasis, and repetition directs readers from an interpretation based on image or metaphor to the symbolic intent of the poet. Determining the symbol within the context of a poem is an essential part of analysis. Consider the following poem:

THE ROAD NOT TAKEN

Two roads diverged in a yellow wood,
And sorry I could not travel both
And be one traveler, long I stood
And looked down one as far as I could
To where it bent in the undergrowth;

Then took the other as just as fair,
And having perhaps the better claim,
Because it was grassy and wanted wear;
Though as for that the passing there
Had worn them really about the same,

And both that morning equally lay
In leaves no step had trodden black.
Oh, I kept the first for another day!
Yet knowing how way leads on to way,
I doubted if I should ever come back.

I shall be telling this with a sigh
Somewhere ages and ages hence:
Two roads diverged in a wood, and I—
I took the one less traveled by,
And that has made all the difference.

—*Robert Frost (1874–1963)*

In its first three stanzas, Frost's poem describes a place in the woods where a road forks and the speaker ponders which direction to take. The imagery is vivid; consequently, the road and its appearance are clear. The first three stanzas include the following visual images:

a yellow wood
the undergrowth
grassy
leaves

Frost further develops the symbolic nature of the poem at the end of the third stanza. Here the speaker suggests that, while wishing to save the road not taken for another day, the realization is inescapable that "way leads on to way." In essence, the choice of one road will determine the future roads that one encounters. This is true of roads and also true of other experiences; "road" has begun to suggest something more than its literal meaning. Here the alert reader begins to realize that the poet has something more in mind than an image of a particular forked road. This preliminary judgment is confirmed in stanza four, where the speaker reveals that the result of the choice "has made all the difference."

You might well ask "made all the difference" in what? The answer will not become clear, however, until you realize that the roads diverging in the woods is a symbol. Everything the poem states about roads in the woods is true, but the observations are also true about any great decision in life. We can all look back upon decisions that we have made and feel that the decisions, the road we chose, "has made all the difference." You should see clearly that Frost's poem is symbolic; it is both about roads diverging in the woods and about decisions. From neither can we return to explore what it would have been like to travel the other way, to make a different decision.

Exercise 1.18 Read the following poems and complete the exercises.

A WHITE ROSE

The red rose whispers of passion
And the white rose breathes of love;
Oh, the red rose is a falcon,
And the white rose is a dove.

But I send you a cream-white rosebud,
With a flush on its petal tips;
For the love that is purest and sweetest
Has a kiss of desire on the lips.

—*John Boyle O'Reilly (1844–1890)*

What does each of the following symbolize in O'Reilly's poem:

    the white rose
    the red rose
    the rosebud

In two or three sentences, identify the symbol in the poem below and explain its meaning.

A Noiseless Patient Spider

A noiseless patient spider,
I mark'd where on a little promontory it stood isolated,
Mark'd how to explore the vacant vast surrounding,
It launched forth filament, filament, filament, out of itself,
Ever unreeling them, every tirelessly speeding them.

And you O my soul where you stand,
Surrounded, detached, in measureless oceans of space,
Ceaselessly musing, venturing, throwing, seeking the spheres to connect them,
Till the bridge you will need be form'd, till the ductile anchor hold,
Till the gossamer thread you fling catch somewhere, O my soul.

—Walt Whitman (1819–1892)

The use of symbols is not unique to poetry, of course. Much of the world's great literature is filled with symbolism. Symbols possess multiple meanings and this is partly what makes literature rewarding to experience again and again; it is possible to find new meanings and different interpretations upon each rereading, even with old and often-read literary favorites. Perhaps it is, in part, this symbolic quality that makes novels such as Herman Melville's *Moby Dick* live for generations.

Lesson Seven: **Allusion**

As connotation is beyond denotation, so **allusion** encourages readers to consider either history or another work of literature apart from the one being read. Like connotation, allusion adds meaning beyond the literal interpretation. Through the use of an allusive reference, readers can make connections that greatly enhance their understanding of the author's intended meaning. Sometimes the allusion is crucial to grasping the purpose of the selection.

In the Garden

In the garden there strayed
A beautiful maid
As fair as the flowers of the morn;

The first hour of her life
She was made a man's wife,
And was buried before she was born.

—*Anonymous*

This brief anonymous poem seems, at first reading, to contain a **paradox**. How, after all, can a beautiful maid be married when she is but an hour old, and how can she die before she is born?

The paradox is answered by an allusion to the Book of Genesis in the Old Testament. In the story of creation, Eve is said to have been created, therefore, never born, and immediately married to Adam. The understanding of this poem presupposes a familiarity with the Bible story, for without that understanding the seeming paradox can never be resolved.

Exercise 1.19 Read the following selection.

QUATRAIN

Jack, eating rotten cheese, did say
Like Samson I my thousands slay;
I vow, quoth Roger, so you do.
And with the self-same weapon too.

—*Benjamin Franklin (1706–1790)*

1. What other text is alluded to in this poem?
2. Write a prose summary of this poem as it relates to the allusion.

Allusions to literature found in poetry most frequently refer to Greek mythology, the Bible, and Shakespeare. However, these are by no means the only references for allusions. Allusions to works of ancient art and other poems are often present. Since they are commonly employed, it is helpful to have at least a casual familiarity with these works, or much of a specific text's richness may pass unnoticed.

Some literary allusions are quite subtle and demand critical thinking and a research on the part of readers. See if you can find the allusion in this Robert Frost poem:

"OUT, OUT—"

The buzz-saw snarled and rattled in the yard
And made dust and dropped stove-length sticks of wood,
Sweet-scented stuff when the breeze drew across it.
And from there those that lifted eyes could count

Five mountain ranges one behind the other
Under the sunset far into Vermont.
And the saw snarled and rattled, snarled and rattled,
As it ran light, or had to bear a load.
And nothing happened: day was all but done.
Call it a day, I wish they might have said
To please the boy by giving him the half hour
That a boy counts so much when saved from work.
His sister stood beside them in her apron
To tell the "Supper." At the word, the saw,
As if to prove saws knew what supper meant,
Leaped out at the boy's hand, or seemed to leap—
He must have given the hand. However it was,
Neither refused the meeting. But the hand!
The boy's first outcry was a rueful laugh,
As he swung toward them holding up the hand
Half in appeal, but half as if to keep
The life from spilling. Then the boy saw all—
Since he was old enough to know, big boy
Doing a man's work, though a child at heart—
He saw all spoiled. "Don't let him cut my hand off—
The doctor, when he comes, don't let him, sister!"
So. But the hand was gone already.
The doctor put him in the dark of ether.
He lay and puffed his lips out with his breath.
And then—the watcher at his pulse took fright.
No one believed. They listened at his heart.
Little—less—nothing!—and that ended it.
No more to build on there. And they, since they
Were not the one dead, turned to their affairs.

—*Robert Frost (1874–1963)*

If you only considered the lines of this poem and overlooked the title, then you will have missed the allusion. It is all too common to ignore titles and, in this case, it is of utmost importance. You will notice, first, that the title is in quotation marks. Quotation marks are used when writing out the titles of poems in essays, but not when the title is at the head of the poem itself. Consequently, these quotation marks are a clue that the poet is quoting another source. Where in history or literature is the expression, "Out, Out" used?

If this quotation is not familiar, then you might search online or consult some secondary source like *Familiar Quotations* by John Bartlett. In the index of *Familiar Quotations*, under "out," the phrase "out brief candle" is listed. On that page, in the middle of a longer quotation, is the allusion you are looking for.

MACBETH:

To-morrow, and to-morrow, and to-morrow,
Creeps in this petty pace from day to day,
To the last syllable of recorded time,
And all our yesterdays have lighted fools
The way to dusty death. **Out**, **out** brief candle!

Life's but a walking shadow, a poor player
That struts and frets his hour upon the stage
And then is heard no more: it is a tale
Told by an idiot, full of sound and fury,
Signifying nothing.

—*William Shakespeare (1564-1616), Macbeth, Act V, Scene V*

The theme of this passage, spoken by Macbeth just after he learns of his wife's death, is the meaninglessness and brevity of life. The philosophy of Macbeth's speech, coupled with the content of Frost's poem, reveals a universal comment about the human condition. The poem's content is a specific incident, but the allusion indicates that the poet has broader concerns than the death of one boy on a Vermont farm. Frost is writing about life and death everywhere. This universality is common in poetry and is one of its overarching attributes.

Although Frost's reference is subtle, it illustrates the power of allusion to suggest so much with so few words. Also, it illustrates that the use of allusion presupposes a knowledgeable reader, which gives validity to the reading of older texts. It is important to remember that, while attention to allusion enhances the meaning of certain poems, a missed reference does not completely preclude one's appreciation of a work.

Exercise 1.20 Read the following selections.

FIRE AND ICE

Some say the world will end in fire,
Some say ice.
From what I've tasted of desire
I hold with those who favor fire.
But if it had to perish twice,
I think I know enough of hate
To say that for destruction ice
Is also great
And would suffice.

—*Robert Frost (1874–1963)*

Frost alludes to Dante's *The Divine Comedy* in his poem "Fire and Ice." How does an allusion to Dante's descriptions of hell's punishments develop the meaning of this poem?

in Just-

in Just-
spring   when the world is mud–
luscious the little
lame balloonman

whistles   far   and wee

and eddiandbill come
running from marbles and
piracies and it's
spring

when the world is puddle-wonderful

the queer
old balloonman whistles
far   and   wee
and bettyandisbel come dancing

from hop-scotch and jump-rope and

it's
spring
and
    the

        goat-footed

balloonMan   whistles
far
and
wee

—*e. e. cummings (1894–1962)*

In the poem above, Cummings's "goat-footed balloon man" is an allusion to the Greek demigod Pan, a satyr with the body of a man but the legs and feet of a goat. How does knowing this allusion change the meaning of the poem?

Lesson Eight: **Irony**

When something is said to be **ironic**, it is meant that the expected outcome is not what eventually occurred. In fact, irony implies that, instead of an expected outcome, the exact opposite occurs. When used in poetry, irony most often invokes a humorous or sardonic response in the reader.

There are three main types of irony, which are found in both poetry and prose alike.

Situational Irony

In **situational irony,** a discrepancy exists between what is expected and what actually happens.

OZYMANDIAS

I met a traveller from an antique land
Who said: Two vast and trunkless legs of stone
Stand in the desert . . . Near them, on the sand,
Half sunk, a shattered visage lies, whose frown,
And wrinkled lip, and sneer of cold command,
Tell that its sculptor well those passions read
Which yet survive, stamped on these lifeless things,
The hand that mocked them, and the heart that fed:
And on the pedestal these words appear:
"My name is Ozymandias, king of kings:
Look on my works, ye Mighty, and despair!"
Nothing beside remains. Round the decay
Of that colossal wreck, boundless and bare
The lone and level sands stretch far away.

—Percy Bysshe Shelley (1792–1822)

In Shelley's poem, the irony lies in the discrepancy between what Ozymandias expects, that we will look on his many works and despair at their sight, and what actually occurs, that nothing is left of his works; a traveler will see only ruins and endless sands. Ozymandias's command furthers the sense of irony in that not only is the wreckage of his sculpture the opposite of a mighty king's legacy, but his final words cannot acknowledge this.

Verbal Irony

As its name suggests, **verbal irony** is the contradiction of what is said with what is meant. We use verbal irony to emphasize a point humorously or sarcastically.

> OF ALPHUS
>
> No egg on Friday Alph will eat,
> But drunken he will be
> On Friday still. Oh, what a pure
> Religious man is he!
>
> —*Anonymous, Sixteenth Century*

Here it is easy to identify the irony in the poem. The speaker shows two of Alph's behaviors; first, his pious act of not eating an egg on Friday, and secondly, his choice to drink himself to drunkenness the same day. By giving the example of Alph's drunkenness, the speaker of the poem shows the conflict between his actions; getting drunk does not qualify Alph to be a religious man. In fact, it means exactly the opposite of what is stated in the last two lines: "Oh, what a pure/ Religious man is he!"

Dramatic Irony

Another kind of irony, **dramatic irony**, is most often found in plays, where the audience knows something a character does not. In poetry, dramatic irony is created when the reader has information not known to the speaker of the poem. This technique highlights a specific truth emerging from conflicted realities.

The dramatic irony in Thomas Hardy's poem, "The Workbox," occurs with the growing knowledge that the wife in the poem obviously knew John Wayward much better than she admits to her husband; the reader gradually becomes cognizant of the wife's unfaithfulness, while the speaker remains unaware.

> THE WORKBOX
>
> "See, here's the workbox, little wife,
> That I made of polished oak."
> He was a joiner*, of village life;
> She came of borough folk.

He holds the present up to her
As with a smile she nears
And answers to the profferer
"Twill last all my sewing years!"

"I warrant it will. And longer too.
'Tis a scantling that I got
Off poor John Wayward's coffin, who
Died of they knew not what.

"The shingled pattern that seems to cease
Against your box's rim
Continues right on in the piece
That's underground with him.

"And while I worked it made me think
Of timber's varied doom:
One inch where people eat and drink,
The next inch in a tomb.

"But why do you look so white, my dear,
And turn aside your face?
You knew not that good lad, I fear,
Though he came from your native place?"

"How could I know that good young man,
Though he came from my native town,
When he must have left far earlier than
I was a woman grown?"

"Ah, no. I should have understood!
It shocked you that I gave
To you one end of a piece of wood
Whose other is in a grave?"

"Don't, dear, despise my intellect,
Mere accidental things
Of that sort never have effect
On my imaginings."

Yet still her lips were limp and wan,
Her face still held aside,
As if she had known not only John,
But known of what he died.

—*Thomas Hardy (1840–1928)*

*fine carpenter

Exercise 1.21 Identify and explain the irony in each of the following poems. (Note there may be more than one example in each.) Write down the lines of the poem where you find these examples.

EPIGRAM

As Thomas was cudgel'd one day by his wife,
He took to the street, and fled for his life:
Tom's three dearest friends came by in the squabble,
And sav'd him at once form the shrew and the rabble;
Then ventured to give him some sober advice –
But Tom is a person of honor so nice,
Too wise to take counsel, too proud to take warning,
That he sent to all three a challenge next morning:
Three duels he fought, thrice ventur'd his life;
Went home, and was cudgel'd again by his wife.

—*Jonathan Swift (1667–1745)*

MY LAST DUCHESS

Ferrara

That's my last Duchess painted on the wall,
Looking as if she were alive. I call
That piece a wonder, now: Frà Pandolf's hands
Worked busily a day, and there she stands.
Will't please you sit and look at her? I said
"Frà Pandolf" by design, for never read
Strangers like you that pictured countenance,
The depth of passion of its earnest glance,
But to myself they turned (since none puts by
The curtain I have drawn for you, but I)
And seemed as they would ask me, if they durst,
How such a glance came there; so, not the first
Are you to turn and ask thus. Sir, 'twas not
Her husband's presence only, called that spot
Of joy into the Duchess' cheek: perhaps
Frà Pandolf chanced to say, "Her mantle laps
Over my Lady's wrist too much," or, "Paint
Must never hope to reproduce the faint
Half-flush that dies along her throat:" such stuff
Was courtesy, she thought, and cause enough
For calling up that spot of joy. She had
A heart—how shall I say?—too soon made glad.
Too easily impressed: she liked whate'er

44

She looked on, and her looks went everywhere.
Sir, 'twas all one! My favor at her breast,
The dropping of the daylight in the West,
The bough of cherries some officious fool
Broke in the orchard for her, the white mule
She rode with round the terrace—all and each
Would draw from her alike the approving speech,
Or blush, at least. She thanked men,—good! but thanked
Somehow—I know not how—as if she ranked
My gift of a nine-hundred-years-old name
With anybody's gift. Who'd stoop to blame
This sort of trifling? Even had you skill
In speech—(which I have not)—to make your will
Quite clear to such a one, and say, "Just this
Or that in you disgusts me; here you miss,
Or there exceed the mark"—and if she let
Herself be lessoned so, nor plainly set
Her wits to yours, forsooth, and made excuse,
—E'en then would be some stooping; and I choose
Never to stoop. Oh, sir, she smiled, no doubt,
Whene'er I passed her; but who passed without
Much the same smile? This grew; I gave commands;
Then all smiles stopped together. There she stands
As if alive. Will't please you rise? We'll meet
The company below, then. I repeat,
The Count your master's known munificence
Is ample warrant that no just pretence
Of mine for dowry will be disallowed;
Though his fair daughter's self, as I avowed
At starting, is my object. Nay, we'll go
Together down, sir. Notice Neptune, though,
Taming a sea-horse, thought a rarity,
Which Claus of Innsbruck cast in bronze for me!

—Robert Browning (1812–1889)

Lesson Nine: **Other Literary Techniques**

P oetry and prose share literary techniques in their structure. The difference between the two executions of these techniques lies in the conciseness of poetry. However, concise or extended, it is important to understand what an author is attempting to convey through literary devices, such as the ones described below.

Allegory—a metaphoric genre, or device, briefly appearing within another genre, in which abstract ideas or concepts are represented as people, objects, or situations. Often, concepts behind these representations are easily identified; sometimes, however, they are hard to grasp, provoking thoughtful questions rather than supplying definite answers. The three passages below use allegory to express an idea or concept.

MATTHEW 13:24–30

24. Another parable put he forth unto them, saying, The kingdom of heaven is likened unto a man which sowed good seed in his field:

25. But while men slept, his enemy came and sowed tares* among the wheat, and went his way.

26. But when the blade was sprung up, and brought forth fruit, then appeared the tares also.

27. So the servants of the householder came and said unto him, Sir, didst not thou sow good seed in thy field? from whence then hath it tares?

28. He said unto them, An enemy hath done this. The servants said unto him, Wilt thou then that we go and gather them up?

29. But he said, Nay; lest while ye gather up the tares, ye root up also the wheat with them.

30. Let both grow together until the harvest: and in the time of harvest I ill say to the reapers, Gather ye together first the tares, and bind them in bundles to burn them: but gather the wheat into my barn.

* weeds

—Bible, King James Version

Now they began to go down the hill into the Valley of Humiliation. It was a steep hill, and the way was slippery; but they were very careful, so they got down pretty well.

…Then said Mr. Great-Heart, "We need not to be so afraid of this valley; for here is nothing to hurt us unless we procure it to ourselves. 'Tis true, Christian did here meet with Apollyon, with whom he also had a sore combat; but that fray was the fruit of those slips that he got in his going down the hill. For they that get slips there must look for combats here; and hence it is that this valley has got so hard a name. For the common people, when they hear that some frightful thing has befallen such an one in such a place, are of an opinion that that place is haunted with some foul fiend or evil spirit; when, alas, it is for the fruit of their doing that such things do befall them there."

—John Bunyan (1628–1688),
The Pilgrim's Progress, Part II, The Fifth Stage

A Man Hides in a Well

A man who has committed a crime is fleeing; the guards are close behind. He comes upon a dry well into which are growing some vines. Desperate, he tries to hide himself by descending into the well on the vines. As he descends, he sees a deadly snake in the bottom; consequently, he decides to cling to the vines for safety. After a time, as his arms begin to tire, he notices two mice, one white and one black, gnawing at the vines. If the vines break, he will fall on the snake and perish. Suddenly, upon looking upward, he sees a bee-hive just above his head. Occasionally a drop of honey falls from the hive. The man, forgetting all his danger, tastes the honey with delight.

—the teachings of Buddha

Allegory is a useful technique because it creates an entirely metaphoric canvas for the author. Where other forms of metaphor are short and are used to emphasize a point by brief comparison, allegory pulls the reader into an entirely symbolic setting. It is less frequently used in poetry, but a notable example is "The Faerie Queene," by Edmund Spenser (1552–1599). This incomplete epic poem uses fantastical imagery in an allegory praising Elizabeth I and Tudor rule.

Other Forms of Metaphor—in addition to the examples on pages 30–32, there are several other forms of implied comparisons.

Personification—giving human characteristics to non-human things such as abstract ideas, animals, or inanimate objects.

I Wandered Lonely as a Cloud

I wandered lonely as a cloud
That floats on high o'er vales and hills,
When all at once I saw a crowd,
A host, of golden daffodils,
Beside the lake, beneath the trees,
Fluttering and dancing in the breeze.
Continuous as the stars that shine
And twinkle on the milky way,
They stretched in never-ending line
Along the margin of a bay:
Ten thousand saw I at a glance,
tossing their heads in sprightly dance.
The waves beside them danced; but they
Out-did the sparkling waves in glee;
A poet could not but be gay,
In such a jocund company;
I gazed—and gazed—but little thought
What wealth the show to me had brought:
For oft, when on my couch I lie
In vacant or in pensive mood,
They flash upon that inward eye
Which is the bliss of solitude;
And then my heart with pleasure fills,
And dances with the daffodils.

—*William Wordsworth (1770–1850)*

Apostrophe—addressing an object as though it were living, or speaking as though an absent person were present. Another Wordsworth poem provides an example of a speaker addressing an absent person.

London, 1802

Milton! thou should'st be living at this hour:
England hath need of thee: she is a fen
Of stagnant waters: altar, sword and pen,
Fireside, the heroic wealth of hall and bower,
Have forfeited their ancient English dower
Of inward happiness. We are selfish men;

Oh! raise us up, return to us again;
And give us manners, virtue, freedom, power.
Thy soul was like a Star and dwelt apart:
Thou hadst a voice whose sound was like the sea;
Pure as the naked heavens, majestic, free,
So didst thou travel on life's common way,
In cheerful godliness; and yet thy heart
The lowliest duties on itself did lay.

—*William Wordsworth 1770–1850)*

Synecdoche—a figure of speech in which a part is representative of a whole, or a whole is representative of a part. For example, "all hands on deck" means "all men on deck."

Unpleasing to a <u>married ear</u>!

[In the context of the poem "Spring," married ear represents the married man. See page 120.]

I should have been a pair of <u>ragged claws</u>
Scuttling across the floors of silent seas.

["Claws" represent a crab. See "The Love Song of J. Alfred Prufrock," page 240.]

Metonymy—use of a word in place of another word that is closely associated with it. This is different from synecdoche in that, where synecdoche requires a direct physical link between the interchanging words, metonymy requires only a logical connection.

The boy's first outcry was a rueful laugh,
As he swung toward them holding up the hand
Half in appeal, but half as if to keep
The <u>life</u> from spilling.

["life" and blood are interchanged. See Frost's poem on page 37.]

Other Types of Irony—Though these types of irony are less frequent in literature, it is helpful to be aware of them.

Socratic Irony—Pretense of ignorance in a discussion to expose an opponent's fallacious logic.

Romantic Irony—Writers creating a serious mood only to make light of themselves.

Irony of Fate—The difference between what a human's hopes and expectations are and what is decreed by the gods, fate, fortune, or sheer chance.

Paradox—a contradiction that is nevertheless true.

ICE AND FIRE

What more miraculous thing may be told,
That fire, which all things melts, should harden ice,
And ice, which is congeal'd with senseless cold,
Should kindle fire by wonderful device?

—*Edmund Spenser (1552–1599)*

Hyperbole—deliberate, often ironic, exaggeration.

The sea him lent those bitter tears,
Which at his eyes he always wears;
And from the winds the sighs he bore,
Which through his surging breast do roar.;
No day he saw but that which breaks
Through frighted clouds in forkèd streaks,
While round the rattling thunder hurled,
As at the funeral of the world.

—*from "*The Unfortunate Lover*" by Andrew Marvelle (1621–1678)*

Understatement—intentional, often ironic, lack of emphasis; the opposite of hyperbole.

SONNET 130

My mistress' eyes are nothing like the sun;
Coral is far more red than her lips' red:
If snow be white, why then her breasts are dun:
If hairs be wires, black wires grow on her head.
I have seen roses damasked, *red and white,
But no such roses see I in her cheeks;
And in some perfumes is there more delight
Than in the breath that from my mistress reeks.
I love to hear her speak, yet well I know
That music hath a far more pleasing sound:
I grant I never saw a goddess go,—

My mistress, when she walks, treads on the ground.
    And yet, by heaven, I think my love as rare
    As any she belied with false compare.

—*William Shakespeare (1564–1616)*

Though not techniques for creating meaning as seen above, the following devices produce the sound, meter, and rhythm that contribute to poetry's impact.

Alliteration—the repetition of similar consonant sounds in the beginnings of nearby words.

THE EAGLE

He <u>c</u>lasps the <u>c</u>rag with <u>c</u>rooked hands;
<u>C</u>lose to the sun in <u>l</u>onely <u>l</u>ands,
Ringed with the azure world, he stands.
The wrinkled sea beneath him crawls;
He watches from his mountain walls,
And like a thunderbolt he falls.

—*Alfred, Lord Tennyson (1809–1892)*

Assonance—the repetition of internal vowel sounds. This sound device, like alliteration and consonance, helps to build rhythm and meter within a poem.

And so, all the night tide, I lie down by the side
of my darling, my darling, my life and my bride

—*from "Annabel Lee" by Edgar Allen Poe (1809–1849)*

Consonance—the repetition of consonant sounds within a short area of the poem.

"While I nodded, nearly napping, suddenly there came a tapping..."

—*from "The Raven" by Edgar Allen Poe (1809–1849)*

Onomatopoeia—the use of words whose sound closely resembles the sound of the event or object names.

Examples: buzz, swoosh, sizzle, hiss, splat, beep

Post-Assessment

Circle the letter of the correct answer for each statement.

I. Most poetry is intended to be
(A) spoken
(B) heard
(C) printed
(D) memorized
(E) thrilling

2. Within the genre of poetry, there exists different
(A) units
(B) strains
(C) forms
(D) practices
(E) divisions

3. Most poetry involves
(A) description of emotional experience
(B) the poet's ideas on morality
(C) the sense of touch
(D) true experience
(E) love

4. When writers employ imagery, they are appealing to a reader's
(A) logic
(B) emotion
(C) feelings
(D) senses
(E) reason

5. A word's connotation is its meaning
(A) as written in a contemporary dictionary
(B) to only one character in the poem
(C) defined by using only synonyms
(D) devoid of emotion
(E) beyond its dictionary definition

6. **Metaphor is a form of comparison that**
   (A) uses the words "as" and "like"
   (B) makes a direct comparison between unlike things
   (C) shows the intended meaning of the words to be the opposite of their expected meaning
   (D) refers to a historical event or other work of literature
   (E) represents abstract ideas as people

7. **Images, metaphors, and symbols**
   (A) never appear in the same poem
   (B) are rarely used in everyday speech
   (C) often overlap
   (D) depend upon dictionary definitions of words
   (E) are the basis of syntax in poetry

8. **Poets are able to make reference to events, people, or places in history or previous literature by using**
   (A) metonymy
   (B) allusion
   (C) hyperbole
   (D) irony
   (E) synecdoche

9. **The use of allusion presupposes**
   (A) familiarity with drama
   (B) course work
   (C) an interest on the part of the reader
   (D) knowledge of history and other literature
   (E) the reader's naiveté

10. **When writers' meanings are the opposite of what is expected, they are called**
   (A) tone
   (B) allegories
   (C) denotation
   (D) simile
   (E) ironic

UNIT TWO

Analyzing Fiction

Of all literary genres, fiction is the most widely read by modern readers. People read **fiction**—short stories and novels about imaginary characters and events—to be entertained, to escape, to learn, and to study the craft of writing. Traditionally, fiction has appeared in both literary journals and books, and this has been extended to electronic formats.

Fictional works appeal to different readers for various reasons. While a short story can be read in one sitting and its effect is considerably more immediate than a novel's, the time it takes to read a novel and delve into the characters and events is alluring to some readers. Like other literary forms, fiction is translated into many languages and becomes a component of shared thought.

Fiction has unique characteristics, and to know them is to enhance one's understanding and appreciation of the form. These characteristics are imbedded within literary techniques and draw readers in, asking them to engage in the work. To know these characteristics is to enhance the reading experience.

Objectives:

AFTER COMPLETING THIS UNIT, YOU WILL BE ABLE TO:

1. Identify the elements of plot structure;

2. Understand how authors create probability;

3. Assess a story's setting and its contribution to the plot, mood, and theme;

4. Examine how authors reveal the characters in their stories;

5. Identify themes in literary works;

6. Determine a work's point of view and discuss its effectiveness;

7. Distinguish between romanticism, realism, naturalism, existentialism, modernism, and magical realism.

Lesson One: **Plot**

Plot is probably the most obvious element of fiction for the reader to observe, and analyzing plot is an excellent place to start understanding any fictional work. On its simplest level, **plot** is a sequence of actions that embody some sort of **conflict**, which is one force opposing another. The plot's action is composed of the changing balance of forces in the story's events. The reader's interest in a story is centered first on this struggle. Conflicts may be divided into five chief types:

1. The individual against nature:

   The Open Boat—Stephen Crane

2. The individual against the gods:

   Oedipus—Sophocles

3. The individual against self:

   Les Miserables—Victor Hugo

4. The individual against another individual:

   Hamlet—William Shakespeare
   The Three Musketeers—Alexandre Dumas
   (Most stories of action and love)

5. The individual against society:

   Brave New World—Aldous Huxley
   1984—George Orwell

Exercise 2.1 Explain the conflict in each of the following short stories:

"To Build a Fire," by Jack London (page 267)
"Lavatory Buddhahood," by Yasunari Kawabata (page 298)

The ancient Greek philosopher Aristotle stated that every story must have a beginning (before which nothing matters), a middle, and an end (after which nothing matters). Simple as this sounds, it ensures readers' interest, and, generally, most stories follow this pattern. A story's beginning, called the **exposition**, introduces characters and their relationships to one another and their environment. This initially helps readers to orient themselves in the novel.

Even though the characters may initially be involved in actions or events with which we are unfamiliar, the situation quickly develops into a conflict to which we can relate.

Once the conflict begins to develop, the largest section of a story begins: the complication. The **complication** is most commonly filled with rising and falling action, which builds suspense. This continues until the peak of the action, known as the **climax**, when it becomes apparent where the plot's progression is headed. The final portion of the story indicates the conflict's settlement in the **resolution**. In some stories, there is a **dénouement**, in which all the loose ends are neatly wrapped up. In others, writers leave the conflicts unresolved.

You should note that some modern writers adopt an ironic attitude toward what they consider the artificial certainties of plot in a chaotic world, arguing that, like life, plot isn't always so simple. Modernist writers, for example, take this stance.

Exercise 2.2 In one sentence each, summarize the exposition, the complication, the climax, and the resolution of "To Build a Fire" (page 267) by Jack London.

> Exposition
>
> Complication
>
> Climax
>
> Resolution

Exercise 2.3 In one sentence each, summarize the exposition, the complication, the climax, and the resolution of "Lavatory Buddhahood" (page 298) by Yasunari Kawabata.

> Exposition
>
> Complication
>
> Climax
>
> Resolution

Probability

Sometimes simply understanding the plot's structure is all we want from a book or a movie. We only want entertainment and escape—we do not wish to delve deeper into the story or look at all of the techniques the writer is employing in order to achieve a certain overall effect. In analyzing a work of literature, however, plot structure does not tell you very much about the story. What is helpful and leads toward a deeper understanding is an analysis of a story's **probability**—the likelihood of its events.

As readers, we are aware that fiction is only a representation of life and not really life itself. Because of this, writers need to make their stories seem probable in order for us to be fully convinced by the work. We want to believe in the events and the characters; we use life in order to gauge the accuracy of the work and are disinclined to believe anything that seems excessively fantastic or implausible.

As Samuel Taylor Coleridge observed, writers can rely on a uniquely human capability: the willing suspension of disbelief. This is our ability to pretend that the events we read in a book or view in a drama or film are actually happening right before our eyes. This phenomenon allows us to cry, to be horrified, to fear, or to love—in short, to be emotionally affected by what we read or view. We want the fiction to be believable so that we may care and fear for the characters.

Of course, we are likely to grant writers of romantic fiction somewhat more leeway than we would grant to realistic writers. In either case, writers must work hard to create within their plots a feeling of consistency and coherence. Without this, readers are likely to see the story as implausible and abandon the work, feeling it unworthy of their time. The way in which writers achieve this much-needed believability is through *chronology*, *motivation*, and *foreshadowing*.

Chronology

Chronology, the arrangement of events in time, is an important element for establishing a story's credibility. If the events appear to progress too swiftly, a story will not seem to portray truth. In actuality, it is not the amount of time in which the story occurs that is of most importance, but rather the effect of this perceived passage of time. You may have seen television shows in which two people meet, survive an ordeal, find true love, and live happily every after in a matter of minutes. These events might seem credible for a longer program—one that takes place over a series of episodes—but thirty minutes leaves us not only breathless, but unconvinced.

The same situation is true for fiction. Sufficient time must appear to pass for the story's events to seem probable; if it does not, the story loses its credibility. It is not the number of words in a piece or the number of events that occur in a story that imply a passage of time to the reader; it is the chronological techniques employed by the author that help us perceive time and solidify the credibility of a story's progression.

Several techniques for creating a sense of time passing are available to writers. The most important of these is the manner in which the author unfolds the story. For example, simple narration—storytelling—covers considerable ground swiftly; therefore, if a writer wishes to create the impression of the passage of time, another writing style should be employed. Dramatized narration, which includes dialogue, moves a plot more slowly; consequently, the reader, having to take more time to read the passage, feels that the story time has also been extended. When a writer employs pure analysis and description, the action of a story stops altogether and time seems to stand still.

A skillful writer can control an unlikely passage of time in ways that make the characters, events, and an entire work more plausible. For example, in James Joyce's *Ulysses,* the author devotes a very long novel to the events of a single day in Dublin, Ireland. This is accomplished by using both dialogue and description, creating a sense of the richness and complexity of one day viewed through the thoughts and feelings of a variety of characters.

Motivation

Why do characters in a story behave as they do? This is a common question readers ask themselves, because they not only want to know what happens in a story, but also why it happens. Unless a story suggests the motivation behind its characters' behaviors and its events, it may seem improbable. There are several ways for writers to establish motivation:

1. Analysis—the narrator explicitly tells readers the motives for actions.
2. Dialogue—characters themselves or other characters report motives to one another.
3. Personality—characters act as we would expect people of their temperament to behave, therefore allowing us to make inferences about the motivation behind their actions.

No matter which way it is expressed, a character's motivation must come from within the story. The work of fiction must be an entity unto itself and not depend upon outside justification for the motives inherent in the plot. If a reader must search for motivation outside of the story, its effect is diminished. To make a story's characters resemble real people, their behavior must not be questioned; readers must feel that if they knew real people like the fictional characters, they would react and behave in a similar manner. Otherwise, the story loses probability.

At the same time, you need to be aware that in fiction, as in life, motivation can sometimes be disguised or uncertain. In such cases, probability may be retained, even when a story deals with the more bizarre or irrational forms of human behavior. In Truman Capote's *In Cold Blood*, Capote spins a web of objective, naturalistic detail around an ultimately unanswerable question of motivation: Why were these murders committed? The fact that Capote employs fiction to depict events that actually happened but whose motivation could not be explained reinforces our awareness that probability can sometimes—paradoxically—be maintained, even when characters' actions do not make sense.

Foreshadowing

The element of surprise, Samuel Taylor Coleridge concluded, is not nearly as satisfying as expectation. By this, Coleridge meant that readers enjoy being able to predict what will happen to a character and have their predictions affirmed, such as when two characters in love finally, after much tribulation, end up uniting. Expectation, or suspense, is created by a plot device known as **foreshadowing**—hints or clues that point the reader to what will happen later in the story. If readers have been led to expect something, they feel satisfaction when it occurs.

Foreshadowing can be accomplished in several ways. In mystery stories, for instance, a knife or any other weapon introduced early in the story will most certainly reappear in the story and play a crucial role in the later action. Foreshadowing can also occur in more subtle ways. In Kurt Vonnegut's *Slaughterhouse-Five*, the protagonist Billy Pilgrim lives through the cataclysmic World War II bombing of Dresden, Germany, which creates a sudden, disastrous rupture in the reality of his everyday life. This sense of a sudden break in reality prepares readers for the later leap into complete fantasy, when Billy Pilgrim, shattered by his wartime experiences, is transported seemingly without warning to the imaginary planet Tralfamadore. This result is satisfying not because of the character's fate, but because our expectation—even though stretched and challenged by seemingly fantastic events—are ultimately realized within the context of the story. A story's probability is enhanced when foreshadowing hints at the final outcome. Critical readers are those who are alert to foreshadowing hints, and thus are the most rewarded by discovering them.

Another useful function of foreshadowing is the preparation of the reader for the final outcome. Without this preparation, the conclusion to the story might be quite confusing. In *Moby Dick*, for instance, the mechanics of a whaleboat's operation are described early and in vivid detail. This gives the reader the knowledge to fully comprehend just what is occurring in the story's final chapters, as Captain Ahab becomes tangled in the harpoon line. Without the earlier foreshadowing detail, either the action would have to be interrupted for explanation or readers might be confused about how Ahab confronts his fate. This foreshadowing in *Moby Dick* allows the action, at its most exciting point, to move forward uninterrupted and with complete probability.

Exercise 2.4 Find several examples of foreshadowing in "To Build a Fire" (page 267) and summarize their use.

Lesson Two: **Character**

Characters are the people found within fiction; more simply put, characters are the author's cast. Writers reveal characters in several ways, and understanding these techniques can show you not only how to look at characters, but also how the author intends for readers to see them. Some characters are revealed through the same techniques that people are revealed in life:

1. We learn about them based upon the actions they take or avoid;
2. We learn about them by what they say and how they respond in dialogue;
3. We make judgments about them based upon their appearances, backgrounds, families, or mannerisms;
4. We learn to know characters by what others say about them.

We can also learn about characters based upon what and how they think. This is not a method by which we can learn about real people; we are not given permission to see the inner thoughts of people in everyday life. However, in fiction, this is a technique that allows us to learn more about the inner workings of a character—specifically, his or her private thoughts.

Usually, writers reveal their characters through a variety of these devices, but the methods employed are determined, to a large extent, by the story's point of view. In turn, the point of view chosen by the author determines whether a reader will learn an immense or limited amount of information about the story's characters. (See Lesson Five, page 69.)

After you determine the way in which characters are revealed in a particular story, it is important to understand how individual characters function. What does each bring to the story? Why is each included? It is not difficult to answer these questions for main characters, as it is often their actions which contribute to the development of the plot.

Protagonists

The **protagonist**, or main character, is usually the character on whom the story is centered. Because of this, it is either his or her actions or experiences that form the plot. There are as many literary examples of protagonists as there are examples of literary works—more, perhaps, since novels or stories often have more than one protagonist. Frequently, works are named after their protagonists, such as "Young Goodman Brown" (page 249) or *Jane Eyre*. Protagonists sometimes act as narrators, as in "The Yellow Wallpaper" (page 278).

Protagonists are regularly paired with **antagonists** who act against, or antagonize, them. In "Young Goodman Brown," the antagonist is easily identified: It is the devilish man in the woods. However, an antagonist is exposed more subtly in "The Yellow Wallpaper": It is the narrator's husband, John. Literature does not always have easily identifiable antagonists, but their presence is essential.

Heroes and Heroines

Heroes and **heroines** are characters noted for their noble qualities, such as courage, moral excellence, and self-sacrifice for the greater good. Often they go on a journey of brave and selfless intent. Examples of heroes and heroines can be seen in the title characters below:

- *Oedipus*: courageously acts against a curse that he was unwittingly fulfilling
- *Jane Eyre*: self-sacrificing, serves others as a governess
- *The Little Mermaid*: courageous enough to go on a journey for love, sacrificing the security of her home

Minor Characters

The importance of main characters in a story is usually apparent, but readers need to analyze the importance of minor characters as well. Often, these characters are vital to moving the plot forward. An example of this can be found in Jane Austen's *Pride and Prejudice*, where the misadventures of heroine Elizabeth Bennett's sisters provide many plot twists. Occasionally, minor characters are present in fiction simply to create the illusion of a populated setting. This can help increase a text's authenticity, especially if the setting is in an urban area.

Sometimes minor characters serve an essential role in fiction because their presence can help shed light on the main character's personality. Once in a while, a minor character is the sympathetic confidant who draws the main character into conversation, thereby allowing the reader to learn more about the plans or events of the story.

Another function of a minor character is that of a **foil**. The term derives from the archaic custom of dueling with pairs of foils, or rapiers, which superficially appear to be the same, but may be quite different upon close analysis. Foils are characters intended to be contrasted, either in behavior or attitude, to the main character. Foils don't antagonize as much as reveal, through opposition, the protagonist's character traits. In Shakespeare's *Hamlet*, for example, the young Laertes is contrasted to Prince Hamlet. The personality and attitude of Hamlet are made all the more clear through the contrast. In *Hamlet*, as in fiction, foils are used to enhance a reader's understanding of the hero.

Exercise 2.5 Choose the main character from "The Story of an Hour" (page 265) or "Lavatory Buddhahood" (page 298) and, in a paragraph, explain how this character is revealed. Can you identify the antagonists or foils in each text?

Lesson Three: **Setting**

The setting in fiction is the location where the events occur, as well as the time or era of the action. More than that, however, the setting establishes the atmosphere and mood of the story. You might note, for example, how important setting is to certain types of stories. Ghost stories are often set in dark, lonely places: old castles or ancient houses, preferably located on cliffs overlooking barren and rocky shorelines. These settings enhance the unnerving mood useful to the horror genre. However, a serene setting for a horror story can sometimes build suspense through irony.

The significance of setting is well illustrated in "The Legend of Sleepy Hollow."

> "Not far from this village, perhaps about two miles, there is a little valley, or rather lap of land, among high hills, which is one of the quietest places in the whole world. A small brook glides though it with just a murmur enough to lull one to repose; and the occasional whistle of a quail or tapping of a woodpecker is almost the only sound that breaks upon the uniform tranquility.
>
> From the listless repose of the place, and the peculiar character of its inhabitants, who are descendants from the original Dutch settlers, this sequestered glen has long been known by the name of SLEEPY HOLLOW…"

Here, author Washington Irving uses setting to create an atmosphere of tranquility. He cleverly uses this atmosphere to enhance the mood of the story through irony; without a serene, calm setting, the horrid events that occur in Sleepy Hollow would seem less shocking. It is this ironic juxtaposition of the setting and the action that gives the story its suspense.

In contrast, there are authors who use setting to directly reflect the actions of the characters. Notice how the setting establishes an atmosphere of impending doom in the following excerpt:

> The room in which I found myself was very large and lofty. The windows were long, narrow, and pointed, and at so vast a distance from the black oaken floor as to be altogether inaccessible from within. Feeble gleams of encrimsoned light made their way through the trellised panes, and served to render sufficiently distinct the more prominent objects around; the eye, however, struggled in vain to reach the remoter angles of the chamber, or the recesses of the vaulted and fretted ceiling. Dark draperies hung upon the walls. The general furniture was profuse, comfortless, antique, and tattered. Many books and musical instruments lay scattered about but failed to give any vitality to the scene. I felt that I breathed an atmosphere of sorrow. An air of stern, deep, and irredeemable gloom hung over and pervaded all.

> —*from "The Fall of the House of Usher" by Edgar Allan Poe (1809–1849)*

Here, the "comfortless" furniture adds to the comfortlessness of the characters and the story.

The details of setting may also reveal something about the characters in a story: personality traits, personal habits, social status, and interests. This subtle development of characters through setting is especially effective because the traits and interests are implied rather than explicit. This makes the characters seem all the more real, since we gain opinions about people and their habits through impressions.

In some stories, the setting is so closely related to the plot that the events appear to be a direct result of the setting. For instance, the Mississippi River governs many of the actions in Mark Twain's *Huckleberry Finn*. Likewise, stories that have a limited environment, such as "The Yellow Wallpaper" (page 278), are often inseparable from their settings.

The setting may also take on a symbolic function that is beyond a simply realistic description of where and when the story takes place. In Stephen Crane's story, "The Open Boat," the great, impersonal, superior sea is a natural power that is indifferent to the four men in a small dinghy who are desperately trying to reach shore after a shipwreck. The philosophical nature of the story is symbolized by the setting. Setting, then, may be simply where a story takes place, or it may relate to the characters, the plot, or the ideas on symbolic levels.

Exercise 2.6 In two or three sentences, describe how the setting in "To Build a Fire" (page 267) contributes to each of the following:

    Plot

    Atmosphere

    Ideas

Lesson Four: **Theme**

n fiction, **theme** is the overarching idea, either stated or implied, that the author wishes most to convey to the reader. Sometimes referred to as a **central thought**, theme is concerned with a story's purpose. It is important to make a distinction between a story's theme and a story's **topic**, which is a subject presented by a literary work. When looking at a piece of fiction, such as Nathaniel Hawthorne's "Young Goodman Brown" (page 249), the topic may be as simple as "good and evil." However, the theme must cover more than the topic. The theme is, in fact, a comment the author makes about the topic. A possible theme for Hawthorne's story is, "it is human nature to encompass both good and evil." Here, the theme is a comment on the topic of good and evil. Theme is not essential to the telling of a story; not all stories have themes, and some have more than one.

Theme is present in fiction only when the author specifically works to create a unified piece and explore some significant truths with it. Occasionally, writers incorporate a philosophy or concept as the central idea and construct a story that is designed to illustrate its truth, as with Charles Dickens's novels *Bleak House* and *Hard Times*. In other cases, the author uses the theme as a pillar for the action of the story, such as in Tolstoy's *War and Peace*.

While it can be beneficial to isolate a story's theme in order to examine and discuss it, the theme of a story is never the only meaning or significance of a work. Whole meaning is the sum total of a story's elements, while theme is just one element. When authors dwell excessively on a theme, they run the risk of overemphasizing ideas; the result is a fiction that appears **didactic**—written solely to teach. Didactic fiction seems to preach and, therefore, appeals to a smaller audience.

Theme is often confused with the moral of the story; it is important to note that theme and moral are not synonymous. The term moral means the practical lesson drawn from the story, while theme examines the story's topic.

Sometimes it is difficult to recognize a story's theme or themes. However, there are three ways in which readers can more readily discern the central thought of a story. First, theme may be discovered by closely analyzing the characters' conflicts. These conflicts—what they are and how they are resolved—give insight as to the true theme of the story. Second, finding and expanding on the topic may point to a theme. Lastly, theme may be confirmed by reading the author's other writings. This would be a helpful approach, for example, in discovering Ernest Hemingway's recurrent theme of a man illustrating his virtue by bravely facing death alone.

Exercise 2.7 Read the short story "The Story of an Hour" (page 265) by Kate Chopin. In no more than two or three sentences, identify the theme of the story. Then, list the hints or clues that led you to the theme.

Exercise 2.8 Read the short story "The Masque of the Red Death" (page 245), by Edgar Allan Poe. In no more than two or three sentences, identify the theme of the story. Then, list the hints or clues which led you to the theme.

Lesson Five: **Point of View**

Another way to begin examining theme in fiction is to determine a story's point of view. In its technical sense, **point of view** means the way the story's narrator relates to the fictional characters and the story; it is the perspective from which the story is told. In fiction, it also establishes the tone of a work. **Tone** represents a writer's or a speaker's implied attitude toward the subject, audience, or self.

Sometimes referred to as a story's angle or focus, point of view is meticulously planned by an author to reveal character or plot. For example, if a story is told solely in dialogue—this occurs in fiction, but is most common in drama—there is no narrator between the action and the audience. As a result, the reader or viewer plays an important role in filtering the information presented by the characters in dialogue.

If, however, a story contains any descriptive material in addition to dialogue, it has a point of view. For example, in Washington Irving's "The Legend of Sleepy Hollow," the reader is told "I recollect that, when a stripling, my first exploit in squirrel shooting was in a grove...." This except reveals that the narrator, or "I," views events through his own perspective. Because it has the bias of a personal account, the same event would, more often than not, be viewed entirely differently through another character's perspective. The author is completely cognizant of the biased or unbiased narrator; in all stories, writers use point of view purposefully to achieve a desired effect.

As a reader, you must be careful that you do not confuse the narrator's view with the author's view; they are not the same, even when the narrator employs the first-person pronoun "I." For instance, no matter how well Hamlet speaks or what opinions he may hold, it is not necessarily Shakespeare's views being expressed. We cannot attempt to know the author's view; we only have the text to work with.

Primary Viewpoint Styles

Whenever a story begins, readers expect to be able to clearly see how narrators relate to it, and to know into which characters' minds they can see. There are four basic points of view from which an author may choose in order to tell the story:

1. **First-Person**—One of the characters tells the story through his or her individualistic, subjective viewpoint. Referring to himself or herself as "I," the narrator tells the reader what he or she thinks or feels about the events, but can only speculate about the thoughts or inner feelings of any other character. This often creates an intimate feeling between the reader and the first-person narrator.

2. **Third-Person Limited**—Someone other than a character in the story tells the reader the tale. This narrator, an observer, refers to the characters in the story with the pronouns "he" or "she," and can see inside characters' minds. However, this narrator chooses to reveal the inner workings of only one character; therefore, the reader is told what one character thinks and feels, but not the thoughts or feelings of any other characters, resulting in a limited viewpoint. This point of view is still subjectively biased, but in a special way known as **concentrated subjectivity**: The bias is limited to one character.

Jane Austen employs third-person limited in *Pride and Prejudice*; the reader only knows the thoughts of the main character, Elizabeth Bennett. Ernest Hemingway's *The Old Man and The Sea* is also written in third-person limited narration. In this story, the narrator retells the action that the main character experiences. The narrator is a person who is outside of the action, thus creating the feel that the narrator is a type of reporter.

3. **Third-Person Omniscient**—The narrator is both all-seeing and all-knowing, choosing to tell everything to the reader. The omniscient point of view allows the reader access into the minds of each character, referred to as "he" or "she," so that their thoughts and feelings are understood. This creates a more objective, less biased viewpoint, as characters' thoughts, feelings, and emotions are not intentionally left out of the story.

4. **Third-Person Objective**—The narrator, who is outside of the story, reveals the external qualities of the characters. Objective descriptions lack the subjectivity of a personal account, such as in Jane Austen's *Sense and Sensibility*. Third-person objective description focuses on the factual account of where the characters are and what they are doing. The reader is told what the characters—"he" or "she"—look like and what they say and do, but never what they think or how they feel. No matters of the subjective—thoughts and feelings—are included in this viewpoint; the narrator reports only what is seen and what is said, without revealing opinions.

Other Viewpoint Styles

Occasionally, writers employ techniques that are different from the four standard points of view. Two of these alternative techniques are second-person and stream-of-consciousness narration.

Second-Person—In this instance, the pronoun "you" is used throughout. For example:

> What a singular moment is the first one, when you have hardly begun to recollect yourself, after starting from midnight slumber! By unclosing your eyes so suddenly, you seem to have surprised the personages of your dream in full convocation round your bed, and catch one broad glance at them before they can flit into obscurity. Or, to vary the metaphor, you find yourself, for a single instant, wide awake in that realm of illusions, whither sleep has been the passport, and behold its ghostly inhabitants and wondrous scenery, with a perception of their strangeness, such as you never attain while the dream is undisturbed.

—from "The Haunted Mind" by Nathaniel Hawthorne (1804–1864)

The second-person point of view is more commonly used in nonfiction writing, such as instructional texts, manuals, and guidebooks. Traditionally, it has not been prevalent in literature, and is rarely used for entire books. Though there are a few early examples of second-person narration, such as passages from Melville's *Moby Dick* and short works by Hawthorne, its wider use has only occurred recently with modernist and post-modern writers such as Albert Camus, Günter Grass, William Faulkner and Angela Carter.

Sometimes the narrative is still from the point of view of the protagonist, other times the narrator appears to be addressing the reader. One effect of second-person is to draw the reader into feeling that he or she is personally participating in the action, perhaps even as the protagonist. Used effectively, the second-person voice can be a powerful device when authors need to distance protagonists from the current action or emotions, or break out of the narrative flow and provide an alternative commentary. The danger for writers is that this point of view may seem implausible, simply a distracting disruption.

Stream of Consciousness—Another fictional point of view, especially popular during the twentieth century, is stream of consciousness. This represents the greatest effort to involve the reader in fiction because it attempts to express a character's unexpressed, unspoken, and unstructured thoughts. A highly subjective, first-person writing style, the stream-of-consciousness point of view strives to link the written word to thought patterns in a way that reflects the casual thought processes of the natural world. When the character, whose consciousness the reader is within, is acting or thinking randomly, the words upon the printed page appear to be irrational, unfocused, and illogical. Furthermore, it asks the reader to make sense out of the jumble. Perseverance and close analysis on the part of the reader will usually bring logical sense to stream-of-consciousness writing; the insights that you gain can make the effort more than worthwhile.

Exercise 2.9 In two or three sentences, analyze the point of view in "The Yellow Wallpaper" (page 278).

Exercise 2.10 What are the points of view in "To Build a Fire" (page 267) and "Lavatory Buddhahood" (page 298)? Which point of view is more subjective and which is more objective? Why?

Shifts in Point of View

Sometimes point of view shifts within a work. In Henry Roth's 1934 novel, *Call It Sleep,* the narration is presented through a variety of techniques. In the passage below, the *actions* of the main character, David Schearl, are told by a third-person narrator, but his *thoughts* are expressed through stream-of-consciousness narration.

> Reluctantly, he neared his doorway, climbed the iron stoop, reluctantly, entered the hallway, sighed. Gee! Used to be darker. Funny. Gee! Look! Look! Is a light! In the corner where baby carriages- No. Looks like though. On the stairs too. Ain't really there. Inside my head. Better is inside.

By shifting the point of view, the author is allowing the reader to see the changes David experiences internally that mark his ascent into adulthood. This technique allows readers an even more intimate, subjective, view.

Exercise 2.11 Identify and analyze the point of view in "A White Heron" (page 258). Where does it shift and how does it change the tone of the story?

Multiple Points of View

Occasionally a work of fiction is written from more than one first-person point of view. Unlike shifts in point of view, this **multiple point of view** style regularly revisits one character's point of view, but jumps to other characters leaving multiple narrators to tell the story. In Virginia Woolf's *To the Lighthouse*, the stream-of-consciousness point of view shifts among each character, thus creating the effect of third-person omniscient—the reader sees into each character's mind, but the effect is more subjective and achieved more uniquely.

Since all stories, except those of pure dialogue, need a narrator from whose viewpoint a story's elements unfold, an author must choose the point of view with extreme caution. For an author, this choice determines, to a large extent, a story's impact upon the reader. If an author chooses to use one of the third-person points of view, the author risks making the action seem distant or remote to readers. However, if the author wants this distance and if, in fact, this distance is essential to the telling of the story, an author would choose this point of view to accentuate the remoteness.

Lesson Six: **Literary Movements**

When asked why they prefer fiction to other literary genres, modern readers often say that they find fiction to be more realistic. Readers see a more direct connection from fiction to their day-to-day lives. This portrayal of the true-to-life in literature can be deceptive to those who are unaware of its construction; no short story or novel actually portrays truth or reality because the very nature of fiction leads to distortion. Fiction is, after all, a work of imagination and creativity.

Fiction can promote distortion in two obvious ways: the emphasis can be on either the emotional or the clinical aspects of experience. When the story emphasizes the emotional aspects, we refer to the work as **romantic**; when it emphasizes the clinical, we refer to it as **naturalistic**; and when the emphasis is a balance between the two that attempts to mirror reality, we refer to it as **realistic**. Each is a different perception of what is real, and each has, at one time or another, become so popular in literature and art that entire cultural eras have been called by these terms.

Examining literary movements is an excellent way for readers to begin to understand the general conditions under which a work was written. Though all the works within a given movement are unique, grouping texts together strengthens all of the works' importance and reveals a set of shared ideals by writers during a specific time period.

Romanticism

Romanticism is a term that has been applied to the principles and characteristics of the **Romantic Movement**, at its height from about 1770 to 1850. The main emphasis of romanticism in both literature and art was the promotion of imagination, sentiment, and individualism in artistic expression. The Old French and medieval historical romances of the seventeenth century, such as King Arthur and the Knights of the Round Table and *The Romance of the Forest* were concerned exclusively with fanciful and far-fetched adventures that were distant from familiar life. Over time, the term "romantic" itself came to denote things that were unreal or opposed to fact. During the next century the term came to mean extravagantly fictitious stories or scenes that are pleasing but deliberately far from everyday life, and in which emotion is emphasized ahead of reason and originality is valued over tradition.

The interests of the romantics included a concern for nature and a return to the simple life. These interests had positive connotations: The romantics elevated the simple, nature-centered life, as well as the past, and they were negatively disposed toward the present. As a result, romantic writers chose subject matter for their fiction that was unfamiliar, remote, out-of-doors, and in the past. Nathaniel Hawthorne wrote about the Puritans; however, he told his stories from his vantage point of the mid-nineteenth century. Herman Melville's novels *Typee* (1846), *Omoo* (1847), and *Mardi* (1849) are each set in Eastern Polynesia among native peoples; these works were published to great success.

Another aspect of romantic fiction focuses upon the unnatural and horrific. Novels such as Mary Shelley's *Frankenstein* are fanciful and highly imaginative, though not idealistic. The Brontë sisters also employed the unnatural aspects of romanticism, such as ghosts and moody settings. In Charlotte Brontë's *Jane Eyre*, Jane believes she sees her uncle's ghost while she is locked in the bedroom where he died. In Emily Brontë's *Wuthering Heights*, Heathcliff is haunted by the ghost of his lost love Cathy, which drives him almost mad.

While many works are easily categorized as belonging to one literary movement, such as romanticism, some authors defy such narrow definition. Jane Austen (1775–1817), for example, exhibits some aspects of romanticism; many of her novels are set in the country with characters walking or riding for hours just to reach a near destination. However, her writings focus on finely observed—and often unflattering—portraits of the society that surrounds her protagonists, rather than the fantastic events that are common to romanticism.

Works and authors associated with Romanticism:

Frankenstein—Mary Shelley (1797–1851, British)

The Scarlet Letter—Nathaniel Hawthorne (1804–1864, American)

The Tell-Tale Heart—Edgar Allan Poe (1809–1849, American)

Jane Eyre—Charlotte Brontë (1816–1855, British)

Primitivism

Primitivism, a sub-branch of romanticism, is concerned with the idea that the early conditions of society are the superior situation for human life. It is thought that this simple life is purer and less corrupt than life in current society. Those who subscribe to this view conclude that primitive humans, living close to nature, do not suffer the evil influences of urban society. Primitive humans are, accordingly, more nearly perfect, thus nobler than civilized humans. Moreover, since gods reveal themselves more completely in nature, primitives are closer to the gods and, therefore, essentially moral; they are not confronted with the evils of self-imposed limitations on freedom that exist for city dwellers.

Human behavior, the Primitivists believed, is naturally prone to good. People less corrupted by modern society, by this reasoning, are quite superior: "noble savages." Part of the enchantment with noble savages arose in response to the accounts of voyagers and the discovery of the South Seas; consequently, unspoiled life became the theme of much primitivist fiction.

Still, a note of tension is often discernible in accounts of outsiders who confront primitive societies. A thin line between enthusiasm and abhorrence can be perceived in Melville's *Typee*, for instance. Tomo, the protagonist, is decidedly uneasy; are his Polynesian captors treating him well in order to initiate him into their midst by tattooing his face and body, or are they planning to have him for dinner? While primitive societies may be uncorrupted, some works of primitivism expose the dangerous aspects of mixing city dwellers with "noble savages."

Like primitive peoples, children were idealized as being closer than adults to divine beings. Children at birth are, of course, as close to nature as they can or will ever be. Thus, the more educated and conforming children become, the less natural they are and the farther they drift from a state of perfection. Civilization, in this view, is inherently unnatural and therefore evil. For example, Pearl, in Hawthorne's *The Scarlet Letter*, is a primitive child who seems to be far more uninhibited and natural in the forest than when she is in the civilized, Puritan village; it is as if Hawthorne uses this juxtaposition to expose the primitivist view.

William Blake also emphasized the idea that children—unchanged by a corrupt adulthood and education—are more natural and, therefore, more pure. In order to emphasize this divide, Blake wrote specifically about the difference between experienced children and inexperienced children. In his *Songs of Innocence and Songs of Experience*, Blake separates these two phases of life in order to look back with nostalgia on childhood.

Works and authors associated with Primitivism:

Typee (glorification of the primitive)—Herman Melville (1819–1891, American)

Walden (celebration of natural beauty and the simple life)—Henry David Thoreau (1817–1862, American)

Uncle Tom's Cabin (idealization of the child and childhood)—Harriet Beecher Stowe (1811–1896, American)

Exercise 2.12 Read "The Masque of the Red Death" (page 245), by Edgar Allan Poe, and discuss the aspects of romanticism that occur in the story.

Exercise 2.13 Write a paragraph in which you contrast romanticism and primitivism.

Realism

After decades of romantic literature and the spread of the Industrial Revolution, writers became interested in achieving **verisimilitude**, which represented a shift in the way people thought about fiction and the way writers approached it. Writers like Stephen Crane in "The Open Boat" and Kate Chopin in "The Story of an Hour" (page 265), wished to create the appearance of reality within their work by using material that could plausibly occur in the reader's life; this desire represented the aspirations of **realism**.

Beginning as a movement in the late nineteenth century, the emphasis in fiction became accuracy, especially in background information. Viewed in one way, realism was a reaction to the flights of imagination that characterized romantic writing. Realists wanted to portray an image of life as it really was. In doing this, they saw themselves as arriving at a more perfect and better crafted work of art.

The main emphasis of the realists became the presentation of events so specific that the details were nearly photographic. Authors went on at great length about seemingly insignificant details, such as Jack London in "To Build a Fire." Quite the opposite of the romanticism, with its imaginary conception of experience, realism became directly concerned with social and psychological problems. The characters in realistic fiction suffer frustration from an environment that is often presented as sordid and depraved, as in Upton Sinclair's *The Jungle*, a novel set in the bloody Chicago stockyards. This novel does not spare details but rather describes the stench and gore with such vividness that it continues to make readers cringe. While romanticism emphasizes idealized beauty or fantastical horror, realism emphasizes the actuality of everyday life and everyday people in a fictional setting with fictional events; thus, their themes differ markedly.

While the differences between romance and realism seem quite substantial, they share important qualities when they are compared with history or journalism. What makes realists different from reporters is emphasis. Frequently, the realistic writer's fictional experiences are more vividly memorable than a newspaper account of the same or a similar event.

> John Kitchell of Daytona came running down the beach, and as he ran the air was filled with clothes. If he had pulled a single lever and undressed, even as the fire horses harness, he could not seem to me to have stripped with more speed. He dashed into the water and dragged the cook. Then he went after the captain, but the captain sent him to me, and then it was that he saw Billy Higgins lying with his forehead on sand that was clear of the water, and he was dead.
>
> —*from Stephen Crane's newspaper account of the Commodore's sinking*

Then he saw the man who had been running and undressing, and undressing and running, come bounding into the water. He dragged ashore the cook, and then waded toward the captain; but the captain waved him away and sent him to the correspondent. He was naked—naked as a tree in winter; but a halo was about his head, and he shone like a saint. He gave a strong pull, and a long drag, and a bully heave at the correspondent's hand. The correspondent, schooled in the minor formulae, said, "Thanks, old man." But suddenly the man cried, "What's that?" He pointed a swift finger. The correspondent said, "Go."

In the shallows, face downward, lay the oiler. His forehead touched sand that was periodically, between each wave, clear of the sea.

—from "The Open Boat" by Stephen Crane (1871–1900)

Here, you can see where Crane's newspaper article differs from his realist description of the same event. The simple introduction of a character in his article, "John Kitchell of Daytona," is far more factually based than his short story's introduction: "the man who had been running and undressing, and undressing and running." Furthermore, Crane's short story allowed him to employ literary techniques, such as the simile in his line, "He was naked—naked as a tree in winter." Historical accounts, as opposed to realism, are not afforded the descriptive advantages of literary devices and techniques. In other words, historical accounts focus on relaying information, whereas literature focuses on the technique by which that information is relayed.

Neither romance nor realism, you should note, is, after all, absolute truth. Realism is closer to romanticism than to historical accounts. As a matter of fact, some of the most notable modern fiction is a skillful merging of romanticism and realism. These works contain sufficiently accurate detail to give the reader the feeling of authenticity, while the subject and characters themselves are remote, exotic, adventurous, mysterious, capable of dealing with the unfamiliar, and predisposed to emphasize the imagination. Such works as William Golding's *Lord of the Flies* or Leo Tolstoy's *Anna Karenina* demonstrate this combination of romanticism and realism.

Works and authors associated with Realism:

Silas Marner—George Eliot (Mary Ann Evans 1819–1880, English)
Madame Bovary—Gustav Flaubert (1821–1880, French)
The Fortress of Solitude—Henry James (1843–1916, American)
The Adventures of Tom Sawyer—Mark Twain (Samuel Clemens 1835–1910, American)
The House of Mirth—Edith Wharton (1862–1937, American)

Naturalism

Naturalism is an extreme form of realism. In complete revolt against romanticism, naturalists take the philosophical position that all phenomena can and should be presented as the natural result of the cause-and-effect principles of science, especially those of chemistry and physics. Naturalists deny the existence of anything miraculous or supernatural and, consequently, exclude it from their writing. In art, and especially in literature, naturalists believe that the methods of scientific transcription of nature should be employed. According to naturalist authors, fiction should become little more than a series of objective reports; it should not be filled with emotion or irrational thought.

If early literary movements were placed on a scale from pure fantasy to reporting, they would follow this order:

LITERARY MOVEMENTS

Fantasy ▸ Romanticism ▸ Primitivism ▸ Realism ▸ Naturalism ▸ Reporting

Influenced by the theories of biological determinism espoused by Charles Darwin and the economic determinism of Karl Marx, literary **naturalism** strives for the treatment of the human condition with scientific objectivity. From the writer's or reader's point of view, then, naturalistic fiction includes more details and is less selective about which of those details to include than in realism. Humans, in this view, are as equally controlled by their instincts and passions as by their economic and social environment. Accordingly, a naturalistic writer often makes few or no moral judgments. Much of naturalistic fiction is pessimistic, such as Norman Mailer's *The Naked and the Dead*, which follows a World War II regiment in the South Pacific whose members question their superior officers and the integrity of fellow soldiers. Mailer's work epitomizes naturalism's capability to portray victims and misfortune in nonjudgmental terms.

Whereas romanticism was emphasized during the eighteenth and most of the nineteenth centuries and primitivism reached its zenith in the late eighteenth century, realism was influential during the late nineteenth and early twentieth centuries. Naturalism, as a branch of realism, was a prominent literary movement from the late nineteenth century through the mid-twentieth century.

Scientist and Philosophers associated with Naturalism

> Charles Darwin (1809–1882, British)
> Thomas Huxley (1825–1895, British)
> Herbert Spencer (1820–1903, British)
> Karl Marx (1818–1883, Prussian)

Works and authors associated with Naturalism

> *The Dream (Le Rêve)*—Emile Zola (1840-1902, French)
> *Sister Carrie*—Theodore Drieser (1871-1945, American)
> *Dubliners*—James Joyce (1882–1941, Irish)
> *The Old Man and the Sea*—Ernest Hemingway (1899–1961, American)

Exercise 2.14 Read the short story "To Build a Fire" (page 267), by Jack London and list the characteristics of realism and naturalism that appear in London's story.

Modernism

French filmmaker Jean-Luc Godard said it best, regarding **modernism**: "A story should have a beginning, a middle, and an end…but not necessarily in that order." While naturalism looks at the cause and effects of science on an individual's experience in the world, modernist writers were concerned with the structures existing in society and how those structures affected individuals' thoughts and actions. They saw the concepts of hierarchy, religion, morality, and their supporting institutions as ideas within a corrupt society that should be questioned and even done away with. In literature, as in art, modernists strove to break away from these ideas and continuously questioned their essentiality.

This questioning allowed modernist writers to postulate and create alternate forms of reality within the confines of literature. They believed that subjectivity was essential to understanding reality and that objectivity was impossible. In order to relate this to readers, modernists used stream-of-consciousness narration to construct multiple accounts of the same experience, thereby making an objective truth implausible.

One of the best known examples of this technique can be found throughout the novel *Mrs. Dalloway* by Virginia Woolf. In this story, Woolf examines the consciousness of each of her characters during one day. Each have different ideas, thoughts, and emotions attached to the main event in the story: Mrs. Dalloway's party. The fact that there is more than one way of seeing the event creates conflicts, which is exactly what modernist writers strived to do. These conflicts show both the existence of multiple realities and the importance of viewing them in order to arrive at a clearer picture of the truth.

Works and authors associated with Modernism

In Search of Lost Times (Remembrance of Things Past)—Marcel Proust (1871–1922, French)

The Waves—Virginia Woolf (1882–1941, British)

"The Wasteland"—T. S. Eliot (1888–1965, American, British)

Ulysses—James Joyce (1882–1941, Irish)

As I Lay Dying—William Faulkner (1897–1962, American)

Existentialism

In contrast to modernism's focus on the effects of institutions on individuals, **existentialism** asserts that human beings are responsible for giving their individual lives meaning. This responsibility, however, comes with a burden: the knowledge that all people are capable of controlling their own happiness or grief. Existentialist philosophy demands, therefore, a personal commitment from each person.

This commitment to a life of meaning is necessary to overcome the irrational nature of the human condition, and to view it—the experience of living—as the origin of universal fears. The only way to overcome the feelings of anxiety, loneliness, and despair, all of which result from living in an absurd universe, is the commitment to create meaning by taking some significant action. This action is self-imposed; it has nothing to do with the scientific restrictions of naturalism and everything to do with the individual and his or her choices.

The knowledge that people have free will and are completely responsible for themselves and their choices becomes a source of great anxiety for those who subscribe to this thought. This anxiety has led some literary existentialists to write of their feelings of alienation and despair—a sense of nothingness. On a more positive note, existentialist philosophy does allow for the possibility of improvement. If individuals can consciously create their own values and act authentically upon commitments originating from within themselves, they can define meaning for their lives and reject the source of their despair: the human condition.

As a literary and philosophical movement, existentialism began in the nineteenth century, became further defined and explored during the first part of the twentieth century, and achieved wide popularity after World War II—a time when the burden of human suffering was particularly heavy.

Existentialists have found literature to be especially useful as a medium for expressing their focus on the responsibility of the individual. Considered one of the first existential novels, Fyodor Dostoyevsky's *Notes From Underground* delves into the thoughts of a bitter civil servant whose loneliness is so absolute that he goes unnamed throughout the novel. Albert Camus examines the consciousness of an individual who has killed another person and sits waiting for his own death in *The Stranger*.

Many modern writers, such as Ernest Hemingway, combine a naturalistic depiction of detail with an existentialist sense of free will; this blending of movements illustrates that authors are not restricted to writing in one movement, but can utilize the ideas of different movements to their advantage. In this way, they are better able to convey their themes and ideas effectively and efficiently.

Philosophers associated with Existentialism

> Søren Kierkegaard (1813–1855, Danish)
> Friedrich Nietzsche (1844–1900, German)
> Jean-Paul Sartre (1905–1980, French)
> Simone de Beauvoir (1908–1986, French)

Works and authors associated with Existentialism

> *Nausea*—Jean-Paul Sartre (1905–1980, French)
> *The Brothers Karamazov*—Fyodor Dostoyevsky (1821–1881, Russian)
> *Metamorphosis*—Franz Kafka (1883–1924, Czech)
> *The Stranger*—Albert Camus (1913–1960, French)

Exercise 2.15 Write a paragraph in which you contrast modernism and existentialism.

Magical Realism

During the modernist movement, another group of writers, chiefly from South America, gained credibility as a group whose literature was creating a new movement: **magical realism**. Like modernists, magical realists aimed to expose their view of truth through different techniques in their literature. They included minute details, in the belief that these would increase the story's authenticity and resemblance to how life is experienced. They also used stream-of-consciousness point of view, in order to relay to readers that multiple accounts of the same event should be expected and acknowledged.

What differed between magical realism and modernism was that the magical realists began to look at the inclusion of dreams, myths, legends, and other indicators of the fantastic as essential to their characters. Without these elements, magical realists felt they were not presenting an authentic version of reality. The dreams and myths included in their texts are often fantastic, meaning that the unexpected is accepted. These elements are often interwoven within the text, so that the dream world and the waking world are difficult and sometimes impossible to separate.

An example of this can be found in María Luisa Bombal's *La última niebla,* where the protagonist marries her cousin, Daniel, who is cold toward her and often discusses his dead first wife. This causes the protagonist to invent a man she can love, one who is able to make her happy as her indifferent husband cannot. In this novel, Bombal purposely makes it difficult to tell if the lover is real or created through the protagonist's imagination. Either way, the idea of the lover lets the protagonist escape her true reality—an unhappy marriage to a relative. The idea that a dream, memory, or fantastical creation from a character's mind has validity in a character's life is what separates these writers from modernists. By including the fantastic, magical realism created and influenced a generation of writers who were unafraid to include these rationally "unreal" elements that are a part of many real individuals' lives.

Works and authors associated with Magical Realism

The Shrouded Woman (La Mortajada)—María Luisa Bombal (1910–1980, Chilean)

Ficciones—Jorge Luis Borges (1899–1986, Argentinean)

One Hundred Years of Solitude—Gabriel García Marquez (b. 1927, Colombian)

The Box—Günter Grass (b. 1927, German)

The Magus—John Fowles (1926–2005, British)

It is important to note that the literary movements mentioned in this lesson are not the only ones; there are others—large and small—to which works of literature belong. Regardless of how many literary movements you are familiar with, knowledge of the movements discussed in this unit will give you an excellent foundation for beginning a critical analysis of an individual literary work.

Post-Assessment:

Circle the letter of the correct answer of each question.

I. Which of the following is NOT a basic area of conflict in fiction?

(A) The individual against nature

(B) The individual against history

(C) The individual against another individual

(D) The individual against self

(E) The individual against the gods

2. Foreshadowing can

(A) prepare the reader for the final outcome,

(B) substitute for a plot,

(C) never be used in realistic fiction,

(D) cause a story to lose probability,

(E) make the characters resemble real people.

3. In literature, a foil is a character who

(A) spoils the main character's plans,

(B) duels constantly,

(C) is a fool,

(D) is intended to be contrasted with a main character,

(E) functions as a listener.

4. Theme is concerned with

(A) a story's plot,

(B) a story's purpose,

(C) point of view,

(D) the overemphasis of ideas,

(E) entertaining diversions.

5. The omniscient point of view

(A) gives the narrator god-like powers of seeing and knowing all,

(B) gives the narrator no clear view of all the characters,

(C) is objective,

(D) tells only what characters look like and what they do,

(E) is stream of consciousness.

6. A first-person narrator

(A) sees all and reports what characters think,

(B) reports what is in only one other character's mind,

(C) refers to himself or herself as "I"

(D) links thought patterns together subjectively,

(E) uses the pronoun "you" frequently.

7. Stream of consciousness

(A) is omniscient,

(B) is objective,

(C) is a nineteenth century technique,

(D) links thought patterns together subjectively,

(E) refers to the setting.

8. Romanticism may be characterized by an interest in

(A) the true to life,

(B) the cause-and-effect principles of science,

(C) objective presentation,

(D) fate determined by the environment,

(E) nature and a return to the simple life.

9. Which of the following is NOT a characteristic of primitivism?

(A) Glorification of the primitive

(B) Celebration of natural beauty

(C) Emphasis on scientific detail

(D) Idealization of childhood

(E) Desire to return to a simple life

10. Naturalists

(A) revolted against romance,

(B) believe all phenomena is a result of the cause-and-effect principles of science,

(C) deny the existence of anything miraculous or supernatural,

(D) feel that humans are controlled by their passions and not by their environment,

(E) all of the above.

UNIT THREE

Analyzing Drama

Drama is another form of literary fiction; it is not meant to be merely read, but to be seen and performed as well. It is through the immediacy of the theatrical experience that drama takes on an aura that radically separates it from other literary genres. Herein lies part of the fascination of the stage performance over the book: the book's imagery is abstract—in the mind—while the play's imagery is present and alive. A play's imagery is effective because the actors convince the audience that the action transpiring before their eyes is both real and significant. If the members of the audience are convinced, they are transported to a level of consciousness that makes drama, for many people, a thrilling literary experience.

Whether you are seeing a play performed or reading it silently, you'll find that the written play includes many elements and devices of both poetry and fiction. Recognizing and understanding these elements leads to a deeper appreciation of this compelling genre, which includes subgenres such as comedic drama, verse, and tragedy.

Objectives

AFTER COMPLETING THIS UNIT, YOU WILL BE ABLE TO:

1. Identify the central conventions of drama;

2. Be familiar with dramatic poetry;

3. Identify literary elements in dramatic poetry;

4. Define catharsis;

5. Distinguish among the component parts of tragedy;

6. Distinguish between classical and modern tragedy;

7. Analyze a short play for its dramatic characteristics.

Lesson One: **Elements of Drama**

Although drama includes many of the same techniques that other literary genres employ, such as foreshadowing, metaphor, and allegory, some profound differences exist. While authors of short stories, novels, and plays all have stories to tell, writers of plays have different technical options at their disposal. In ancient Greek and Shakespearean dramas, a chorus sometimes narrates part of the story. Modern playwrights, however, cannot typically tell audiences everything about what characters look like, what they think, or why they do what they do; all these must be shown, and they are shown through the interpretations of actors and the playwright's minimal stage directions. Out of these limitations come the **central conventions of drama,** which state as follows:

1. The playwright is outside the action;
2. Characterization is achieved through speech and action;
3. Verbal tone contributes to a line's meaning;
4. Characters' thoughts may be suggested by a line's content and its delivery.

A play, like fiction, needs to be plausible. To be convincing, a play must be unified in time and space. Many plays throughout history have emulated the structure of ancient tragedies (page 99) to create this unity; most dramatic works, with the exception of some modern plays, have a chronological progression from beginning, to middle, to end.

A play's subject matter typically commences near the end of an action. In other words, since the audience wants to see the action at its climactic point, the action starts close to that point. *Hamlet*, for instance, begins with the sighting of the ghost of Hamlet's father, not with the elder Hamlet's death or even with the plot that led to his death. Rather, the play starts at the point where the ghost sets into motion the action that precipitates the climax. In order to keep the audience's interest, playwrights often limit their plays to a realistic time span and restrict setting changes to what is absolutely necessary.

Literary Elements

Since a modern play seldom runs longer than three hours, its action is often compressed. Even what seems to be minor action must contribute to the meaning of the whole. As a result, the playwright's use of metaphor and symbolism are often less subtle than the novelist's. Consequently, the playwright's figures of speech seem more obviously attached to the play's meaning.

Figurative Language

In the following excerpt from Shakespeare's *A Midsummer Night's Dream*, you can observe his use of poetic devices. Here, Helena, who is in love with Demetrius, is greeted by Hermia, who receives the love of Demetrius but does not return it. Helena is consumed by jealousy, which is revealed both literally and figuratively.

> *HERMIA*: God speed fair Helena! whither away?
>
> *HELENA*: Call you me fair? that fair again unsay.
> Demetrius loves your fair: O happy fair!
> Your eyes are lode-stars; and your tongue's sweet air
> More tuneable than lark to shepherd's ear,
> When wheat is green, when hawthorn buds appear.
> Sickness is catching: O, were favour so,
> Yours would I catch, fair Hermia, ere I go;
> My ear should catch your voice, my eye your eye,
> My tongue should catch your tongue's sweet melody.
> Were the world mine, Demetrius being bated,
> The rest I'd give to be to you translated.
> O, teach me how you look, and with what art
> You sway the motion of Demetrius' heart.

Helena's speech reveals her longing to be more like Hermia, so that she might win the heart of Demetrius. However, there are deeper meanings which can be understood by simply reading the speech as if it were a poem. Metaphorically, Helena compares Hermia's allure to a disease. The reader or viewer is given a comparison that gives new meaning to Helena: her desperation. Shakespeare employs imagery when he writes, "and your tongue's sweet air/ More tuneable than lark to shepherd's ear,/ When wheat is green, when hawthorn buds appear." With this imagery, Helena exposes a complicated aspect of her relationship with Hermia: she is jealous of Hermia for being the object of Demetrius's affection, but she does not dislike Hermia. In fact, she flatters her foil through poetic imagery, exposing that the only person Helena finds lacking is herself. When reading or listening to a verse play, it is important to pay attention to these poetic elements in order to capture the full intent of a line as well as its effect on your understanding of the characters themselves.

Tone

The rewards of reading drama are enhanced directly in proportion to readers' skill and experience in perceiving the author's tone, or attitude. In *Death of a Salesman*, playwright Arthur Miller's point of view, written as parenthetical stage directions, gives readers important clues about the characters before the play even begins. About his characters, Miller writes, "[Willy Loman] is past sixty years of age, dressed quietly. Even as he crosses the stage to the doorway of the house, his exhaustion is apparent.... Most often jovial, [Linda] has developed an iron repression of her exceptions to Willy's behavior—she more than loves him, she admires him...." This point of view holds great authority; before one line is spoken, Miller has set the tone.

Tone is also created by the way in which a character speaks his or her lines. Readers must become alert to even very subtle shifts in tone, lest the meaning be either misinterpreted or lost.

Verbal Irony

Verbal irony is the contradiction of what a character says and what he or she really means; it most often results in a humorous or sarcastic effect. In drama, it is created both by the intonation of the speaker and the content of his or her speech.

A famous example of verbal irony, laced with sarcasm, occurs in Shakespeare's *Julius Caesar*, when Mark Antony, orating over the body of the murdered Caesar, says of one of the chief assassins, "Brutus is an honorable man." The crowd (and the audience) soon see that Antony means just the opposite.

Dramatic Irony

Dramatic irony occurs when the audience or reader knows something a character does not. The viewer may know that a character is making a mistake because he or she does not have the information that, ironically, the viewer has. A classic example of dramatic irony occurs in Sophocles's play *Oedipus*, when Oedipus curses whoever caused the plague in the city of Thebes; the audience knows, as Oedipus does not, that he has cursed himself as he is the one who caused it.

Lesson Two: **Dramatic Poetry**

"The purpose of playing [acting], whose end, both at first and now, was as is, to hold, as 'twere, the mirror up to Nature."

—William Shakespeare (1564–1616): Hamlet, Act III, Scene II

D ramatic poetry—poetic language or verse spoken by characters in a play—has its origins in ancient Greece. In its earliest forms, it consisted of a single actor delivering a monologue to music, often accompanied by a chorus of singers and dancers. Throughout the centuries dramatic poetry evolved into a production of actors, and while the content of the plays were still written metrically, the musical element was, for the most part, lost.

Sixteenth-century England saw the flowering of dramatic verse, and its many iconic plays are still performed today. Among many famous Elizabethan playwrights, Christopher Marlowe (1564–1593) is known as the father of English tragedy. His most famous play, *The Tragical History of Doctor Faustus*, was published in 1604, eleven years after his death. Another dramatist, Ben Johnson (1572–1637), is best known for *The Alchemist* and *Every Man in His Humour.*

The best known Elizabethan playwright is William Shakespeare. He wrote thirty-seven plays in his lifetime, ranging from tragedies to histories to comedies. His works exemplified dramatic poetry in its highest form, combining plot, verse, meter, rhyme, and poetic devices into acclaimed masterpieces of the English language. Shakespeare's works require that the reader or viewer not only understand the literal meaning of his verses, as well as his many allusions to mythology, literature, and biblical passages, but also the intricacies of his figurative language, brought about by poetic devices such as metaphor, simile, and symbol.

Verse

Modern audiences often find dramatic verse difficult to understand because of its unfamiliar rhythms and rhymes. However, reading verse with knowledge of its structure and variations makes it easier to comprehend. Shakespeare's dramatic poetry is primarily written in iambic pentameter (see page 14): Each line is ten syllables, every second syllable is stressed. When rhymed, these ten-syllable lines are called rhymed verse; when unrhymed, they are called blank verse. Shakespeare wrote in both rhymed and blank verse, often in the same play, but his blank verse is, perhaps, most renowned. *Romeo and Juliet* is an example of a work written in both verse styles. Below are two of Juliet's speeches, one written in rhymed verse and the other in blank verse.

Rhymed Verse:

"Good pilgrim, you do wrong your hand too much,
Which mannerly devotion shows in this;
For saints have hands that pilgrims' hands do touch,
And palm to palm is holy palmers' kiss."

Blank Verse:

"Is there no pity sitting in the clouds,
That sees into the bottom of my grief?
O, sweet my mother, cast me not away!
Delay this marriage for a month, a week;
Or, if you do not, make the bridal bed
In that dim monument where Tybalt lies."

By using both rhymed and blank verse, Shakespeare is able to explore the effects of each. When Juliet speaks in rhyme in Act I, Scene V, she is carefully flirting with Romeo. Rhymed verse has an effect of formality, and on their first meeting, she would naturally present herself in a formal manner. Furthermore, rhymed verse implies premeditation in speech: it is a thoughtful mode of communication in which each line is purposefully worded to create the rhyming effect of the whole. This adds continuity and a sense of predictability to the speech. In contrast, Juliet's speech from Act III, Scene V, is an emotional plea. Here, the blank verse implies a lack of formality; she is speaking to her mother with disarming honesty, and the blank verse serves to mirror Juliet's directness.

Prose Poetry

While Shakespeare wrote his plays primarily in iambic pentameter, there are many instances of prose poetry—verse without meter or rhyme—in his dramas. Orlando's speech from *As You Like It* is an instance of Shakespeare employing prose.

ORLANDO:

As I remember, Adam, it was upon this fashion
bequeathed me by will but poor a thousand crowns,
and, as thou sayest, charged my brother, on his
blessing, to breed me well: and there begins my
sadness. My brother Jaques he keeps at school, and
report speaks goldenly of his profit: for my part,
he keeps me rustically at home, or, to speak more
properly, stays me here at home unkept; for call you
that keeping for a gentleman of my birth, that
differs not from the stalling of an ox? His horses
are bred better; for, besides that they are fair
with their feeding, they are taught their manage,
and to that end riders dearly hired: but I, his
brother, gain nothing under him but growth; for the
which his animals on his dunghills are as much
bound to him as I. Besides this nothing that he so
plentifully gives me, the something that nature gave
me his countenance seems to take from me: he lets
me feed with his hinds, bars me the place of a
brother, and, as much as in him lies, mines my
gentility with my education. This is it, Adam, that
grieves me; and the spirit of my father, which I
think is within me, begins to mutiny against this
servitude: I will no longer endure it, though yet I
know no wise remedy how to avoid it.

Shakespeare uses prose in this monologue, it may be interpreted, in order
to highlight Orlando's lack of education, either in schooling or culture. Blank
and rhymed verse, along with prose, are often used as cultural standards in
Shakespeare's work; kings and queens speak in rhymed verse, while rustics
speak in prose. Here, Orlando is of high rank, but due to his brother's denying
him an education, he is characterized as a peasant through prose.

Exercise 3.1 Read this short passage from Act IV, Scene I of William Shakespeare's *Much
Ado About Nothing*. Is it written in rhymed verse, blank verse, or prose? What do you
think Shakespeare intended with his choice?

BENEDICK:

I swear by it that you love me; and I will make
him eat it that says I love not you.

Punctuation

When reading dramatic poetry, it is not only important to pay close attention to poetic devices and the style of the verse, but also to make yourself aware of the punctuation used in each line. Dramatic poetry was intended to be heard rather than read, and punctuation is a tool to that end. It is worthwhile to read a play aloud, as a class or individually, in order to explore how punctuation affects the way you read a line—the way the playwright intended the line to be read.

With a simple pause, a playwright can alter the meaning of a line. For instance, the three witches of Shakespeare's *Macbeth*, known as the Weird Sisters, chant together before the first appearance of Macbeth himself. Punctuation is key to knowing how Shakespeare intended their speech to be read and understood.

WEIRD SISTERS:

The weird sisters, hand in hand,
Posters of the sea and land,
Thus do go about, about:
Thrice to thine and thrice to mine
And thrice again, to make up nine.
Peace! the charm's wound up.

By using commas, Shakespeare implies a short pause, while continuing the rhythm of the line. Colons, used after the second "about" in line three, imply more of a stop than a pause. Not a complete stop, though—merely a longer breath between words. However, a period, seen in line five, or an exclamation mark, seen in line six, each signify a complete stop in the rhythm of speech. Pauses and stops reflect an impediment to momentum: A pause is less severe than a stop. They are also useful in emphasizing certain words. For instance, "Peace!" is emphasized by the exclamation mark following it. Without that punctuation, a reader would simply say "Peace" without any emphasis; with the exclamation point, a reader is asked to shout it. When reading dramatic verse, or any play for that matter, it is important to be guided by the punctuation; it is the closest readers can get to a playwright's original intent.

Exercise 3.2 Following are two versions of Juliet's monologue. Read aloud and, if possible, record the first version. Next, analyze the punctuation in the second version and recite the passage again. What differences do you hear between the two? How does focusing on punctuation change your second reading and its meaning? (If you are unable to record your voice, have a classmate listen to both readings and note the changes observed before and after the punctuation was analyzed.)

1.

Thou knowest the mask of night is on my face
Else would a maiden blush bepaint my cheek
For that which thou hast heard me speak to-night
Fain would I dwell on form fain fain deny
What I have spoke but farewell complement
Dost thou love me I know thou wilt say 'Ay'
And I will take thy word Yet if thou swear'st
Thou may prove false At lovers' perjuries
They say Jove laughs O gentle Romeo
If thou dost love pronounce it faithfully

2.

Thou knowest the mask of night is on my face;
Else would a maiden blush bepaint my cheek
For that which thou hast heard me speak to-night.
Fain would I dwell on form, fain, fain deny
What I have spoke; but farewell complement!
Dost thou love me? I know thou wilt say 'Ay';
And I will take thy word. Yet, if thou swear'st,
Thou may prove false. At lovers' perjuries,
They say Jove laughs. O gentle Romeo,
If thou dost love, pronounce it faithfully.

—*William Shakespeare (1564–1616), Romeo and Juliet, Act II,*
Scene 2

Lesson Three: **Tragedy**

Many feel that the highest form of drama is **tragedy**: plays involving unhappy events and often the downfall of the main character. From its beginnings in ancient Greece down to today's tragic drama, tragedy has had wide appeal. Aristotle (384–322 BCE), a Greek philosopher, postulated a philosophic theory regarding tragedy's appeal. Aristotle believed that literature, and all art for that matter, is an imitation of reality. As such, literature presents a heightened and harmonious exercising of peoples' feelings. This exercising of emotions results in their enlargement and refinement, which leads to the ability to form a more perfect total person, thus reconciling and integrating emotion and intellect through art. This, according to Aristotle, has an ethically desirable effect upon the total well-being of each individual. Part of this positive effect entails the purging of emotion, a process which is called **catharsis** (*katharsis*).

Specifically, Aristotle believed catharsis cleanses the emotions of fear and pity. This is accomplished in tragic drama, for example, by first exciting, and then releasing emotions; it excites in order to purify. The Greek view, as Aristotle expressed it, gave catharsis credit for the removal of disturbing, painful elements by purifying them in tragedy. This almost medicinal idea seems to fit well not only into Greek culture, but into modern ideas of the arts as well. Part of the fascination with drama would seem to be that the audience identifies with the characters, fears for them as they proceed toward the inevitable, and pities them as they plummet into the catastrophe.

Classical tragedy has three basic components as it proceeds:

1. a beginning (introduction; antecedent action)
2. a middle (suspense; climax; reversal)
3. an end (catastrophe; dénouement)

Beginning

1. *Introduction (the play's opening)*: Tragedy usually begins with one of five basic openings: a speech given by a major character, small talk between minor characters, a speech given by a chorus, a recited prologue, or an exchange between major characters.

2. *Antecedent Action*: In order to explain the present action of a play's characters, events that occur prior to the opening action must be explained. These events are the antecedent action.

Middle

1. *Suspense*: As with any longer work of literature, something must be curious or sufficiently enthralling to maintain the self-discipline to read on or, as in the case with drama, to come back after the intermission. Without a doubt, one of the most effective methods of maintaining reader and viewer interest is through suspense. Suspense intrigues the audience by creating curiosity, uncertainty, or excitement; it heightens emotions, a prerequisite for catharsis.

The playwright may increase suspense through the technique of foreshadowing. Sometimes foreshadowing is accomplished in drama by dwelling on something that will be important later. By seeing hints that mirror later events, the audience's curiosity is stimulated and suspense is enhanced. **Dramatic irony** (page 42) may also be used to build suspense.

2. *Reversal*: The dramatic turning point, or **reversal**, for the protagonist is that point at which it is discovered that the expected fate is not the fate that will transpire. Often, during the beginning and the middle of a play, plans are made, character relationships established, and certain events are anticipated. Then, suddenly, a dramatic reversal reveals that the main character's expectations will not be fulfilled. For example, Romeo, thinking that Juliet is dead, kills himself. Hamlet, seeking vengeance and the throne, is himself the object of vengeance, resulting in his death. The reversal is sometimes an odd twist of fate or, at other times, a logical outgrowth of a character's personality; in any case, the technique is dramatic and contributes to a play's cathartic value.

3. *Climax*: An often misunderstood term, the dramatic **climax** is not at the end of a play, nor is it usually near the catastrophic events. Rather, the dramatic climax is that point at which the catastrophe becomes inevitable. In many plays, such as in Shakespeare's tragedies, the climax comes during Act III—directly in the middle of the play. For example, in *Hamlet's* rising action, there are exposition, antecedent action, character introduction, and conflict. All of these contribute to what Aristotle called "the complications," and result in mounting tension. The rising action peaks at the climax, after which begins the falling action. From this falling action, the tragedy proceeds rapidly toward disaster.

End

Catastrophe and Dénouement: Closely related in tragedy, the catastrophe and dénouement come at or near the end of a play. The **catastrophe** is that point at which the protagonist, and often allies and loyal friends, die. **Dénouement** is a general term, which means unraveling or untangling. The dénouement is where the plot action ends and any unanswered questions are explained. A dénouement is necessary to the achievement of a satisfying drama so that members of the audience do not leave the theater puzzled about any part of the dramatic story.

Exercise 3.3 In one paragraph, describe Aristotle's view of what effect tragedy has upon those who read or view it. In what ways does a drama you have recently seen meet the requirements of tragedy?

Exercise 3.4 Create a graph that shows the phases of the three basic components of classical tragedy as a work proceeds.

Lesson Four: **The Modern Play**

Modern tragedy, while similar to classic tragedy in structure, has undergone certain shifts in focus. Contemporary emphasis has changed what the ancient Greeks called fate (the will of the gods) to a greater concern with social, cultural, or political milieu. In other words, the modern fates are "society," "the system," or whatever other force or entity playwrights believe controls people's destinies. Moreover, the characters in classic tragedy deeply care about what happens to tragic protagonists because their deaths change the fortunes of all people in a society. Modern protagonists, by contrast, do not usually have the fortunes of society resting upon their shoulders. In fact, their lives or deaths often seem to have little impact upon the societies in which they live.

These are not the only differences between classical drama, such as tragedy or verse, and modern drama. Drama has witnessed literary movements, just as poetry and fiction have. While ancient drama focused upon gods and legends, by the end of the medieval era drama had begun to abandon exclusively religious-themed plot lines. Seventeenth-century English drama was dually centered on comedy and tragedy, and was then followed by the romanticism of nineteenth-century works.

During the late nineteenth century, antirealism became the dramatic fashion. Playwrights felt that a greater truth could be found in the abstract rather than in naturalism, with its focus on reality and the cause-and-effect principles of science. Modern drama has undergone a number of shifts, from symbolist drama, which is a dream-like production, to absurdism, which employs illogical and irrational elements to compose its plot. A return to realism has dominated contemporary drama, although aspects of other movements are often incorporated.

Reading a Dramatic Work

Plays derive much of their impact from the fact that members of the audience are affected by one another. Humor in a play, for example, may bring more intensified responses because the whole group is reacting not only to the humor, but to the other members of the audience. Moreover, watching something happen along with others, makes it appear more realistic. Although the audience only watches, individual members participate in the action by identifying with the emotions being portrayed before them.

If you read a play aloud, perhaps in a classroom, an audience's response will not suggest the importance of a character's line or action. While stage directions are always vital in interpreting a play, tone and flow become important when hearing a play read aloud. By assessing a speaker's tone, you will have a better understanding of the line's intention: Was it meant to be whispered or shouted, said sarcastically or sincerely? You can also analyze the flow of conversation when hearing a play aloud. Is there frequent back-and-forth banter, or is the play littered with monologues that slow down the conversational quality of the dialogue? While this aspect of drama can be examined when reading silently, it is easier to assess flow when hearing a play read aloud.

Reading on Your Own

Reading a play in class is not always possible; sometimes you will be asked to experience a playwright's work by reading it on your own. This, however, can have advantages. A fuller understanding of dramatic verse or any figurative language can be easier to attain when the reader can slow or stop the action to study metaphors, ironies, allusions, or other literary elements that may escape meaning when delivered quickly by an actor. When reading alone, you may find it helpful to read aloud—that way, you can analyze the verbal tone of the lines, along with their content.

If you read a play silently by yourself, you must pay close attention to the parenthetical stage directions. These authorial notes will become valuable assets to your understanding of the play, as well as its individual characters. For example, if you are reading *The Stronger* and you ignore stage directions, you will have no comprehension of Miss Y's character, since she has no spoken lines. Furthermore, without Mrs. X's small gestures, noted parenthetically, you will not grasp the intricacies of her patronizing and often nervous movements.

The Stronger

Characters:

MRS. X, an actress, married

MISS Y, an actress, unmarried

A WAITRESS

SCENE: *The corner of a ladies' cafe. Two little iron tables, a red velvet sofa, several chairs. Enter MRS. X, dressed in winter clothes, carrying a Japanese basket on her arm.*

MISS Y: Sits with a half-empty beer bottle before her, reading an illustrated paper, which she changes for another.

MRS. X: Good afternoon, Amelia. You're sitting here alone on Christmas eve like a poor bachelor!

MISS Y: (Looks up, nods, and resumes her reading.)

MRS. X: Do you know it really hurts me to see you like this, alone, in a cafe, and on Christmas eve, too. It makes me feel as I did one time when I saw a bridal party in a Paris restaurant, and the bride sat reading a comic paper, while the groom played billiards with the witnesses. Huh, thought I, with such a beginning, what will follow and what will be the end? He played billiards on his wedding eve! *(MISS Y starts to speak)* And she read a comic paper, you mean? Well, they are not altogether the same thing.

(A WAITRESS enters, places a cup of chocolate before MRS. X and goes out.)

MRS. X: You know what, Amelia! I believe you would have done better to have kept him! Do you remember, I was the first to say "Forgive him?" Do you remember that? You would be married now and have a home. Remember that Christmas when you went out to visit your fiancé's parents in the country? How you gloried in the happiness of home life and really longed to quit the theatre forever? Yes, Amelia dear, home is the best of all—next to the theatre—and as for children—well, you don't understand that.

MISS Y: (Looks up scornfully.)

(MRS. X sips a few spoonfuls out of the cup, then opens her basket and shows Christmas presents.)

MRS. X: Now you shall see what I bought for my piggywigs. *(Takes up a doll.)* Look at this! This is for Lisa, ha! Do you see how she can roll her eyes and turn her head, eh? And here is Maja's popgun.

(Loads it and shoots at MISS Y.)

MISS Y: (Makes a startled gesture.)

MRS. X: Did I frighten you? Did you think I would like to shoot you, eh? On my soul, if I don't think you did! If you wanted to shoot me it wouldn't be so surprising, because I stood in your way—and I know you can never forget that—although I was absolutely innocent. You still believe I intrigued and got you out of the Stora theatre, but I didn't. I didn't do that, although you think so. Well, it doesn't make any difference what I say to you. You will believe I did it. *(Takes up a pair of embroidered slippers.)* And these are for my better half. I embroidered them myself—I can't bear tulips, but he wants tulips on everything.

MISS Y: (Looks up ironically and curiously.)

MRS. X: *(putting a hand in each slipper)* See what little feet Bob has! What? And you should see what a splendid stride he has! You've never seen him in slippers! *(MISS Y laughs aloud.)* Look! *(She makes the slippers walk on the table. MISS Y laughs loudly.)* And when he is grumpy he stamps like this with his foot. "What! damn those servants who can never learn to make coffee. Oh, now those creatures haven't trimmed the lamp wick properly!" And then there are draughts on the floor and his feet are cold. "Ugh, how cold it is; the stupid idiots can never keep the fire going." *(She rubs the slippers together, one sole over the other.)*

MISS Y: (Shrieks with laughter.)

MRS. X: And then he comes home and has to hunt for his slippers which Marie has stuck under the chiffonier—oh, but it's so sinful to sit here and make fun of one's husband this way when he is a kind and good little man. You ought to have had such a husband, Amelia. What are you laughing at? What? What? And you see he's true to me. Yes, I'm sure of that, because he told me himself—what are you laughing at?—that when I was touring Norway that brazen Frederika came and wanted to seduce him! Can you fancy anything so infamous? *(pause)* I'd have torn her eyes out if she had come to see him when I was at home. *(pause)* It was lucky that Bob told me about it himself and that it didn't reach me through gossip. *(pause)* But would you believe it, Frederika wasn't the only one! I don't know why, but the women are crazy about my husband. They must think he has influence about getting them theatrical engagements, but he is connected with the government. Perhaps you were after him yourself. I didn't use to trust you any too much. But now I know he never bothered his head about you, and you always seemed to have a grudge against him someway.

(Pause. They look at each other in a puzzled way.)

MRS. X: Come and see us this evening, Amelia, and show us that you're not put out with us—not put out with me at any rate. I don't know, but I think it would be uncomfortable to have you for an enemy. Perhaps it's because I stood in your way (more slowly) or—I really—don't know why—in particular.

(Pause. MISS Y stares at MRS. X curiously.)

MRS. X: (*thoughtfully*) Our acquaintance has been so queer. When I saw you for the first time I was afraid of you, so afraid that I didn't dare let you out of my sight; no matter when or where, I always found myself near you—I didn't dare have you for an enemy, so I became your friend. But there was always discord when you came to our house, because I saw that my husband couldn't endure you, and the whole thing seemed as awry to me as an ill-fitting gown—and I did all I could to make him friendly toward you, but with no success until you became engaged. Then came a violent friendship between you, so that it looked like all at once as though you both dared show your real feelings only when you were secure—and then—how was it later? I didn't get jealous—strange to say! And I remember at the christening, when you acted as godmother, I made him kiss you—he did so, and you became so confused—as it were; until—now! (*Rises suddenly.*) Why are you silent? You haven't said a word this whole time, but you have let me go on talking! You have sat there, and your eyes have reeled out of me all these thoughts which lay like raw silk in its cocoon—thoughts—suspicious thoughts, perhaps. Let me see—why did you break your engagement? Why do you never come to our house anymore? Why won't you come to see us tonight?

(MISS Y appears as if about to speak.)

MRS. X: Hush, you needn't speak—I understand it all! It was because—and because—and because! Yes, yes! Now all the accounts balance. That's it. Fie, I won't sit at the same table with you. (*Moves her things to another table.*) That's the reason I had to embroider tulips—which I hate—on his slippers, because you are fond of tulips; that's why (throws slippers on the floor) we go to Lake Malarn in the summer, because you don't like salt water; that's why my boy is named Eskil—because it's your father's name; that's why I wear your colors, read your authors, eat your favorite dishes, drink your drinks—chocolate, for instance; that why—oh—my god—it's terrible, when I think about it, it's terrible. Everything, everything came from you to me, even your passions. Your soul crept into mine, like a worm into an apple, ate and ate, bored and bored, until nothing was left but the rind and a little black dust within. I wanted to get away from you, but I couldn't; you lay like a snake and charmed me with your black eyes; I felt that when I lifted my wings they only dragged me down; I lay in the water with bound feet and the stronger I strove to keep up the deeper I worked myself down, until I sank to the bottom, where you lay like a giant crab to clutch me in your claws—and there I am lying now.

I hate you, hate you, hate you! And you only sit there silent—silent and indifferent; indifferent whether it's new moon or waning moon, Christmas or New Year's, whether others are happy or unhappy; without power to hate or to love; as quiet as a story by a rat hole—you couldn't scent your prey and capture it, but you could lie in wait for it! You sit here in your corner of the café—did you know it's called "The Rat Trap" for you?—and read the papers to see if misfortune hasn't befallen someone, to see if someone hasn't been given notice at the theatre, perhaps; you sit here and calculate about your next victim and reckon on your changes or recompense like a pilot in a shipwreck. Poor Amelia, I pity you, nevertheless, because I know you are unhappy, unhappy like one who has been wounded, and angry because you are wounded. I can't be angry with you no matter how much I want to be—because you come out the weaker one. Yes, all that with Bob doesn't trouble me. What is that to me, after all? And what difference does it make whether I learned to drink chocolate from you or someone else? (*Sips a spoonful from her cup*) Besides, chocolate is very healthful. And if you taught me how to dress—tant mieux!—that has only made me more attractive to my husband; so you lost and I won there. Well, judging by certain signs, I believe you have already lost him; and you certainly intended that I should leave him—do as you did with your fiancé and regret; but, you see, I don't do that—we musn't be too exacting. And why should I take only what no one else wants?

Perhaps, take it all in all, I am at this moment the stronger one. You received nothing from me, but you gave me much. And now I seem like a thief since you have awakened and find I possess what is your loss. How could it be otherwise when everything is worthless and sterile in your hands? You can never keep a man's love with your tulips and your passions—but I can keep it. You can't learn how to live from your authors, as I have learned. You have no little Eskil to cherish, even if your father's name was Eskil. And why are you always silent, silent, silent? I thought that was strength, but perhaps it is because you have nothing to say! Because you never think about anything! (*Rises and picks up slippers.*) Now I'm going home—and take the tulips with me—your tulips! You are unable to learn from another; you can't bend—therefore, you broke like a dry stalk. But I won't break! Thank you, Amelia, for all your good lessons. Thanks for teaching my husband how to love. Now I'm going home to love him. (*Goes.*)

—*August Strindberg (1849–1912)*

Exercise 3.5 What is the antecedent action of "The Stronger"?

Exercise 3.6 After listing some facts about either Mrs. X or Miss Y, write a description of one of them.

Exercise 3.7 In one paragraph, describe how the tone of Mrs. X changes from the beginning of the play to the end. How did you recognize this?

Exercise 3.8 Identify the literary techniques that Strindberg has employed in his one-act play.

Analyzing a Dramatic Work

Playwrights put great meaning in the simplest of lines—time and space constraints ensure that each word is used for a reason. When judging a play as a text, you can use similar analytical approaches to those of poetry or prose, focusing on a chronological understanding of the plot, literary techniques, and the theme or themes that emerge from the play.

- Analyze characters' particular diction or syntax—what does this tell you about them?
- How does time seem to pass? In a short story or novel, time can pass by the narrator simply saying so. If there is no narrator, or chorus, in a play to explain the passing of time, how do dialogue or scene changes express time? How, in general, is the continuity of time achieved?
- How does the setting affect the overall meaning of the play? How does it contribute to the characters' actions? What mood does the setting create? How is this reflected in the overall meaning of the play?
- What themes can you find? How did you identify them—through use of metaphor, irony, or through a series of similar events and outcomes? What kind of effect do these themes have on your understanding of the play?

Post-Assessment

Circle the letter of the correct answer for each statement.

I. The most important difference between plays and other literary forms is that
(A) plays are an individual experience.
(B) plays are a group experience
(C) plays cannot use metaphor and imagery
(D) plays are not considered literature
(E) plays are seen and heard as well as read

2. Which of the following is NOT a convention of drama?
(A) Characterization is through speech and action.
(B) Tone is part of meaning.
(C) The playwright is outside the action.
(D) Characters' thoughts may not be suggested.
(E) Mood may be suggested by lighting.

3. According to the Greek philosopher Aristotle, literature is
(A) a lie, thus sinful
(B) an imitation of reality
(C) a fruitless waste of energy
(D) a mere diversion for the wealthy
(E) an escape into fantasy

4. Which of the following is not part of tragedy?
(A) antecedent action
(B) suspense
(C) narration
(D) reversal
(E) catastrophe

5. Which term best matches the following explanations?

_____ Explains events that occur prior to the play's beginning

_____ The emotional tension that sustains interest

_____ Hints about the outcome

_____ Point at which catastrophe becomes inevitable

_____ The unraveling or untangling of the plot action

    (A) suspense
    (B) dénouement
    (C) climax
    (D) foreshadowing
    (E) antecedent action

PART TWO

Approaches to Literary Analysis

UNIT FOUR

Contextual Analysis

Quite often, an understanding of literature is enhanced by looking outside of the text in order to arrive at a more accurate perspective of the content within. When we look outside of the work in order to find meaning, it is known as placing the work in context. Put simply, **contextual analysis** situates the text in the time and place it was created by acknowledging the author's linguistic, social, and historical environment.

In the view of contextual analysis, comprehending language—including the connotation and syntax of the words in the work's era—is essential to literary understanding. Allusions and the influences of literary movements around the author's time also give clues to the text's milieu. Furthermore, historical knowledge is especially helpful: the author's biography, as well as the history of the larger society from which the writing arose. These combined concerns help students, teachers, and scholars arrive at a fuller understanding of the text.

The reader also brings to literature his or her own context—the lens of personal experience. To understand how a work may be viewed and interpreted subjectively, we begin our study of context with reader response analysis.

Objectives

AFTER COMPLETING THIS UNIT, YOU WILL BE ABLE TO:

1. Identify the main elements of Reader Response;

2. Understand the importance of language—linguistic connotation, syntax, and genre characteristics—in analyzing a work of literature;

3. Assess the socio-historical perspective of examining literature, which includes an author's biographical information and the text's historical context;

4. Have an understanding of different ways to execute a contextual analysis.

5. Write a contextual analysis of a literary selection.

Lesson One: **The Reader's Context**

The first context in which we can place a work of literature is our-selves; by examining our own subjective responses to a text, we create meaning in the literature we read. It is, in part, our impressions of and reactions to a work of art, shaped by our personal experiences and culture, that create meaning within a text. The form of criticism that focuses on the reader's personal reaction to a text is known as **reader response**

Reader response is a theory of criticism first introduced in the 1960s and 1970s. C. S. Lewis popularized this analysis approach in his book *An Experiment In Criticism*, which looks at how individual readers select, respond, and derive meaning from literature. The idea behind this theory is that there is no single way readers are supposed to respond to a text. Instead, reader response theory presupposes that each reader has his or her individual way of reacting to literature based on personal experience or culture, regardless of the response intended by the author.

These individual responses often have commonalities created by readers' shared contexts. For example, the way in which women respond to a text may be similar, thus creating a group response to a given piece of writing. These responses—whether grouped or isolated—are what help create meaning in a text.

An example of this can be seen in one student's reaction to the text *To Kill A Mockingbird*. This student was asked to comment on the theme of gender presented in the novel—in particular, what issues of gender roles are faced by the character of Scout.

> Jem's attitude towards Scout is starting to get ridiculous. In one example from chapter four, Jem pushes Scout in the tire and it rolls out of control, making Scout fall out and the tire roll inside the Radley gate:
>
> "Jem looked at me furiously, could not decline, ran down the sidewalk, treaded water at the gate, then dashed in and retrieved the tire."
>
> "See there?" Jem was scowling triumphantly. "Nothin' to it. I swear, Scout, sometimes you act so much like a girl it's mortifyin'."
>
> Every time Scout doesn't want to do something, Jem plays the gender card. "Quit acting like a girl!" he always says. It's so annoying! Being a kid and hanging out with the guys, I used to get the same exact thing. When I was little and I acted like a boy, the boys were

the first to point out that I didn't belong and was supposed to act more like a girl. But it's not like girls didn't react, too. My friends who were girls liked to play with dolls, not outside where there was mud and bugs. When I stepped out of the female norm, I was considered a tomboy, a name which implies that, by playing outdoors and not with dolls, I had transformed genders.

I believe that throughout their lives, both females and males experience this with their own gender and the opposite gender. Both males and females are asked not to overstep their gender boundaries because it causes anxieties from their counterparts.

Here, the student informally responds to a sociological aspect of the novel, while using her personal understanding, as well as the text, as a reference. This student's childhood experiences may be similar to those of other female readers, which will in turn contribute to developing a shared meaning within a group. It is important to remember that reader response theory relies on the reader's own life experiences for literary understanding, but the emphasis of the analysis must remain on the text to reach understanding.

Conflicting viewpoints are sometimes expressed as to whether the meaning of a work can depend solely upon the individual's response to a text. Some scholars and theorists believe that by using certain techniques and devices, an author is able to produce a controlled response in readers. Other academics believe that while the text employs these methods in order to produce a response, achieving the same reaction in all readers is improbable.

Exercise 4.1 Read "The Snake" (page 291) and write a response about why you think Dr. Phillips enjoys working alone and what that says about his character. Cite specific examples from the text that support your answer. Next, explain how this compares to the character of the woman. Are these two characters complimentary or contradictory? Explain your answers using specific examples from the text, but rely on your personal response to the piece.

Lesson Two: **Language as Context**

Reader response analysis focuses on the reader's frame of reference; however, traditional contextual analysis relies on knowledge of the author and his or her era. Among the aspects of contextual analysis is language; an author's diction often reveals much about the text itself as a work from a particular time and place. Elements such as linguistic connotation, allusion, syntax, and genre characteristics can also aid in placing a work in its milieu, or the world of the story, thereby better understanding it.

Linguistic Connotation

Linguistic connotation, or the study of a word's meaning during the time in which it was written, is a distinct tool of criticism that requires both the desire to acquire a deeper meaning of texts and the ability to research the history of a word's meaning. While it is usually not too difficult to determine the denotation, the definition of a word based upon dictionaries and other documents available from the period of interest, determining a word's connotation is often challenging.

If you are unfamiliar with a word's connotation from the perspective of the time it was written, the meaning of a line may be misinterpreted and the intent of the author misunderstood. For example, in Shakespeare's tragedy *Hamlet*, Prince Hamlet, frustrated with his mother's hasty remarriage after the death of his father, takes out his bitterness upon Ophelia. Seeing his mother's actions as indicative of all women, Prince Hamlet tells Ophelia in Act III, Scene I,

"Get thee to a nunnery. Why wouldst thou be a breeder of sinners?"

Some sources have suggested that the term "nunnery" means that Hamlet is suggesting that Ophelia remove herself from temptation by placing herself in religious confinement. By entering a convent, she would not turn into a sinner, which is what Prince Hamlet feels both he and his mother have become. Though the imagery of a "nunnery" as a convent is an effective way to explain Hamlet's growing misogyny, it fails to impart the viciousness that has begun to cloud his thoughts. Likewise, the word "nunnery" defined as a convent may not explain Ophelia's obvious revulsion at such a suggestion.

If you look at the slang of Shakespeare's day, you will discover that, while the denotation of "nunnery" did mean convent, the common slang connotation of a "nunnery" during Elizabethan times was that of a brothel. To read the term "nunnery" as a suggestion that Ophelia go to a brothel dramatically changes the imagery and significance of the lines.

This connotation is not only indicative of Hamlet's state of mind but also shares a direct connection to Hamlet's earlier comment: that Polonius, Ophelia's father, is a fishmonger. In Elizabethan slang, a fishmonger is not a seller of fish but of women. The connotations of these two terms—nunnery and fishmonger—in the period in which they were written reveal that Hamlet believes his mother's sin to be a sexual one: She married without a suitable period of mourning, and she married her brother-in-law, a union Hamlet views as incestuous. By discovering the connotations of words within a text at the time in which they were written, readers are able to arrive at a deeper understanding of the literature's intended meaning.

Exercise 4.2 Read the following poem.

SPRING

When daisies pied and violets blue
And lady-smocks all silver-white,
And cuckoo-buds of yellow hue
do paint the meadows with delight,
The cuckoo then, on every tree,
Mocks married men; for thus sings he
"Cuckoo!"
Cuckoo, cuckoo!" O word of fear,
Unpleasing to a married ear!
When shepherds pipe on oaten straws,
And merry larks are ploughmen's clocks,
When turtles tread, and rooks, and daws,
And maidens bleach their summer smocks,
The cuckoo then, on every tree,
Mocks married men; for thus sings he,
"Cuckoo!
Cuckoo, cuckoo!" O word of fear,
Unpleasing to a married ear!

—*William Shakespeare (1564–1616)*

"Cuckoo" is the origin for the word "cuckold," which dates from the thirteenth century. It is a term for a man with an unfaithful wife. Cuckoo birds are known for laying their eggs in other birds' nests. The poem ends each stanza by stating that the cuckoo is "unpleasing to the married ear."

As one interested in linguistic connotation, answer the following questions:

1. What does knowing the connection between "cuckoo" and "cuckold" reveal about the poem?
2. How does reading the poem without an understanding of this linguistic connotation change its meaning?

Exercise 4.3 In the following selection, look at the bracketed words and write down the connotations you associate with them. Then, use a dictionary to discover the etymology and connotation of the word in the time and place in which it was first used by the poet. Make sure to use dictionaries available online and in print in order to find the best possible choice. Write down which connotation fits the poem best, based on the time period in which it was written. Does this change the meaning of a line or the entire poem?

> The [weird sisters], hand in hand,
> Posters of the sea and land,
> Thus do go about, about:
> Thrice to thine and thrice to mine
> And thrice again, to make up nine.
> Peace! the charm's wound up.
>
> —*William Shakespeare (1564–1616), Macbeth, Act I, Scene III*

Syntax

The way in which words are arranged in a phrase or sentence refers to a text's syntax. Scholars believe syntax—the grammatical rules based on the language in which a work is written—is what writers use to create different rhetorical effects. Syntax can vary greatly by author, time period, language, and location; therefore, it may reveal important information about the work itself.

One of the best examples of analyzing syntax can be seen through the examination of a sonnet. Throughout history, the structure of a sonnet has evolved; there are Italian, Shakespearean, and modern versions of this type of poem, and each has a specific syntactical structure. By identifying the type of sonnet and the syntactical structure used by the author, a reader can gain knowledge of the meaning of the poem in the time and place in which it was written.

These fourteen-line poems have different rhyme schemes, depending on which type of sonnet is being written. A Shakespearean or English sonnet's lines rhyme in an a-b-a-b-c-d-c-d-e-f-e-f-g-g structure, where each letter represents a line and matching letters represent lines ending in a rhyme. However, there are different styles; the Italian sonnet, for instance, is written a-b-b-a-a-b-b-a-c-d-e-c-d-e. As you can see, the place and the time a piece was written can dictate its form.

Exercise 4.4 Based on the rhyme scheme, which sonnet version best describes the following poem?

Sonnet 130

My mistress' eyes are nothing like the sun;
Coral is far more red than her lips' red;
If snow be white, why then her breasts are dun;
If hairs be wires, black wires grow on her head.
I have seen roses damask'd, red and white,
But no such roses see I in her cheeks;
And in some perfumes is there more delight
Than in the breath that from my mistress reeks.
I love to hear her speak, yet well I know
That music hath a far more pleasing sound;
I grant I never saw a goddess go;
My mistress, when she walks, treads on the ground:
And yet, by heaven, I think my love as rare
As any she belied with false compare.

Exercise 4.5 Use your knowledge of linguistic connotation and syntax to analyze and compare the following poems. Copy any words that are unfamiliar and research their meanings. What does this tell you about the time and place these poems were written?

Barbara Allan

It was in and about the Martinmas time,
When the green leaves were a-falling,
That Sir John Graeme in the west country
Fell in love with Barbara Allan.

He send to his man down through the town,
To the place where she was dwelling,
"O haste and come to my master dear,
Gin ye be Barbara Allan.

O hooly, hooly rose she up,
To the place where he was lying,
And when she drew the curtain by—
"Young man, I think you're dying."

O it's I'm sick, and very, very sick,
And tis a' for Barbara Allan."
"O the better for me ye's never be,
Tho' your heart's blood were a-spilling.

"O dinna ye mind, young man," said she,
"When ye as in the tavern a-drinking,
That ye made the health gae round and round,
and slighted Barbara Allan."

He turned his face unto the wall,
and death was with him dealing:
"Adieu, adieu, my dear friends all,
And be kind to Barbara Allan."

And slowly, slowly raise she up,
And slowly, slowly left him;
And sighing, said she cou'd not stay,
Since death of life had reft him.

She had not gane a mile but twa,
When she heard the dead-bell ringing,
When she heard a dead-bell geid,
It cry'd, Woe to Barabara Allan.

"O mother, mother, make my bed,
O make it soft and narrow,
Since my love died for me today,
I'll die for him tomorrow."

—*Anonymous*

BARBARA ALLEN

In Scarlet Town, where I was born,
There was a fair maid dwelling,
Made every youth cry "Well away!"
Her name was Barbara Allen.

All in the merry month of May,
When green buds they are swelling,
Young Jimmy Green on his death bed lay
For the love of Barbara Allen.

He sent his man unto her there,
To the town where she was dwelling;
"O you must come to my master dear,
If your name be Barbara Allen.

"For death is printed on his face
And o'er his heart is stealing;
O haste away to comfort him,
O lovely Barbara Allen!"

"If death is printed on his face
And o'er his heart is stealing,

Yet little better shall he be
For the love of Barbara Allen."

So, slowly, slowly, she came up,
And slowly she came nigh him;
And all she said when there she came,
"Young man, I think you're dying."

He turned his face unto her straight,
With deadly sorrow sighing:
"O lovely maid, come pity me!
I'm on my death bed lying."

"If on your death bed you do lie,
What need the tale you're telling?
I canno keep you from your death:
Farewell, " said Barbara Allen.

He turned his face unto the wall,
And deadly pains he fell in:
"Adieu, adieu to all,
Adieu to Barbara Allen."

She turned herself around about
And spied the corpse a-coming:
"Lay down, lay down the corpse, " said she,
"That I may look upon him."

With scornful eyes she did look down,
Her cheeks with laughter swelling;
While all her friends cried out amen [for amain],
"Unworthy Barbara Allen!"

When he was dead and laid in grave,
Her heart was struck with sorrow:
"O mother, mother, make my bed,
For I shall die to-morrow.

Hard-hearted creature him to slight
He who loved me so dearly!
O had I been more kind to him,
When he was alive and near me!"

On her death bed as she did lay,
She begged to be buried by him,
And sorely repented of that day
That she e'er did deny him.

"Farewell, ye virgins all, " she said,
"And shun the fault I've fell in;
Henceforward take warning by the fall
of cruel Barbara Allen."

*One was buried in the high churchyard,
The other in the choir;
On one there grew a rose bush,
On the other grew a brier.

*They grew and they grew to the high steeple top,
Till they could grow no higher;
And there they locked in a true-lover's knot,
For true lovers to admire.

—*Anonymous*

*Floating stanzas—they "float" from one version to another.

Allusion

Allusion is of importance to contextual analysis because it reveals more of the meaning and the intent of an author's poem or story. By understanding a work's allusions, you have a better chance of capturing the author's complete intent, which may be associated with the literary movements at the time of the writing. This brief excerpt from "The Raven" illustrates this concept in contextual analysis.

> Open here I flung the shutter, when, with many a flirt and flutter,
> In there stepped a stately Raven of the saintly days of yore.
> Not the least obeisance made he; not a minute stopped or stayed he,
> But, with mien of lord or lady, perched above my chamber door—
> Perched upon a bust of Pallas just above my chamber door—
>   Perched, and sat, and nothing more.
>
> Then the ebony bird beguiling my sad fancy into smiling,
> By the grave and stern decorum of the countenance it wore,
> "Though thy crest be shorn and shaven, thou," I said, "art sure no craven,
> Ghastly grim and ancient Raven wandering from the Nightly shore—
> Tell me what thy lordly name is on the Night's Plutonian shore!"
>   Quoth the Raven, "Nevermore."

—*from "The Raven" by Edgar Allan Poe (1809–1849)*

Allusions throughout "The Raven" are useful in creating the ambience that Poe intended for the poem. In the fifth line of the excerpt above, he includes the image of a raven perching on "the bust of Pallas." Pallas refers to Pallas Athena, the Greek goddess of wisdom. With this allusion, we view the speaker as a wise man, but the juxtaposition of the raven makes us wonder if the raven knows things the speaker does not. Poe's imagery darkens when, in the fifth line of the second stanza, he writes that the raven has come from "the Night's Plutonian shore." Here, the allusion is to Pluto, the Roman god of the underworld, implying that the raven is some sort of messenger from the afterlife. Through the use of allusion, Poe has created in "The Raven" a mysterious and eerie atmosphere, which is associated with romanticism.

Literary Movements

Beyond syntax, linguistic connotation, and allusion, subject and theme provide additional clues to a literary work's context. For example, a poem or story written in the romantic era may focus on nature, an idealized past, emotion, the unnatural, and, frequently, the horrific. However, the realist movement that followed did not share the concerns of romanticism, nor its subject matter. You may wish to review "Literary Movements" (page 74) when you consider the following poems.

Exercise 4.6 Read the following poems.

THE WORLD IS TOO MUCH WITH US

The world is too much with us, late and soon,
Getting and spending, we lay waste our powers;
Little we see in nature that is ours;
We have given our hearts away, a sordid boon!
This sea that bares her bosom to the moon
The winds that will be howling at all hours
And are up-gathered now like sleeping flowers;
For this, for everything, we are out of tune;
It moves us not.—Great God! I'd rather be
A Pagan suckled in a creed outworn;
So might I, standing on this pleasant lea,
Have glimpses that would make me less forlorn;
Have sight of Proteus rising from the sea;
Or hear old Triton blow his wreathed horn

—*William Wordsworth (1770–1850)*

IN A STATION OF THE METRO

The apparition of these faces in the crowd;
petals on a wet, black bough.

—*Ezra Pound (1885–1972)*

1. What is each poem's syntax in relation to its form?

2. What tone is the author presenting in each poem? What images are used to convey the overall feeling?

3. What literary movement is associated with each poem's theme?

4. What allusions does "The World Is Too Much With Us" employ, and how do they create meaning within the poem?

5. How does the syntax of "In a Station of the Metro" contribute to the poem's imagery?

Lesson Three: **Historical Analysis**

"There is no private life which is not determined by a wider public life."

—George Eliot (1819–1880)

Though deceptively simple in name, historical analysis includes more than the mere knowledge of events that occurred at or around the date of a work's creation. Historical analysis is also concerned with the intellectual and social environment out of which literature is produced; in addition to historical events, you must also consider social, political, economic, and religious contexts at the time a work was written. This type of analysis adheres to the belief that authors do not create a work in an intellectual and social vacuum; consequently, even those who write in isolation must be influenced by the world in which they live.

Within the process of historical analysis, there are two distinct areas of analysis: the immediate environment, or the author's biography; and the larger environment, or the events and culture at the time of the writing. Studying these different areas in tandem can contribute considerably to the understanding of literature.

Biographical Context

Authors' biographies are often quite helpful in attempting to fully understand a work because authors usually write about what they know. Furthermore, a familiarity with other writings by the same author can offer insight to a reader—their biographical information includes their life's work. For example, the knowledge that John Milton was blind is invaluable to understanding his poetry, as is the knowledge that he was the Latin secretary for Oliver Cromwell, the leader of the English Puritan revolution. Without this knowledge, a reader may overlook allusions and metaphors in Milton's work that would otherwise seem obvious.

While some critics object to what they view as over-dependence upon matters extraneous to the literature itself, it is hard to dispute the argument that some familiarity with an author's life and other writing can aid in the understanding of a particular piece of literature.

Exercise 4.7 Read the following poem and answer the questions that follow.

My cocoon tightens, colors tease,
I 'm feeling for the air;
A dim capacity for wings
Degrades the dress I wear.

A power of butterfly must be
The aptitude to fly,
Meadows of majesty concedes
And easy sweeps of sky.

So I must baffle at the hint
And cipher at the sign,
And make much blunder, if at last
I take the clew divine.

—*Emily Dickinson (1830-1886)*

1. What do you think the poem says about the religious background of the author?
2. Is this poem ironic based on the author's religious background?

The Larger Environment

Many scholars believe the socio-historical circumstances of a period have a direct connection to the writers and the works they create. For example, Charles Dickens's novel, *Bleak House*, concerns the fates of several families entangled in a court case that progresses with agonizing slowness through Chancery Court in London; your familiarity with the corruption and long delays typical of the legal system in mid-nineteenth-century England can greatly enhance your understanding of the book and the issues that Dickens is addressing. Likewise, your knowledge of the condition in which books like Dickens's were produced (*Bleak House* first appeared in eighteen monthly installments) can help you understand some of the ways in which Dickens's characters are presented, and his close relationship with his readers, who waited eagerly for each installment.

Remember, no one is able to produce any type of art in an intellectual or social void; all people, including writers, are influenced by the time in which they live. One might reflect upon the very recent changes in attitude toward such issues as national security, marriage, and the educational system. It is difficult to see how any contemporary writer could write about those subjects and not be influenced by current attitudes and recent events.

Historical events and societal conditions are particularly important for such works as "The Chimney Sweeper" (page 10), by William Blake, which refers to the conditions of child labor, and Nathaniel Hawthorne's "Young Goodman Brown" (page 249), which references the responsibilities of religious officials. Sometimes the historical influence is subtler, but it can offer insight nonetheless.

Exercise 4.8 Read the two poems below and research their authors' biographies. Write a paragraph explaining why one of the poems may be better understood through historical and biographical information than the other.

THE MAN HE KILLED

Had he and I but met
By some old ancient inn,
We should have sat us down to wet
Right many a nipperkin!*

But ranged as infantry,
And staring face to face,
I shot at him as he at me,
And killed him in his place.

I shot him dead because—
Because he was my foe,
Just so; my foe of course he was;
That's clear enough; although

He thought he'd list, perhaps,
Off-hand-like—just as I—
Was out of work—had sold his traps—
No other reason why.

Yes; quaint and curious war is!
You shoot a fellow down
You'd treat, if met where any bar is,
Or help to half-a-crown.

—*Thomas Hardy (1840-1928)*

*half-pint cup

Dulce et Decorum est

Bent double, like old beggars under sacks,
Knock-kneed, coughing like hags, we cursed through sludge,
Till on the haunting flares we turned our backs
And towards our distant rest began to trudge.
Men marched asleep. Many had lost their boots
But limped on, blood-shod. All went lame, all blind;
Drunk with fatigue; deaf even to the hoots
Of gas-shells dropping softly behind.

Gas! GAS! Quick boys!—An ecstasy of fumbling,
fitting the clumsy helmets just in time,
But someone still was yelling out and stumbling
And flound'ring like a man in fire or lime…
Dim through the misty panes and thick green light,
As under a green sea, I saw him drowning.
In all my dreams, before my helpless sight,
He plunges at me, guttering, choking, drowning.

If in some smothering dreams you too could pace
Behind the wagon that we flung him in,
And watch the white eyes writhing in his face,
His hanging face, like a devil's sick of sin;
If you could hear, at every jolt, the blood
come gargling from the froth-corrupted lungs,
Obscene as cancer, bitter as the cud
Of vile, incurable sores on innocent tongues,—
My friend, you would not tell with such high zest
To children ardent for some desperate glory,
The old Lie: Dulce et decorum est
Pro patria mori.*

—*Wilfred Owen (1895-1918)*

*Latin, from the Roman poet Horace, meaning, "It is sweet and fitting to die for one's country."

Lesson Four: **Writing the Contextual Analysis**

C ontextual analysis looks outside of the text in order to find meaning in a literary work. Its goal is to establish the milieu of a work through study of language, the author's biography, and socio-historical aspects at the time of its writing. When writing a contextual analysis, each of the following questions is important:

- Does the work contain words with significant linguistic connotations?

- What biographical information about the author might change the meaning of the text for you?

- What knowledge of events, societal conditions, or political situations at the time might help to better understand the text?

- What literary movement characterizes the work?

Exercise 4.9 Write a contextual analysis of "To Build a Fire" (page 267). For help with planning and writing an analysis, see Unit Nine, "Writing an Analysis" (page 215).

Post-Assessment:

Circle the letter of the correct answer of each question.

I. Serious literature achieves its status
   (A) through subtlety of expression
   (B) by presenting ideas of moral or emotional significance
   (C) by its association with a famous author
   (D) through uplifting characters
   (E) by being very popular

2. Reader response analysis requires
   (A) biographical information and an interest in literature
   (B) knowledge of historical events to derive meaning
   (C) the meaning of the words beyond their dictionary definitions
   (D) a reader looking at his or her individual response in order to create meaning and understanding of a literary work
   (E) citations referring to outside works

3. Linguistic connotation is concerned primarily with
   (A) today's meanings of the words in a story
   (B) the meanings of the words in a selection at the time they were written
   (C) how emotional the words are in a selection
   (D) why certain words were chosen for a story
   (E) the denotation of the words in a story

4. Socio-historical analysis is executed through examining a combination of
   (A) other works of the author and scholars' criticism
   (B) biographical information about the author and the history of the time in which the work was written
   (C) events in the time the work was written and literary criticism
   (D) one's perspective on the text and the biographical information on the author
   (E) the effect of the work at the time of its publication

5. A work's theme can be contextualized by looking its

(A) technical elements

(B) author's preferences

(C) literary movement

(D) school of thought

(E) literary devices

UNIT FIVE

Formalist Analysis

Formalists believe that if a work of literature is worthwhile at all, it should be able to stand on its own merit. This means that readers should not have to be familiar with an author's previous work, the history or era in which the literature was written, or the biographical profile of the author. Instead, readers should be able to understand, to analyze, and to appreciate a work based on the "whole" that its separate literary elements create. **Formalism**, then, requires that analyzing and, thus, creating a deep understanding of a text, comes through one's own critical abilities, based not on personal experience, but developed through comprehension of literary elements and devices.

The formalist approach also asks readers to look closely at a text for complexities of irony, tension, and ambiguity and accepts that a work may contain multiple, even conflicting meanings. By examining a text this way—as an organic whole—readers are able to more fully understand and appreciate a work of literature, according to formalists.

Objectives

AFTER COMPLETING THIS UNIT, YOU WILL BE ABLE TO:

1. Describe the formalist approach to literary interpretation;

2. Identify the aspects of literary analysis irrelevant to the formalist;

3. Better recognize literary elements and devices in a work;

4. Undertake a close reading and annotation of a work;

5. Write a formalist analysis of a literary selection.

Lesson One: **The New Critics**

After World War I, a group of scholars gathered at Vanderbilt University in Nashville, Tennessee, where John Crowe Ransom (1888–1974) was a professor of English. Ransom, along with three of his students—Alan Tate, Robert Penn Warren, and Cleanth Brooks—developed a new philosophy of literary analysis that became known as New Criticism. During the 1930s and 1940s, the ranks of the New Critics, as they became known, grew. By 1941, Ransom had written *The New Criticism*, and the literary theory that we call formalism was launched.

The New Critics, reacting to what they viewed as the excesses of historical analysis, took the position that the truly valuable information of literature can be derived only from within the text itself. Everything else is peripheral, extraneous, and distracting, according to their theory. No matter how interesting authors' lives may be or how intriguing the social significance of their works, these details are irrelevant to the formalists, who are concerned solely with the work itself.

For example, a reader who concentrates upon Virginia Woolf's depression and her eventual suicide, and sees a distinct connection to Clarissa Dalloway's behavior in Woolf's novel *Mrs. Dalloway*, may never fully understand the significance of Clarissa as a character. Likewise, the fact that Kurt Vonnegut, Jr., author of *Slaughterhouse-Five*, was a prisoner of war in Dresden, Germany, when the Allies firebombed it—as was the novel's protagonist, Billy Pilgrim—is interesting information; however, the biographical facts about the authors and their similarities to the protagonists in their literature are without importance to any formalist explication of their writing. It is formalism's contention that only through an examination of a work's form—the unified whole created by every large and small feature of the text—may one derive a deep understanding of the literature as a work of art.

Lesson Two: **The Text Itself**

In order to come to a formalist understanding of a work, you can first look at the text's overall structure: the unifying patterns which shape the work and give its parts a relevance to the whole. Thus, a reader of an epic poem should begin his or her analysis by comparing its structure to that of other epic poems; this comparison will lead to a discovery of how closely the poem conforms to its category. Formalists believe that discovering these similarities and differences will help the reader achieve a greater understanding of the text.

For example, traditional Japanese haiku has a predetermined structure of seventeen syllables in a three-line, 5-7-5 sequence (page 20). Examine the syllable counts of the poem below:

> In my medicine cabinet
> the winter fly
> has died of old age
>
> —*Jack Kerouac (1922–1969)*

This example demonstrates how a poet can make a statement by breaking the rules of a traditional genre of writing. By breaking the strict syllable count of the traditional haiku, Kerouac demonstrated his place as a writer of the Beat Generation—a group of writers who desired to create an American style of writing.

Syntax and Style

Because words are set down on the page in a particular way, the text's syntax (see page 26) forms a structure that has a meaning of its own. Often referred to as an author's style, this pattern of words is one of the most notable elements in a text. In fact, formalists assert that changing even one word or image in a poem, or one line in a text, would alter the meaning of the entire work. Formalists believe that literature has unity built into it that gives it appeal, and that this touches almost everyone who reads it—today as in the past, and undoubtedly into the future.

For many readers, Emily Dickinson's poems have just such an appeal because of her syntax and style, elements for which she is celebrated; no biographical or historical knowledge of Dickinson or her era is needed to appreciate her poetry. "Apparently with no surprise" stands on its own as literary work, with its comment upon the apparent contradiction between faith and beauty and an approving, indifferent Almighty.

> APPARENTLY WITH NO SURPRISE
>
> Apparently with no surprise
> To any happy flower,
> The frost beheads it at its play
> In accidental power.
>
> The blond assassin passes on,
> The sun proceeds unmoved

To measure off another day
For an approving God.

—*Emily Dickinson (1830–1886)*

Semantics and Figurative Language

Formalist analysis emphasizes knowledge of certain literary elements that comprise the work, assuming that each element contributes to the unity and meaning of a text. Actually, these elements are many of the same ones considered important in contextual analysis, but formalists concentrate on them more intensely. By way of review, the major language interests of formalist analysis follow (for a more in-depth review, see page 27).

Semantics, the study of word meanings in language or of communication processes themselves, belongs at the head of any list of formalist interests. Semantics, for instance, is concerned with topics like the ritual use of language, fallacious reasoning, and denotation and connotation. Although formalists are interested in each of these topics, they seem most interested in connotation.

Denotation is the dictionary definition of a word.

Connotation is the meaning of a word beyond its dictionary meaning. Formalism is not concerned with the historical connotations of words, only their present-day associations and the emotional responses they elicit. For example:

> **mother:** beyond a female who has borne a child—mother may suggest security, affection, home, selflessness, and love.

Imagery represents a sensory experience through language. Words or phrases that explain how something looks, feels, tastes, sounds, or smells, appeal to the senses, ultimately make a tangible connection to readers. For example:

> "…as the young man leaned over the cage the forked tongues, black on the ends and pink behind, twittered out and waved slowly up and down."
>
> ["The Snake"]

Metaphor is a direct comparison between things that are unlike. The technique is particularly useful for its power of suggestion. Metaphor can be used in one sentence to punctuate a point or throughout an entire piece, creating an overarching metaphor. For example:

Simple metaphor:	"The person is the rat."
	["The Snake"]
Overarching metaphor:	Charlotte Perkins Gilman's "The Yellow Wallpaper" creates an overarching metaphor in the wallpaper itself; the woman is the wallpaper, confined to one room and trapped in her life's repeating pattern.

A **simile** is a comparison using the words "like" or "as." Similes are much like metaphors in that they draw a comparison between two different objects or ideas. Unlike metaphors, similes allow the two entities to remain distinct instead of drawing a direct comparison; the two things share qualities, but they are not one and the same.

The simile below is from John Donne's poem, "A Valediction: Forbidding Mourning."

> Our souls are therefore, which are one,
> Though I must go, endure not yet
> A breach, but an expansion,
> Like gold to airy thinness beat.

Here, Donne is comparing the expansion of the lovers' souls with the expansion of gold when it is beaten into "airy thinness."

A **symbol** is anything in literature that means more than what it literally is. Often, the meaning of an abstract idea may be represented in a story or poem by some object. An example of symbolism can be seen in Nathaniel Hawthorne's "Young Goodman Brown" (page 249). In this short story, Hawthorne names Goodman Brown's wife Faith, which can be seen as a symbol of Brown's spirituality. When Brown cries, "My Faith is gone!" Hawthorne intends that statement to mean more than the loss of a wife.

Exercise 5.1 Identify the literary element used in each of the following lines:

1. "So twice five miles of fertile ground/ with walls and towers were girdled round"
2. "Then how should I begin/ To spit out the butt-ends of my days and ways"
3. "He watches from his mountain walls,/ And like a thunderbolt he falls."

4. "It was good for my heart:/ there my feelings were ash-gray,/
   the sky tin-gray,/ ash-gray the autumn."

Literary Devices

Beside elements such as connotation, imagery, and figurative language, we can better understand how tension, ambiguity, and multiple interpretations may arise by reviewing the roles that some common literary devices may play.

Irony is created when the anticipated outcome is the opposite of the expectation. Verbal irony is the contradiction of what is said and what is meant; situational irony is an event unfolding contrary to expectations; and dramatic irony is the awareness an audience knows something that a poem's speaker or play's character does not. For example, the excerpt below from "Barbara Allen" (page 123) provides a subtle irony through diction:

All in merry month of May
When green buds they are swelling
Young Jimmy Green on his death bed lay
For the love of Barbara Allen

This stanza is ironic because, while the world is green outside with life blooming in flowers and trees, a boy with the name of Green is lying inside, dying.

A **paradox** is a statement or series of events that seem to have contradictory elements, but contain a potential truth. For example, in Shakespeare's *Julius Caesar*, Caesar says:

Cowards die many times before their deaths;
The valiant never taste of death but once.

While it is, of course, impossible for anyone to die multiple times, cowards will re-experience that which they fear repeatedly because they are unable to confront it.

Tone represents a writer's or speaker's implied attitude toward the subject, audience, or self. An example is the following poem by Walt Whitman.

WHEN I HEARD THE LEARN'D ASTRONOMER

When I heard the learn'd astronomer,
When the proofs, the figures, were ranged in columns before me,
When I was shown the charts and diagrams, to add, divide, and measure them,
When I sitting heard the astronomer where he lectured with much applause in the lecture-room,
How soon unaccountable I became tired and sick,
Till rising and gliding out I wandered off by myself,
In the mystical moist night-air, and from time to time,
Looked up in perfect silence at the stars.

—*Walt Whitman (1819–1892)*

In Whitman's poem, the speaker's tone first expresses weariness for the analytical, scientific view of the heavens, then wonder for the universe experienced through the senses.

Lesson Three: **A Close Reading**

I n order to perform a formalist analysis, the reader must conduct a close reading of the text. A **close reading** of the work asks readers to analyze a work's meaning by isolating its parts to see how they create the whole; the reader must examine a piece of literature closely enough to discover its literary elements, and to recognize its ambiguities and conflicts.

Formalism also looks for multiple interpretations, sometimes conflicting, to find meaning in literature. For example, William Golding's *Lord of the Flies* may be read as (1) a story about the passage of a group of youngsters toward maturity and adulthood; (2) an examination of guilt and responsibility; (3) a commentary on the rights of the individual and the power of the mob; (4) a criticism of world power politics and the use of force as an instrument for the settlement of disputes; or (5) an analysis of philosophical and ideological concepts in conflict with one another. None of these interpretations are incorrect, as long as the close reading has allowed for textual evidence.

Similarly, Charlotte Brontë's *Jane Eyre* may be seen as a story of (1) a heroine in the midst of an unfair society or (2) a young person looking to find a deep and enduring love in an isolated world. Again, neither of these is more correct than the other. Their validity relies solely on the literary evidence found in the close reading.

The multiple meanings found in a text are a result of examining the individual effects of each element in the text; the formalist, then, looks for an overarching idea that will unify these elements. When performing a close reading for a formalist analysis, consider these three questions:

- What literary elements (semantics, imagery, irony, tone, etc.) are found in the work?
- Is contradiction or ambiguity created by these elements?
- What idea about the work holds these elements together?

Annotating a Work

Looking for specific literary elements and techniques in a text, such as simile, irony, and tone, will help you discover different levels of meaning, as well as any possible unification of the text's ambiguities and conflicts. The easiest way to ascertain all of the features employed is to **annotate** the text you are planning to analyze, which means reading through the text several times and looking for the literary elements found. Once you feel you are completely familiar with the work, make notes of what you find either alongside the text or on a separate sheet of paper.

APPARENTLY WITH NO SURPRISE

Apparently with no surprise	
To any happy flower,	2
The frost beheads it at its play	
In accidental power.	4
The blond assassin passes on,	
The sun proceeds unmoved	6
To measure off another day	
For an approving God.	8

—*Emily Dickinson (1830–1886)*

Example of Annotation:

- *Line 1: The word "Apparently" seems ambiguous, since it could be taken literally—it became evident, or conversationally—an offhand remark about something observed from hearsay (e.g., "Apparently, this is a big deal").*

- *Line 2 / 3: "happy flower" implies peace in nature through personification, while the imagery of beheading creates an ironic image of natural destruction.*

- *Line 3 / 4: The frost is playing, which creates an image of jovial work. However, the "accidental power" it possesses causes the "happy flower" (another jovial image) to die. Dickinson is showing a seesawing, happy/sad relationship between natural elements.*

- *Line 5: "The blond assassin" seems to be a metaphor for frost.*

- *Line 6: The sun is "unmoved," not physically—the sun continues to move—but emotionally. This personification of nature creates implied emotional ties between the other natural elements of the poem, but those emotional ties aren't strong enough to keep some elements from destroying others.*

- *Line 7 / 8: God uses the sun as a measuring tool, nothing more. And God approves of what the sun and frost have done to the flowers because a natural course has been taken. There is no emotion in nature—death is a part of life, with nothing sorry about it.*

With this annotation, a reader is able to formulate an overarching idea about the poem and cite evidence for that idea through the identification of literary elements and devices in the text.

Exercise 5.2 Choose a poem from the two selections below. Read the selection several times and, during your final reading, annotate it as you read. List two topics that might be developed into a formalist analysis.

LEAVES FELL

A gust roused the waves,
leaves blew into the water,
the waves were ash-gray,
the sky tin-gray,
ash-gray the autumn.

It was good for my heart:
there my feelings were ash-gray,
the sky tin-gray,
ash-gray the autumn.

The breath of wind brought cooler air,
the waves of mourning brought separation:
autumn and autumn
befriend each other.

*—Juhan Liiv (1864–1913), translated from Estonian by H.L. Hix
& Jüri Talvet*

146

Darkness

I had a dream, which was not all a dream,
The bright sun was extinguish'd, and the stars
Did wander darkling in the eternal space,
Rayless, and pathless, and the icy earth
Swung blind and blackening in the moonless air
Morn came – and went and came, and brought no day,
And men forgot their passions in the dread
Of this desolation; and all hearts
Were chill'd into a selfish prayer for light:
And they did live by watchfires – and the thrones,
The palaces of crowned kings – the huts,
The habitations of all things which dwell,
Were burnt for beacons; cities were consumed,
And men were gathered round their blazing homes
To look once more into each other's face
Happy were those who dwelt within the eye
Of the volcanos, and their mountain-torch:
A fearful hope was all the world contain'd;
Forests were set on fire – but hour by hour
They fell and faded – and the crackling trunks
Extinguish'd with a crash – and all was black.
The brows of men by the despairing light
Wore an unearthly aspect, as by fits
The flashes fell upon them; some lay down
And hid their eyes and wept; and some did rest
Their chins upon their clenched hands, and smiled;
And others hurried to and fro, and fed
Their funeral piles with fuel, and look'd up
With mad disquietude on the dull sky,
The pall of a past world; and then again
With curses cast them down upon the dust,
And gnash'd their teeth and howl'd: the wild birds shriek'd,
And, terrified, did flutter on the ground.
And flap their useless wings; the wildest brutes
Came tame and tremulous; and vipers crawl'd
And twined themselves among the multitude,
Hissing, but stingless – they were slain for food:
And War, which for a moment was no more,
Did glut himself again; – a meal was bought
With blood, and each sate sullenly apart
Gorging himself in gloom: no love was left;

All earth was but one thought – and that was death,
Immediate and inglorious; and the pang
Of famine fed upon all entrails – men
Died, and their bones were tombless as their flesh;
The meagre by the meagre were devour'd,
Even dogs assail'd their masters, all save one,
And he was faithful to a corpse, and kept
The birds and beasts and famish'd men at bay,
Till hunger clung them, or the dropping dead
Lured their lank jaws; himself sought out no food,
But with a piteous and perpetual moan
And a quick desolate cry, licking the hand
Which answered not with a caress – he died.
The crowd was famish'd by degrees; but two
Of an enormous city did survive,
And they were enemies: they met beside
The dying embers of an altar-place,
Where had been heap'd a mass of holy things
For an unholy usage; they raked up,
And shivering scraped with their cold skeleton hands
The feeble ashes, and their feeble breath
Blew for a little life, and made a flame
Which was a mockery; then they lifted up
Their eyes as it grew lighter, and beheld
Each other's aspects – saw, and shriek'd, and died –
Ev'n of their mutual hideousness they died,
Unknowing who he was upon whose brow
Famine had written Fiend. The world was void,
The populous and the powerful was a lump,
Seasonless, herbless, treeless, manless, lifeless,
A lump of death – a chaos of hard clay.
The rivers, lakes, and ocean stood still,
And nothing stirr'd within their silent depths;
Ships sailorless lay rotting on the sea,
And their masts fell down piecemeal; as they dropp'd
They slept on the abyss without a surge –
The waves were dead; the tides were in their grave,
The Moon their mistress had expired before;
The winds were wither'd in the stagnant air,
And the clouds perish'd; Darkness had no need
Of aid from them. She was the Universe!

—*Lord Byron (1788–1824)*

Lesson Four: **Writing the Formalist Analysis**

Formalists seek to understand how literary elements create a unified text. To perform a formalist analysis, readers need to consider how a text was constructed. As previously stated, information such as the author's biography or era is considered irrelevant to formalism. When writing a formalist analysis, each of the following elements is of importance:

- Semantics, including style, syntax, and connotation
- Figurative language, including similes, metaphors, and symbols
- Irony
- Tone

Exercise 5.3 Read "The Snake" (page 291), by John Steinbeck. Reread the work several times, until you are familiar with all of its literary elements. Begin to ask yourself questions about the story as you become more and more familiar with the major events. Concentrate on what happens and why. Think about the characters, the setting, and the language. Following are some questions that you might ask about Steinbeck's story:

1. How does the text portray Dr. Phillips's attitude toward the woman?
2. How does imagery draw a comparison between the snake and the woman?
3. How much time passed during the interaction between Dr. Phillips and the woman? How was that made apparent in the text?
4. What is the tone of the story?
5. What literary devices are most often used to reveal Dr. Phillips's attitude? The woman's? The snake's?

Exercise 5.4 Annotate "The Snake" in the margins of the text or on a separate sheet of paper. Look for literary elements and comment accordingly.

Exercise 5.5 Write a formalist analysis of "The Snake." For help with annotating, planning, and writing an analysis, see Unit Nine, "Writing an Analysis" (page 215).

Post-Assessment:

Circle the letter of the correct answer of each question.

1. The New Critics gathered together
(A) after World War II
(B) after the stock market crash of 1929
(C) after World War I
(D) after John F. Kennedy was elected president
(E) after William Golding won the Nobel Prize for literature

2. The New Critics took the view that the valuable information in literature may be derived only from
(A) the text
(B) the author
(C) the era
(D) psychological symbols
(E) linguistic authenticity

3. The New Critics developed an approach to literature that became known as
(A) symbolic analysis
(B) archetypal analysis
(C) structural analysis
(D) traditional analysis
(E) formalist analysis

4. Which of the following is a concern of formalists?
(A) The relation of a literary work to its era
(B) The relation of the meanings of words in the story to the story's imagery
(C) The use of allusion in literary works
(D) The comparison of the work to other works by the same author
(E) The relation of a literary work to the biography of the author

5. List five literary elements and techniques important to formalism:
(A)
(B)
(C)
(D)
(E)

6. The formalist critic looks for

(A) the anthropological significance of recurring words
(B) evidence that the work has, or will become, a classic
(C) the use of allusions in a literary work
(D) the unifying patterns that shape a work and give its parts a relevance to its whole
(E) all of the above

UNIT SIX

Psychological Analysis

The implications of psychology have long been recognized as important to writers, who have perceived in humans certain unconscious forces, drives, or needs that are significant motivators of behavior. Some of the world's most respected authors have created such penetrating portraits of mental functioning in their literature that their works have been cited as particularly significant in understanding human psychology. Among many others, Sophocles, Shakespeare, Dostoyevsky, Melville, and Hawthorne are studied for their insight into the human psyche through their literature.

Common examples of psychoanalytical readings include viewing a character's unconscious mind as the source of his or her motivations, analyzing characters' defense mechanisms, and even evaluating authors' mental and emotional traits through their writings.

Sigmund Freud is credited with defining the human psyche, thought to be the source of one's thought, behavior, and personality. After Freud and his colleagues probed the inner workings of the human mind and began publishing psychoanalytic discoveries, writers and literary critics began to view literature in strikingly different ways.

Objectives

AFTER COMPLETING THIS UNIT, YOU WILL BE ABLE TO:

1. Understand Freud's theory of the unconscious mind;

2. Describe Freud's concepts of the id, ego, and superego;

3. Identify defense mechanisms, anxieties, and core issues in literature;

4. View a work's literary elements through a psychological lens;

5. Explain the criticisms of Freud and the dangers of an overemphasis on psychology in literary analysis;

6. Write a psychological analysis of a literary selection.

Lesson One: **The Theories of Sigmund Freud**

Sigmund Freud (1856–1939) wrote that it was "not I, but the poets [who] discovered the unconscious." Freud was interested in both psychology and literature and, indeed, he often expressed his indebtedness to literature as the laboratory where one could observe psychological phenomena in operation.

Emphasizing individuals' conflicts, anxieties, and frustrations, psychoanalysis, as postulated by Freud, is primarily concerned with diagnosing, treating, and curing people's emotional problems; it is a therapeutic science rather than a purely experimental discipline. As a result, not all of Freud's theories are applicable to literary study, but the following assertions have been influential in altering the style of much analytical thinking about literature.

The Unconscious Mind

Freud's underlying presupposition is that most of the mental processes of human beings take place in the unconscious mind, a part of the mind wherein a person's psyche influences his or her actions in an unperceived manner. A great example of this can be seen in how we react to a smile. There have been numerous studies showing that, when a person sees an image of a smiling face, the brain fires endorphins, which creates a feeling of euphoria. Therefore, a feeling of happiness is unconsciously transmitted to the brain simply by seeing another person smile. This is an instance of the unconscious mind at work.

Freud asserts that even the most conscious processes quickly become latent, although they may later become conscious, or active. He grouped these processes into what he calls the "preconscious"; he asserted that they are differentiated from those in the "unconscious," which are brought to the conscious mind with the greatest of difficulty or never at all. Freud demonstrated in case studies that human actions are controlled by a psyche over which there exists only the most limited control. He likened the human mind to an iceberg: only the smallest portion of the whole iceberg is visible above the water's surface, as only the smallest portion of the human psyche is accessible to consciousness.

The Psychic Zones: Id, Ego, Superego

To better understand Freud's ideas, we will next look at the psychic zones. Freud asserts that the human mind contains three psychic zones, which control the mental functions that govern motivation.

Id

The **id** is submerged in the unconscious and its function is to fulfill what is called the **primordial life principle**—or, as Freud referred to it, the pleasure principle. Contained within the id are impulses such as aggression and desire, from which comes the individual's psychic energy. Freud describes the id as completely lacking in rational logic, since contrary impulses may exist simultaneously without canceling each other out.

According to Freud, the id knows no ethics or values; it knows no good or evil; it encompasses no morality. Since the id is amoral and lawless, it disregards any religious or legal ethics, social conventions, or other constraints. Concerned solely with instinctual self-indulgence, the id would drive an individual to any length for this pleasure—even to self-destruction, for self-preservation is not an id impulse.

Prior to Freud, these instincts toward excessive pleasure were attributed to outside, often supernatural, forces. In many ways, the old Puritan concept of the devil fits well into the id psychic zone. Small children, not yet imbued with the restraints of society, operate on pure id impulses. They are egocentric, selfish, and solely interested in their own enjoyment. Occasionally, one hears the old phrase that a misbehaving child is "full of the devil." An id character in literature is often one of mystery who tempts protagonists to act against their "better judgment" with an offer that the hero finds difficult to refuse. The temptation for some pleasurable reward is often nearly irresistible, and this can be seen as an illustration of Freud's principles in literature.

Ego

The **ego** is usually thought of as the conscious mind; however, it resides equally in the unconscious as well. Referred to as the reality principle, the ego's function is to govern the id, channeling the id's drives into socially acceptable outlets. Since the id's demands for pleasure are not often immediately obtainable, the ego postpones or even alters the demands into drives that are realistically attainable. The ego's function is, then, to determine when, where, and how the id's demands might best be gratified in ways that are acceptable for the well-being of the individual within the culture. In a well-balanced person, the ego and the id work harmoniously together; when the two are in conflict, repression and neurosis result. In literature, the ego and the id working in balance can be seen when stream-of-consciousness narration reveals a character's id's desires, but the actions of the character are kept in check by his or her ego.

Superego

If the id is the source of the pleasure principle and the ego is reality, then the **superego** is the source of ethics: the morality principle. As a moral, censoring agency, the superego is the home of the conscience and pride. If a society regards a particular id impulse toward pleasure as socially unacceptable and the ego cannot divert the impulse to a satisfactory substitute, then the superego blocks its fulfillment by forcing it back into the unconscious: repressing it. Overt aggression and unacceptable desires are types of impulses that are repressed.

Since the superego is responsive to its own society, however, its inhibitions vary from culture to culture. What is proper and moral in one culture can be improper and immoral in another. This can be seen in literature that refers to Greek mythology. In Greek mythology, romantic relationships between blood relatives were common, whereas those relationships would be unacceptable and repressed in another culture. Allowed to become overactive, the superego can create a guilt complex: an unconscious, brooding sense of guilt.

The initial and, by all accounts, most influential source of the superego is a child's parents. They are the first to impart to the child their moral and ethical values, which is accomplished more by their example than by their instruction. These ethical influences are assimilated and internalized by children early in life; later influences of school, religion, and peer groups have an effect, but they are not nearly as influential as parents are early in a child's life.

Though the three zones of the psyche are very distinct, it is helpful to list their characteristics.

Id—Pleasure principle

- Source of aggression and desire
- Source of energy
- Impulse toward self-indulgence
- Illogical
- Amoral

Ego—Reality principle

- Rational

- Regulates id's drives

- Mediating agency of psyche

Superego—Morality principle

- Protects society

- Censors or represses the id

- Source of conscience and pride

Exercise 6.1 Read William Blake's "A Poison Tree." Identify text that, in your opinion, mirrors Freud's psychic zones. Write several sentences on each psychic zone you identify; make sure to explain that zone's functions.

A POISON TREE

I was angry with my friend.
I told my wrath, my wrath did end.
I was angry with my foe.
I told it not, my wrath did grow;

And I water'd it in fears,
Night and morning with my tears;
And I sunned it with smiles,
And with soft deceitful wiles.

And it grew both day and night
Till it bore an apple bright,
And my foe beheld it shine,
And he knew that it was mine,

And into my garden stole
When the night had veil'd the pole.
In the morning glad I see
My foe outstretched beneath the tree.

—*William Blake (1757–1827)*

Lesson Two: **Core Issues**

One of the most common ways humans manage their problems is to repress them. For instance, if a person's stated reason for never being in a relationship is because they simply "aren't good in relationships," they may be repressing a deeper issue. Freud referred to these deeper issues as **core issues**. Repressing any of the core issues is accomplished by an individual keeping a particular behavior or emotion in their unconscious mind; ironically, it is this very repression that maximizes the core issue's power over the individual.

Defense Mechanisms

Defense mechanisms, or the mental processes of an individual that work to avoid conflict or anxiety, keep the contents of the unconscious mind hidden. The superego's repression is an example of a defense mechanism, but there are other methods of defense available to the unconscious mind. Examples of defense mechanisms include selective perception, selective memory, denial, avoidance, displacement, projection, and regression.

- Selective perception, or perceiving only what one can handle, is a defense mechanism that limits one's complete understanding of an event.
- Selective memory is slightly different from selective perception in that it involves a complete perception of an event at the time, but a partial memory, which involves only what a person is capable of processing.
- Denial is the refusal to admit the veracity of something that is true.
- Avoidance is the act of keeping away from a thought process altogether.
- Displacement is taking one's aggression out on something or someone else, rather than the true source of conflict.
- Projection is ascribing one's problem to someone else and then condemning him or her for it.
- Regression is the temporary return to a former psychological state, whether painful or pleasant, as an escape from some present difficulty.

When examining a work of literature through the lens of psychological analysis, it is easy to identify certain defense mechanisms in characters. The narrator of "The Yellow Wallpaper" (page 278), for instance, is rich with defense mechanisms. She experiences selective perception when observing that her husband, John, chose their new house as a summer vacation home rather than a secluded location to treat her depression. She displaces the fear and aggression fostered by her stifling treatment onto the wallpaper and asks John to change the wallpaper in her room because she finds the walls' patterns menacing. Consequently, she projects those fears onto the wallpaper itself, and begins to despise its smell and vandalize the paper. She experiences selective memory when she chooses not to recall that she has caused the long "smooches" along the wallpaper by crawling along the walls. "The Yellow Wallpaper" is rife with psychological elements; many characters in literature exhibit some form of these defense mechanisms.

Exercise 6.2 Read D. H. Lawrence's "Piano." In a paragraph, identify and explain text that, in your opinion, mirrors Freud's ideas about defense mechanisms.

PIANO

Softly, in the dusk, a woman is singing to me;
Taking me back down the vista of years, till I see
A child sitting under the piano, in the boom of the tingling strings
And pressing the small, poised feet of a mother who smiles as she sings.

In spite of myself, the insidious mastery of song
Betrays me back, till the heart of me weeps to belong
To the old Sunday evenings at home, with winter outside
And hymns in the cosy parlour, the tinkling piano our guide.

So now it is vain for the singer to burst into clamour
With the great black piano appassionato. The glamour
Of childish days is upon me, my manhood is cast
Down in the flood of remembrance, I weep like a child for the past.

—D. H. Lawrence (1885–1930)

Anxiety

Once an individual is aware that he or she is repressing a behavior or an emotion, **anxiety** will most likely occur. According to Freud, anxiety develops from the realization of repression. That realization can expose many core issues, including fear of intimacy, abandonment, death, and betrayal. Throughout literature, anxiety in its myriad forms, including madness, has overtaken characters.

Oedipal and Electra Complexes

Freud's theories of the Oedipal and Electra complexes are controversial. He postulated that during an early phase, all children pass through an **Oedipal complex**—a boy's unconscious rivalry with his father for the love of his mother, or an **Electra complex**—a girl's unconscious rivalry with her mother for the love of her father. Freud further postulates that a frustrated rivalry with a parent may give rise to resentment of parental authority and later manifest itself in an unreasonable hostility toward all authority.

A classic psychological analysis of Shakespeare's *Hamlet*, for example, asserts that the primary source of Prince Hamlet's predicament is not so much moral quandary as Oedipal repression: According to Freudian theory, Hamlet's antisocial behavior may be attributed to repressions, fixations, anxieties, and complexes rooted in his childhood.

Exercise 6.3 Read Edgar Allan Poe's short story "The Masque of the Red Death" (page 245). From a psychological perspective, what defense mechanisms and anxieties are seen in the story?

Dreams

> The dream-thoughts which we first come across as we proceed with our analysis often strike us by the unusual form in which they are expressed; they are not clothed in the prosaic language usually employed by our thoughts, but are on the contrary represented symbolically by means of similes and metaphors, in images resembling those of poetic speech.

—*from On Dreams, by Sigmund Freud*

Because the unconscious is not directly observable by examination, the id is revealed only through deep hypnosis, during unintentional expressions (known as "**Freudian slips**"), or by the analysis of dreams. Unfortunately, even during dreaming the inhibiting power of the superego is functioning; consequently, Freud viewed dreams themselves only as symbols of the unsatisfied or repressed desires of the id. According to Freud, if a dream's symbolic function comes too close to reality, then the dreamer awakens and is unable to recall the dream's content.

Since dreams are expressions of the id and the id is the source of instinctual drives, dreams are, Freud believed, best interpreted in terms of those repressed desires. This theory has led many psychoanalytical literary critics to examine literature for images lending themselves to either female or male symbols. But Freud himself said, "The assertion that all dreams require a sexual interpretation, against which critics rage so incessantly, occurs nowhere in my *Interpretation of Dreams* ... and is in obvious contradiction to other views expressed in it." He further argued that dream images are too personal to use for general interpretation because an individual's dreams are not sufficiently universal; they employ only the individual dreamer's symbols.

The influence of literature and literary elements on Freud's thinking is evident in his naming of dream characteristics:

- Condensation—a single dream represents multiple associations and ideas. (Metaphor)
- Displacement—the emotional significance is separated from its real object to an entirely different one that is acceptable to the ego and super-ego. (Metaphor, symbolism)
- Visualization—a thought is represented by an image. (Imagery, symbolism)
- Symbolism—a symbol stands in for an action, person, or idea in a dream. (Symbolism)

Exercise 6.4 Read "Young Goodman Brown" (page 249) and answer the following questions:

1. What represents the unconscious?
2. Who or what among the characters or in the setting represents psychic zones?
3. What dream symbols can you identify?
4. What is the psychological significance of the fact that Brown dreams the story?

Lesson Three: **Writing a Psychological Analysis**

Freud's ideas are used in two different ways in literary analysis: to examine the motivations of a story's characters and to gain access to the inner workings of the author's psyche using the story and its characters. The first approach concentrates on the psychological result of characters' infancy and childhood problems. While these problems are not themselves described in the literature, the problems' existence is clearly suggested by characters' actions. Emphasizing unconscious motivation for characters' actions, this style of criticism attempts to reveal characters' mental turmoil, fixations, and repressions through their social or antisocial behavior.

The second approach of psychological analysis concentrates on the author by viewing his or her works as an expression of tensions and conflicts produced by frustrated and repressed id drives. Since a literary work springs from the author's imagination, we know that the characters originate in the author's psyche. This approach could be used in Jane Austen's six novels, many of which focus on romantic tensions between members of separate classes or families. It may be interpreted that Austen dealt with these tensions in her own life, thus using her creative work as therapeutic expression of repressed id drives. This second approach requires that a reader have an understanding of multiple works by an author's in order to make a full analytical conjecture.

Psychological criticism asserts that literature, like dreams, is greatly influenced by the unconscious and asks that you examine a work for its literary elements, such as imagery, symbolism, and figurative language. These elements are considered clues to the psyche of a story's characters or that of the author. For any psychological analysis, the following questions maybe helpful:

- How can a character's motivations or actions be explained in psychological terms?

- Are there dreams or symbols in the work that suggest additional meanings?

- What literary elements, such as similes and metaphors, appear in the text, and what is a possible psychological interpretation of their function?

- What does the work suggest about the author's psyche?

Exercise 6.5 Write a psychological analysis of "Young Goodman Brown" (page 249). For help with annotating, planning, and writing an analysis, see Unit Nine, "Writing an Analysis" (page 215).

Post-Assessment:

Circle the letter of the correct answer of each question.

1. **The zone of the human psyche that lacks any rational logic is the**
   (A) id
   (B) ego
   (C) superego
   (D) persona
   (E) preconscious

2. **According to Freud, the ego represents the**
   (A) unconscious
   (B) conscious
   (C) shadow
   (D) desire for idleness
   (E) reality principle

3. **The superego of a psychologically healthy, mature person**
   (A) protects society
   (B) mediates between the ego and the id
   (C) promotes amoral behavior
   (D) is the source of aggression
   (E) reflects the collective unconscious mind

4. **Which of the following might lead to psychological problems?**
   (A) A person who allows the id to dominate the superego
   (B) A conflict between the pleasure principle and morality
   (C) A person who represses id drives
   (D) A frustrated Oedipal stage of development
   (E) All of the above

5. **Freud asserted that dreams are the expressions of**
   (A) the conscious mind
   (B) the conscience
   (C) the ego
   (D) the unconscious mind
   (E) defense mechanisms

6. **Freud viewed dreams as**
   (A) premonitions of what is about to happen
   (B) symbols of unsatisfied id desires
   (C) reflections of past lives
   (D) unsettled images of the ego
   (E) unimportant to psychoanalytic technique

7. **Which of the following is NOT a characteristic of psychological analysis?**
   (A) Dream symbols
   (B) Anxieties
   (C) Repressions
   (D) Fixations
   (E) The collective unconscious

8. **One of the main aims of psychological analysis is to**
   (A) examine characters' behavior
   (B) discover mythic themes
   (C) find metaphors and allusions
   (D) show the relationship of theme to history
   (E) ascertain the original meanings of terms

UNIT SEVEN

Archetypal Analysis

Many contemporary theorists and critics believe that the significance of a work of literature may well lie in its **universality**—its appeal to all peoples regardless of time or culture. These critics believe a work's universality relies on certain situations or images that create similar emotional responses in nearly everybody. For example, Homer's "Odyssey" is considered universal because of one of its main themes: the journey home, or *nostos*. It takes Odysseus approximately twenty years to return home to Ithaca and be reunited with his son and wife. The feelings that accompany the journey, such as struggle, perseverance, and relief, are also universal.

Archetypal analysis, also referred to as myth criticism, is a method of analysis that enhances readers' critical abilities by requiring them to probe literature for symbols, imagery, situations, and themes that suggest recurrent human circumstances. Looking for these common archetypal elements will reveal to the reader both their importance and prevalence in literary works.

Objectives

AFTER COMPLETING THIS UNIT, YOU WILL BE ABLE TO:

1. Describe Carl Jung's characteristics of archetypes;

2. Understand the role of creation stories in societies;

3. Identify archetypal images, characters, and situations in literature;

4. Explain Jung's theory of shadow, anima, and persona;

5. Explain the function of myths in societies;

6. Write an archetypal analysis of a literary selection.

Lesson One: **Archetypes**

Archetype is rooted in the Greek word *arche-tupos*, meaning "first type": the original pattern from which all other copies are made. Archetypal analysis shares some of the basic concepts of other analytical approaches but rejects others. As with formalist analysis, archetypal critics emphasize a close, analytical reading of literature. Unlike the formalist, however, the archetypal analyst rejects the idea that nothing outside the printed page is relevant. As with psychological critics, archetypal critics search the unconscious, but here the interest lies in the **collective unconscious**—those similarities in the unconscious shared by all humans—rather than the unconscious of the individual psyche.

Carl Jung

Archetypal analysis is indebted to Swiss psychologist Carl Jung (1875–1961). Jung agreed with Freud that all humans have an unconscious deep within their psyches, which is unique to each individual. However, Jung further asserted that one aspect of the unconscious mind exists that is the same for everyone. Just as each person's unconscious is the result of unique personal and environmental experience, Jung suggested that the **collective unconscious** is the mental record of all of the experiences of those who have existed previously. Archetypes, according to Jung, represent images or thematic patterns that are repeated so frequently in mythology, religion, and literature that they have taken on a universally symbolic power.

In *Contributions to Analytical Psychology*, Jung writes that there are three basic qualities that characterize archetypes: the primordial, the universal, and the recurrent.

Primordial Characteristics

The most fundamental quality of archetypes is that they are **primordial**; they represent primeval concepts that exist within the origins of the species. Located within the preconscious, that area of the mind from which information can be recalled or remembered, primordial archetypes are not present in the conscious mind. As a result, these are sometimes thought of as expressions of humans' instinctual nature. Be careful, however, about attributing instinctive motivations in humans. Little agreement exists about the importance or extent of human instincts or even what they may be. Most behavioral scientists concur that a human baby is born knowing how to suck and possessing a fear of falling. If you suggest almost anything else as instinctual, however, you will find argument and controversy.

In humans, encoded patterns of the past such as the fear of falling or the fear of drowning are important for the species' survival. These fears are the result of countless experiences of the same kind: experiences that literally began before the development of consciousness. They are innate images of experiences that have been repeated so often that they have formed deep, lasting impressions upon the collective unconscious.

While the exact process of how archetypes are formed has never been satisfactorily explained—is it genetic, cultural, or mystical?—these experiences represent those formed earliest in the development of the human species. Primordial experiences, therefore, are fundamental, original occurrences, repeated so many times that they are mentally imprinted. Consequently, since Jung viewed them as models or prototypes of universal behavior, he named them archetypes.

Universal Characteristics

The second essential quality of archetypes is that they are universal; they are unaffected by time or situation, community or culture. They are as significant to isolated tribal people who believe they are the only human beings in existence as they are to modern people who are electronically connected to the entire globe. From this perspective, humans have changed little in 4,000 years of recorded history, a period which is only an instant in the span of evolutionary time. The psycho-neurological functions of the modern mind remain essentially unchanged from those of Neolithic peoples, the first humans to utilize technology. As a result, we all share similar experiences, emotions, drives, needs, and archetypes with each other and with our ancient ancestors.

Recurrent Characteristics

The third fundamental quality of archetypes is that they are recurrent. Researchers in anthropology, comparative religion, and mythology point to the similarities of narratives among peoples and find that the differences that do exist are mostly attributable to local adaptations. They are universal and, therefore, archetypal.

An example of recurrent characteristics in an archetype can be found in creation stories. All people have been concerned with their origin and the meaning of their existence; it makes little difference where or when they live. When comparing these stories across cultures and time, it is fascinating to discover that the explanations of human origin and worldly creation are strikingly similar.

Exercise 7.1 Read the following explanations for creation. List the common aspects that you find.

Ancient Hebrew (2000 BCE)

1. In the beginning God created the heaven and the earth.

2. And the earth was without form, and void; and darkness was upon the face of the deep. And the Spirit of God moved upon the face of the waters.

3. And God said, Let there be light: and there was light.

4. And God saw the light, that it was good: and God divided the light from the darkness.

5. And God called the light Day, and the darkness he called Night. And the evening and the morning were the first day.

6. And God said, Let there be a firmament in the midst of the waters, and let it divide the waters from the waters.

7. And God made the firmament, and divided the waters which were under the firmament from the waters which were above the firmament: and it was so.

8. And God called the firmament Heaven. And the evening and the morning were the second day.

9. And God said, Let the waters under the heaven be gathered together unto one place, and let the dry land appear: and it was so.

10. And God called the dry land Earth; and the gathering together of the waters called the Seas: and God saw that it was good.

11. And God said, Let the earth bring forth grass, the herb yielding seed, and the fruit tree yielding fruit after his kind, whose seed is in itself, upon the earth: and it was so.

12. And the earth brought forth grass, and herb yielding seed after his kind, and the tree yielding fruit, whose seed was in itself, after his kind: and God saw that it was good.

13. And the evening and the morning were the third day.

    (On subsequent days God [Yahweh, or Jehovah, Elohim] created the sun and moon, the living creatures, and the first humans, Adam and Eve.)

    — Bible, King James version, Genesis 1:1–13

Ancient Mayan (2600 BCE)

There is not yet one person, one animal, bird, fish, crab, tree, rock, hollow, canyon, meadow, forest. Only the sky alone is there; the face of the earth is not clear. Only the sea alone is pooled under all the sky; there is nothing whatever gathered together. It is at rest; not a single thing stirs. It is held back, kept at rest under the sky.

Whatever there is that might be is simply not there: only the pooled water, only the calm sea, only it alone is pooled.

Whatever might be is simply not there: only murmurs, ripples, in the dark, in the night. Only the Maker, Modeler alone, Sovereign Plumed Serpent, the Bearers, Begetters are in the water, a glittering light. They are there, they are enclosed in quetzal feathers, in blue-green.

Thus the name, "Plumed Serpent." They are great knowers, great thinkers in their very being.

And of course there is the sky, and there is also the Heart of Sky. This is the name of the god, as it is spoken.

And then came his word, he came here to the Sovereign Plumed Serpent, here in the blackness, in the early dawn. He spoke with the Sovereign Plumed Serpent, and they talked, then they thought, then they worried. They agreed with each other, they joined their words, their thoughts. Then it was clear, then they reached accord in the light, and then humanity was clear, when they conceived the growth, the generation of trees, of bushes, and the growth of life, of humankind, in the blackness, in the early dawn, all because of the Heart of Sky, named Hurricane. Thunderbolt Hurricane comes first, the second is Newborn Thunderbolt, and the third is Raw Thunderbolt.

So there were three of them, as Heart of Sky, who came to the Sovereign Plumed Serpent, when the dawn of life was conceived:

"How should it be sown, how should it dawn? Who is to be the provider, nurturer?"

"Let it be this way, think about it: this water should be removed, emptied out for the formation of the earth's own plate and platform, then comes the sowing, the dawning of the sky-earth. But there will be no high days and no bright praise for our work, our design, until the rise of the human work, the human design," they said.

And then the earth arose because of them, it was simply their word that brought it forth. For the forming of the earth they said "Earth." It arose suddenly, just like a cloud, like a mist, now forming, unfolding. Then the mountains were separated from the water, all at once the great mountains came forth. By their genius alone, by their cutting edge alone they carried out the conception of the mountain-plain, whose face grew instant groves of cypress and pine.

And the Plumed Serpent was pleased...

—*from Popol Vuh, the Mayan Book of the Dawn of Life, trans. Dennis Tedlock*

While these explanations have some variations, they are remarkably similar and serve to illustrate human concern for creation. All peoples seem to thirst for an understanding of how the universe began and how humans fit into the larger design. Because of this universal curiosity, creation is then a fundamental recurrent archetype. Since stories of creation involve so much more than simply an image or single situation, all of the explanations of a particular people's creation combine to form what is called a **motif**—in this instance, the archetypal motif of creation. Other recurrent archetypal motifs include world destruction, immortality, and heroes and heroines.

Exercise 7.2 Read the following selection. What motif is alluded to in the poem?

THERE WILL COME SOFT RAINS

There will come soft rains and the smell of the ground,
And swallows circling with their shimmering sound;

And frogs in the pools singing at night,
And wild plum trees in tremulous white;

Robins will wear their feathery fire,
Whistling their whims on a low fence-wire;

And not one will know of the war, not one
Will care at last when it is done.

Not one would mind, neither bird nor tree,
If mankind perished utterly;

And Spring herself, when she woke at dawn
Would scarcely know that we were gone.

—*Sara Teasdale (1884–1933)*

Lesson Two: **Images, Characters, and Situations**

Deep within the collective unconscious, archetypes may lurk; we may not even be remotely aware of them, or perhaps they are known to us only in our dreams. In this view, the number of potential archetypes is limited only by the number of recurrent human experiences. The archetypes with which we are most familiar seem to fall naturally into three groups: images and symbols, characters, and situations.

Images and Symbols

Viewed one way, archetypes are universal in their symbolism. In other words, certain images seem to have universal appeal. These images call from within us certain responses and associations that appeal to us in emotional ways quite apart from our intellect.

Exercise 7.3 Write your own associations to the list of archetypal images below.

1. the sun, for example: rising and setting
2. colors, for example: white, red, black, green
3. water, for example: rivers, lakes, oceans, ice
4. shapes, for example: circles, triangles, ovals
5. landscapes, for example: forests, deserts, gardens

If you compare your responses with others, do you find similarities? If so, to what do you attribute them? If not, to what do you attribute your differences? Where have you seen these images in literary works?

Exercise 7.4 Read Robert Frost's poem, "Stopping by Woods on a Snowy Evening," and the excerpt from T. S. Eliot's poem, "The Wasteland," that follows. Identify symbolic images used by each author. What do they convey?

Stopping by Woods on a Snowy Evening

Whose woods these are I think I know.
His house is in the village though;
He will not see me stopping here
To watch his woods fill up with snow.

My little horse must think it queer
To stop without a farmhouse near
Between the woods and frozen lake
The darkest evening of the year.

He gives his harness bells a shake
To ask if there is some mistake.
The only other sound's the sweep
Of easy wind and downy flake.

The woods are lovely, dark and deep,
but I have promises to keep,
And miles to go before I sleep,
And miles to go before I sleep.

—*Robert Frost (1874–1963)*

April is the cruellest month, breeding
Lilacs out of the dead land, mixing
Memory and desire, stirring
Dull roots with spring rain.
Winter kept us warm, covering
Earth in forgetful snow, feeding
A little life with dried tubers.
Summer surprised us, coming over the Starnbergersee
With a shower of rain; we stopped in the colonnade,
And went on in sunlight, into the Hofgarten,
And drank coffee, and talked for an hour.
Bin gar keine Russin, stamm' aus Litauen, echt deutsch.
And when we were children, staying at the archduke's,
My cousin's, he took me out on a sled,
And I was frightened. He said, Marie,
Marie, hold on tight. And down we went.
In the mountains, there you feel free.
I read, much of the night, and go south in the winter.

—*from "The Wasteland," by T. S. Eliot (1888–1965)*

Characters

A number of recurrent, archetypal characters make up the cast in many works of literature, as well as in mythology and religion. These characters share such remarkably similar experiences and behave in such seemingly predetermined manners that their lives appear almost ritualistic in their predictability.

1. The *Hero* or *Heroine*: This is a character noted for his or her noble qualities, such as courage, moral excellence, and self-sacrifice for the greater good (e.g. Oedipus, Jane Eyre, The Little Mermaid). There are many variations, including:

   - The *Princess Heroine* or *Maiden Heroine*: This character has the qualities of the male hero: individualism, intellect, independence. She is unhappy with the status quo, is proactive, and, in the case of the maiden heroine, rejects the suitor (e.g., Cathy from *Wuthering Heights*).

   - The *Rebel Hero*: This a character who openly defies authorities to right an injustice (e.g., Prometheus, Robin Hood).

2. The *Star-Crossed Lovers*: Two characters whose relationship ends with the tragic death of one or both of them (e.g., Romeo and Juliet; Antigone and Haemon; Psyche and Eros).

3. The *Devil*: A character who is the personification of evil. He or she often offers fortune, fame, or power in return for a soul (e.g., Mephistopheles; Beelzebub).

4. The *Temptress*: The woman to whom the protagonist is physically attracted and who ultimately brings about his downfall. She is sometimes seen as representing an alien culture or the unknown (e.g., Delilah, Helen of Troy, Circe, Cleopatra).

5. The *Monster*: A nightmarish creature that stands in the way of the hero's progress and plagues a society. Heroes typically gain their first fame after defeating a monster (e.g., the Sphinx, Circe, Grendel).

6. The *Doppelgänger*: A contrasting counterpart: an evil twin of the hero or heroine who inspires terror on sight (e.g., Mr. Hyde, the counterpart of Dr. Jekyll; Poe's "William Wilson").

7. The *Outcast*: A character who is condemned to wander, usually alone, after committing some crime against society (e.g., Cain; The Ancient Mariner; Odysseus in *The Odyssey*; Rashkolnikov in *Crime and Punishment*).

8. The *Scapegoat:* A person whose death in a public ritual expiates the community's sins (e.g., the victim in "The Lottery," by Shirley Jackson; Piggy in *Lord of the Flies*).

9. The *Intellectual*: A person who is a mathematician, astronomer, scientist, or computer genius and exhibits antisocial, neutral, or pro-social tendencies (e.g., Dr. Frankenstein in Mary Shelley's *Frankenstein*).

10. The *Trickster*: An ambiguous figure who is a fool and a cheat. The trickster assumes many guises, both animal and human, to perform cruel tricks and practical jokes (e.g., Old Man, Coyote, Raven, Br'er Rabbit, Hermes, Cupid).

Other archetypal characters can be identified by what they experience; many of these experiences are varied, but each is important in literature and mythology. Below are additional archetypes you may wish to explore:

- King or Queen
- Mother or Father
- Child or Innocent
- Shaman or Medicine Woman
- Warrior or Amazon
- Guru or Disciple
- Fool or Wise Fool

Exercise 7.5 Identify the archetypal characters in "Ulysses" (page 239) and "Young Goodman Brown" (page 249).

Heroes and Heroines

Probably the most common of the archetypal characters are heroes and heroines. Their lives revolve around adventures that are so familiar you should be able to identify several examples from literature as you read the following list of their lives' major events.

1. A hero's conception is typically unusual; often, by tradition, his mother is a virgin;

2. Frequently, the hero must escape a plot for his death soon after birth;

3. The hero grows to maturity in the home of foster parents after a narrow escape from death, therefore little is known about his childhood, t

4. As a young man, the hero feels a longing for something other than what he has and begins a journey of "initiation";

5. Along the way, the hero encounters temptation, is assisted by mystical beings, and usually travels a road of trials that brings him close to death;

6. The hero finds what he has been searching for and returns home victorious;

7. Settling down, the hero often marries a beautiful princess and becomes king;

8. After a long and often uneventful rule, the hero finds himself no longer in the good graces of the gods, is driven from his kingdom, and mysteriously dies;

9. Although not officially buried, the hero typically has one or more holy graves.

While not all of these events occur in the life of each hero or heroine, the following heroes and heroines clearly embody these ritualistic events:

Hercules	Oedipus
King Arthur	Robin Hood
Beowulf	The Little Mermaid
Jane Eyre	

Exercise 7.6 Read the following story of Oedipus. Using the list of the hero's common life events, identify the predictable events in Oedipus's life.

Oedipus

Shortly after the birth of their first child, Laius and Jocasta, King and Queen of Thebes, travel to Apollo's sanctuary, the Oracle at Delphi, to ask about their infant's destiny. The happy parents are horrified when the Oracle indicates that the child's fate is to murder his father and marry his mother. Feeling that they cannot allow the god's prediction to occur, the parents decide that their child must not be allowed to live. To avoid the wrath of the gods, however, they cannot actually kill him themselves. Rather, they order a servant shepherd of the palace to abandon the baby up on the mountainside: there he can die either from exposure or from wild animals, but the King and Queen cannot be accused of murder.

In order to seal his fate absolutely, the child's feet are pinned together. This mutilation prevents the baby from crawling to safety, keeps him from coming back to haunt his parents after his death, and, they believe, makes him undesirable to save.

The shepherd who is ordered to abandon the child upon the mountain has no stomach for his assignment, however. He chances upon a shepherd from the neighboring city of Corinth and persuades him to take the injured child. This shepherd happens to be employed by the King and Queen of Corinth, Polybus and Merope, who are childless; consequently, when the mutilated infant is presented to them, they are happy to treat his wounds and adopt him as their own. He is the child for whom they have prayed to the gods for years.

Polybus and Merope name their new, adopted son Oedipus, which means swollen-foot, and pretend that he is their natural son, thus heir to the throne of Corinth.

As a young man Oedipus hears persistent rumors that he is adopted. Although his "parents" try to assure him that he is not, he journeys to the Oracle at Delphi to learn the truth from Apollo—the god of truth. The Oracle, in response to Oedipus's question about his parentage, states that he is destined to murder his father and marry his mother. Stunned, the young man immediately determines never to return to Corinth. Upon leaving Delphi he decides to travel to Thebes.

At a narrow crossroads on the Corinth-Delphi-Thebes highway he meets a cantankerous old man on a chariot who will not let him pass. The old man is Laius, King of Thebes, on his way to the Oracle at Delphi to ask Apollo's assistance in ridding the City of Thebes of a terrible monster, the Sphinx.

(The Sphinx, who has the body of a lion, the wings of an eagle, and the head of a woman, stands outside the city gates and asks travelers to answer her riddle—what walks on four legs in the morning, two legs at noon, and three legs in the evening? Anyone who cannot correctly answer the riddle is devoured.)

Old Laius attempts to run down Oedipus at the crossroads, but Oedipus quickly jumps aside and, as the chariot charges by, strikes Laius a killing blow with his staff. Infuriated after killing the old man, Oedipus subdues and kills all but one of King Laius' guards and attendants. The one man escapes to return to Thebes to tell of a whole band of robbers who have ambushed the group and assassinated the King. The city, however, has greater worries because the Sphinx is still on the edge of town killing whosoever fails to answer her riddle.

After the slaughter at the crossroads, Oedipus proceeds toward Thebes. Upon arriving at the city's outskirts, the Sphinx leaps out at him and demands that her riddle be correctly answered or she will devour him. She states her riddle and the wise Oedipus quickly answers it—man crawls upon hands and feet in the morning of life, walks upright on two legs in the noon of life, and walks with the aid of a cane in the evening of life. Her riddle successfully answered, the Sphinx kills herself, and Oedipus is treated to a hero's welcome by the grateful citizens of Thebes. He is given wealth, made king, and given Jocasta, widow of King Laius, in marriage.

Oedipus rules uneventfully for several years, but as his oldest children approach adulthood, a great plague that kills young things strikes the city. Again it is necessary to take some action to save Thebes. Therefore, Creon, Jocasta's brother, is sent to the Oracle at Delphi to find the source of this calamity whereupon a solution might be found.

(The play—"Oedipus," by Sophocles—unfolds at this point as the audience learns, along with Oedipus, this history.)

After the truth is discovered, Jocasta hangs herself; Oedipus blinds himself and is sent into exile. After many years of wandering in the desert, led about by his youngest daughter, Antigone, the gods feel that he has suffered enough. Consequently, they decide to take him directly into the underworld, to the land ruled over by Hades, without having to pass through death. Thus, the earth opens up and Oedipus is taken directly down; he does not die but joins the dead without the unpleasantness of death. The site where the ground opened up to accept him became his holy grave.

Exercise 7.7 Read the following synopsis of Hans Christian Andersen's "The Little Mermaid". Identify the patterns of the heroine in the life of the Little Mermaid. What other archetypal characteristics are present in the story?

The Little Mermaid

Long ago, at the bottom of the sea, there lived a sea king with his older mother and six mermaid daughters. The youngest mermaid daughter, the Little Mermaid, was the most beautiful, and her singing voice was loved throughout the sea. The mermaids' lives were full of playing and singing, and all were happy. The Little Mermaid was happiest when her grandmother was telling her stories about the humans above the sea. Her grandmother told her when she turned fifteen, she could swim up and see for herself. The Little Mermaid was so excited. She would gaze up through the water at night, hoping to get a glimpse of the world outside of the water.

When the Little Mermaid turned fifteen, her grandmother gave her a long string of pearls to wear before she swam to the surface of the sea. When the Little Mermaid lifted her head from the sea, she saw a big ship and swam to a window to see in. Inside, she saw the most handsome prince she could ever imagine. Suddenly, a storm blew through and lightening littered the sky. The sea rose and the Prince's ship broke apart in the crashing waves. The Little Mermaid saw the Prince begin to sink in the sea and dove below to save him. When the Little Mermaid found the Prince, she carried him to the surface and laid him on the sand, kissing his forehead before swimming away from the beach. She hid behind a large rock, watching the Prince lie on the sand.

Soon, a beautiful girl found the Prince while she was walking along the beach. He woke up and smiled at the girl. He didn't know that the Little Mermaid had saved him or that she existed at all. The beautiful girl led the Prince away, and the Little Mermaid felt so heartsick that she swam back home full of sorrow.

After weeks, the Little Mermaid could do nothing but think of the Prince. She found his palace by the sea and swam nearby to watch him look out his window. The Little Mermaid longed for the world above the sea more than ever.

One day, she asked her grandmother, "Do people live forever?" Her grandmother told her that people die, just as mermaids do. She said, when mermaids die, they become foam of the water, but when people die, they have souls that live forever.

The Little Mermaid wondered if she could get a human soul. Her grandmother told her she would be granted a soul only if a human loved her with all his heart and married her. Then his soul would be a part of her body. The Little Mermaid wanted a soul and the love of her Prince, so she swam to the Sea Witch for help. When the witch saw the Little Mermaid, she already knew what the Mermaid wanted: human legs. The witch made a magic drink that the Little Mermaid was to swim to land and drink. Then her tail would split in two and she would have human legs, but the witch said it would hurt terribly when she walked.

Once she became human, the witch said she could never become a mermaid again. If the Prince married someone else, the Little Mermaid would not get a human soul, and she would turn to foam of the sea. The Mermaid agreed and paid the witch with her voice. The Little Mermaid swam to the Prince's palace, sat on his steps, and drank the magic potion. Suddenly, she had two beautiful legs and the Prince was walking toward her. He asked where she came from, but the Little Mermaid could not speak. He took her hand and led her to his palace, but every step she took felt like knives in her feet and legs.

The Prince took good care of the Little Mermaid, giving her fine dresses to wear and inviting her to many parties. Because she could not speak or sing, the Little Mermaid danced for the Prince to show her affection. She danced, even though it hurt so terribly. The Prince loved the Little Mermaid's dancing and they began spending all of their time together.

The Prince told the Little Mermaid that she reminded him of a young girl who saved his life. He said he could never love anyone but that girl. The Mermaid wished she could tell him it was she who saved his life, but she could not speak. One day, the Prince told the Little Mermaid that his parents had arranged a marriage to a princess across the sea. They were both heartbroken, and the Prince kissed the Little Mermaid before he boarded the ship.

When he returned, the Prince was with the beautiful girl who found him on the beach after the Little Mermaid had rescued him. The Prince believed that this girl, the princess he would marry, was the girl who saved him, and he loved her deeply. The Little Mermaid was heartbroken. The Prince and princess were married aboard a ship, and the Little Mermaid danced for the last time, knowing that she would soon turn into foam of the sea.

Before she went to sleep on the wedding ship, the Little Mermaid's sisters swam to the surface of the sea and told her that if she killed the Prince, her tail would grow back and she could live her life as a mermaid. The Little Mermaid took a knife and went to the Prince's room, but when she looked at the Prince that she loved, she threw the knife into the sea and jumped into the water. The Little Mermaid did not turn into sea foam, as she thought she would. Instead, she rose up into the air and sang with the children of the air. They told her that she loved the Prince so deeply that she gave her life to save his, and her soul would live forever.

Situations

Several recurrent archetypal situations have been identified in literature through the use of Jung's analytical techniques. These situations, or thematic patterns, are a combination of what the images suggest (page 178) and what the characters pursue (page 179). In mythic stories, the situation forms the basis for plot. However, the way in which situation is used in literature varies; the order of the situation's events is not absolute, and the presence of all of the situation's stages is not always included. The most common situations in mythology are the initiation, the task, the quest, the fall, and death and rebirth.

Initiation situations are usually concerned with the passage from childhood to maturity or from maturity to the wisdom of old age. They often symbolize an increased awareness of life, its meaning, and its consequences. The initiation itself may be symbolic of those events in a culture that mark one's passage to maturity. In contemporary American society, these symbolic acts involve such situations as acquiring a driver's license, graduating from high school or college, voting for the first time, and getting a job. Examples of initiation can be found in the following classic literature:

- *Adventures of Huckleberry Finn*: running away from home;
- *The Catcher in the Rye*: wandering alone in New York City, drinking alcohol, having a sexual encounter;
- *Jane Eyre*: leaving home, falling in love.

In the **task**, a hero or heroine must perform some extraordinary, difficult feat in order to reassert his or her authority (e.g., Odysseus strings the great bow after all others have failed; the Little Mermaid rescues the prince from drowning).

The **quest** involves a great search for someone or something that will bring about either a returned fertility to the land or a lost order to the world. The quest is more than a task—it's so large that many of the participants often cannot comprehend the end goal (e.g., the quest for the Grail; the quest for the great white whale, Moby Dick; Jason's quest for the golden fleece).

The archetype of the **fall** describes a loss of power, status, or innocence. Accompanying the fall is typically banishment from paradise and relocation to some less desirable place. Resulting from moral misbehavior or disobedience, the punishment sometimes lasts for generations (e.g., Adam and Eve; Hester Prynne; Anna Karenina).

One of the most popular archetypal situations with myth creators and writers involves the **cycles of death and rebirth**. Both nature and life share similar cycles. For example, death imagery suggests fall and winter because the natural environment's vegetation appears to die. Spring and summer, on the other hand, bring new life and rebirth; therefore, these seasons represent birth (or rebirth) and youth.

Exercise 7.8 Look again at Frost's "Stopping by Woods on a Snowy Evening" (page 178) and Cummings's "in Just—" (page 40). What archetypal situations do these poems suggest?

Lesson Three: **Shadow, Anima, and Persona**

Archetypal analysis can also be concerned with the individual human psyche. Unlike Freud, Jung probed literary characters' psyches in order to better understand their manifestations of the collective unconscious, rather than to assess the author's psyche. Jung asserts that there are three aspects present in individual psyches: the shadow is the darker side of the personality wherein reside the elements we often wish to suppress; the anima or animus is the vital life force that gives us creativity and makes us human; and the persona is the face we all put on to show the world.

Shadow

Jung believed that, in addition to the collective unconscious, the mind has a collective subconscious. He referred to the darker part of this region as the **shadow**. In the shadow resides the less pleasant aspects of the personality. Often dangerous, this region belongs to the primitive, uncivilized, pre-evolutionary past of the species. The shadow holds emotions such as jealousy and repressed desires like avarice, aspects which most people would prefer not to recognize as part of their being. In literature, the shadow is represented by such characters as Iago in Shakespeare's *Othello* and Kurtz in Joseph Conrad's *Heart of Darkness*.

Anima and Animus

This is the place
And I am here, the mermaid whose dark hair
streams black, the merman in his armoured body
We circle silently
about the wreck
we dive into the hold.
I am she: I am he

— from "Diving into the Wreck," by Adrienne Rich (1929–2012)

Jung theorizes the existence of an **anima** and **animus**, archetypes that represent the life force, or soul, within everyone. One of their functions is to represent a person's opposite sex within his or her psyche. In other words, in every man's unconscious resides a female image, or anima, that reveals herself in his dreams or in his projections upon others. In women, this life force is referred to as the animus and is a masculine counterpart to her psyche. According to Jung, the anima is responsible for feelings of love, because when a man finds a woman who closely mirrors his anima, he will love her. Likewise, a woman who finds a man who mirrors her inner animus will be inclined to fall in love with him. This, Jung believed, explains the phenomenon of love at first sight.

Keep in mind that the anima or animus is an archetype of the collective unconscious and not the personal unconscious; it does not represent all of the personal influences on an individual of mothers, fathers, sisters, brothers, etc. Because the anima or animus generally represents a background of the psyche close to the unconscious, any person who dwells within his or her contrasexual self—a male living in his female self or female living in her male self—lives in his or her psyche's background, according to Jung.

Some of the characteristics attributed to the anima or animus:

Anima	Animus
• Female principle	• Male principle
• Images of dark, water, earth	• Images of light, fire, air
• Irrational	• Rational
• Intuitive, emotional	• Logical, analytical
• Relating	• Independent, individualistic

Modern critics fault Jung for what they argue are his stereotypes of male and female attributes: For instance, he assigns characteristics of irrationality to women and rationality to men. While Jung's overarching theory may be more predicated on the duality of life he found in the teachings of Taoism, he is perceived as equating culturally acquired gender roles with innate male and female characteristics. (See page 205 in Feminist Analysis for more on Jung's critics.)

Persona

Simply put, the **persona** is the social personality or mask that everyone puts on to face the world. For many people, the persona is quite different from their true self. Jung did not consider the persona to be an archetype, but rather a psychological means to relating. The chief function of the persona is to mediate between the ego and the world outside.

Exercise 7.9 Examine Adrienne Rich's "Aunt Jennifer's Tigers" (page 207). What archetypal elements concerned with the human psyche are present in this poem? Explain your answer for each element in two to three sentences.

Exercise 7.10 Read Nathaniel Hawthorne's "Young Goodman Brown" (page 249). Identify archetypal situations in the story and write two or three sentences summarizing each. Next, identify the shadow, the anima, and the persona. In two or three sentences, explain how each of your identifications fits Jung's theory.

Lesson Four: **Mythology**

A popular misconception about mythology is that it is synonymous with the word "false"—something that is believed only by the naïve and uneducated. In contrast to the popular notion that they are untrue, myths actually make no comment whatsoever on whether a belief is literally true or not. Instead, **myths** are the enduring stories that interpret the mysteries of life and the universe for a group of people. Told as allegories, they strive to answer questions as timeless as the creation and purpose of the universe and all that populates it. With their commentaries on the laws of the universe, they are as applicable to the lives of people now as to peoples in the past.

Edith Hamilton and Joseph Campbell

Mythology was introduced to a wide audience in the twentieth century by two scholars with two very different sets of mythological interests. Edith Hamilton (1867–1963) grew up in Fort Wayne, Indiana, in a family that shared a passion for reading and promoted female aspiration. From an early age she was inspired by the literature of ancient Greece, seemingly preferring its larger-than-life heroines to those of English literature. She wrote *Mythology*, the authoritative text in her area of expertise, in 1942. Critics have noted that her retelling of myths often features power struggles between male and female deities.

Joseph Campbell (1904–1987) began his career with the study of American Indian mythology. This grew into a passion for comparative mythology, with an emphasis on looking at the commonalities in narratives of unrelated cultures throughout the world. He was profoundly influenced by Asian mythology, which inspired him to bring world mythology to a larger, non-academic audience through his book, *The Hero with a Thousand Faces*.

Literary Applications

Greek mythology is important in both poetry and fiction. Geoffrey Chaucer, for instance, relied heavily upon Greek mythology for his collection of short stories, *The Canterbury Tales*, written between 1342 and 1400. Chaucer's "The Knight's Tale" was set in ancient Greece and tells the story of Theseus, the mythological King of Athens. Chaucer's allusions had meaning for his readers, who were also familiar with Greek mythology. Thus, the emotion and impact of Theseus's story was comprehended and people could easily relate to "The Knight's Tale."

Functions of Mythology

Campbell suggested that mythology has four essential functions. First, he asserted that myths reveal the mystery and awe of the universe. Mythology, he said, awakens and instills for each individual a sense of wonder and participation in the mystery of the universe. Across many cultures, this wonder and inquiry in individuals often translates into a personal quest for revelation of the universe.

Second, Campbell said that mythology gives importance to whatever image of the universe is shared by a culture. This includes describing the shape and functioning of the universe. Science also aims to explain the size and shape of the universe; however, it only provides explanations of how certain aspects of life work: it cannot answer fundamental questions about the meaning and purpose of all that is alive.

He further observed that myths pronounce the laws of the universe. Many mythologies support and validate a particular social order. This provides the basis for a moral system, customs, and ethical laws—the laws of life as they are expected to be in a good society. These ethical laws often create socially constructed expectations for how individuals are to live in a certain society. Because there are many different groups of people around the world, myths vary enormously from culture to culture and era to era. For example, the myth of Cain and Abel reinforced the moral code of the Hebrew people by dramatizing how easy it is to fall into the sin of envy and pride. This story suggests that sin is always waiting and thirsting to destroy the unwary. The punishment for those who fail to obey God's will and don't resist envy and pride is banishment from both land and God.

Last, according to Campbell, mythology illuminates life cycles. Myths lay out the path for different stages of an individual's life: birth and the dependency of childhood, the responsibilities of maturity, old age, and the passage into death. Myths teach one how to live at every stage. They aim to guide one through all of life, to recognize where one is on the journey, and how one can keep going. They do the same for the society as a whole.

Myth (Greece)

In the beginning, there was chaos. Chaos divided into two deities, Uranus (overhanging heavens) and Gaea (Mother Earth). Among their children, one group, the mighty Titans, became the rulers of the Universe. Chief among these early gods was Cronus (Father Time), who feared a child born to his wife Rhea (Mother Goddess) would become sufficiently powerful to rise up and usurp his rule. Consequently, he swallowed each of his children at birth (Hestia, Demeter, Hera, Hades, and Poseidon). Eventually, Rhea, tiring of his treachery, concealed a newborn from her husband and substituting in its place a stone, which Cronus swallowed believing it his child. The child, Zeus, was spirited away to Crete, where he was reared and taught to master the thunderbolt, a formidable weapon. Upon reaching maturity, he returned to confront his father and, in the ensuing conflict for power, he mortally wounded Cronus, forcing him to vomit out the swallowed children. Zeus and his brothers and sisters became the first of the Olympian gods of Greece.

For the Greeks, one of the most important images of the universe was the mystical concept of fate, represented by the passage of time. However, only mortals are subject to time; the gods are immune, and therefore immortal.

The story of Cronus (Father Time) swallowing his children is an image that demonstrated for the Greeks, in a visually understandable way, how each individual is ultimately "swallowed up by time." The Olympian gods were not subject to the forces of time, however, because Zeus had fought Cronus and defeated him. Consequently, the gods were immortal: free from the entrapment of time, free from the threat of being swallowed up by time. Through this myth the image of the universe, of which time is an integral part, is given mystical importance.

Myth (Australia)

In the great night before people, there was only Sky and Earth. In the earth dwelt Ungud, in the form of a great snake; in the sky dwelt Wallanganda, the Milky Way. Wallanganda dropped water on the earth, and Ungud made it deep. In the night Ungud and Wallanganda dreamed and life arose on the earth in forms from their dreams. From Wallanganda's dreaming came images that he projected onto rocks and into caves, where the red, white, and black paintings may be seen to this day. Once painted, the forms were multiplied by Wallanganda in the shape of living beings—the animals of the earth. The paintings are the spiritual center of the animals. They are the fathers, while the living beings of each kind are brothers.

Ungud's dreaming created spiritual germs on earth, and he would not let his creations die. At the bottom of the water he discovered Wondjina (anthropomorphic beings that personify rain, represented in cave paintings). Wherever Wondjina went they brought rain, and while the rocks were still wet they lay down upon them periodically and sank into the earth, leaving impressions behind that remain today as rock paintings. Each lake, river, or spring is owned by a specific Wondjina whose image is nearby and who dwells under the water that lies beneath the earth under the painting. These Wondjina create child-germs (which are part of the Wondjina, consequently, part of Ungud). During a dream, a man will find one of these child-germs, which, in a subsequent dream, he projects into his wife's dream, where it assumes human form. The germ is that portion of the spirit that returns at death to the waterhole to await reincarnation.

The rightful inhabitants of a region are all those who are descended from the same Wondjina. The oldest in a region is considered the Wondjina incarnate. During Dream Time (annually), it is his duty to renew (repaint) the cave images before the rainy season. When the painting is done, he fills his mouth with water and blows it onto the image. Later, when rain comes, it is regarded as the Wondjina's, therefore a gift from Ungud.

For the indigenous people of Australia, Dream Time is the time when the people, in ritual and ceremony, re-enact the local founding drama. During the ritual, each individual draws upon the creative power of the drama (especially useful in times of sickness, death, or need) to celebrate the continuity of life. During Dream Time people re-establish their connections with their spiritual lives, "remember" their origins, celebrate their progress along life's journey, and anticipate their reunion with their individual creator (Wondjina) as they await reincarnation. Dream Time is conducted throughout their entire lives.

As varied as different people's mythologies appear, they all seem to serve these four essential functions. Myths accomplish this through the literary technique of allegory (page 46). Many mythic, archetypal metaphors are recurrently recognized (death and sleep; sunlight and consciousness; caves and wombs; waning and waxing of the moon and celestial death and rebirth; snakes shedding their skins and earthly death and rebirth), while others are culturally specific, applicable to only one group of people (e.g., the elephant as an earthbound cloud in Hindu myth). Mythology is, then, the principal narrative that interprets the mysteries of life and the universe, and because of this is as applicable to the lives of people now as to all peoples in the past.

Exercise 7.11 Read "Ulysses" (page 239) and discuss the elements of mythology you find in the work.

Lesson Five: **Writing the Archetypal Analysis**

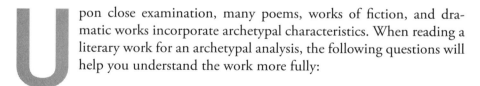pon close examination, many poems, works of fiction, and dramatic works incorporate archetypal characteristics. When reading a literary work for an archetypal analysis, the following questions will help you understand the work more fully:

- What archetypal characters appear in the work?
- Why would the author choose these archetypes over others?
- Are there any archetypal situations or myths that relate to the story?
- How would that situation's or myth's message affect the story's theme?

Exercise 7.12 Write an archetypal analysis of "A White Heron" (page 258). For help with annotating, planning, and writing an analysis, see Unit Nine, "Writing an Analysis" (page 215).

Post-Assessment:

Circle the letter of the correct answer of each question.

1. Archetypal analysis is based upon the work of
(A) Sigmund Freud
(B) Carl Jung
(C) Edith Hamilton
(D) C. P. Snow
(E) Joseph Campbell

2. Which of the following is NOT a characteristic of archetypes?
(A) Primordial
(B) Universal
(C) Recurrent
(D) A defense mechanism
(E) Part of the collective unconscious

3. Groups of mythic situations that together make up a larger, universal story are referred to as archetypal
(A) motifs
(B) images
(C) shadows
(D) animus
(E) initiation

4. Which of the following is not an archetypal image of women?
(A) Earth Mother
(B) Temptress
(C) Working Mother
(D) Heroine
(E) Platonic Ideal

5. The archetypal hero
(A) usually achieves victory over a king or a wild beast
(B) never becomes the king
(C) loses the beautiful princess
(D) has a happy childhood with his parents
(E) has the good graces of the gods throughout his life

6. The part of the psyche called the shadow contains

(A) the ego

(B) the psycho-motor responses

(C) the initiation urge

(D) situations

(E) less pleasant aspects of the personality

7. The anima represents the

(A) anthropomorphic elements

(B) life force

(C) desire for idleness

(D) shadow

(E) male impulse

8. The persona is an aspect of the psyche which is

(A) hidden

(B) satisfied

(C) rational

(D) arbitrary

(E) what others see

9. Archetypes are found in the human psyche in the

(A) personal unconscious

(B) subconscious

(C) collective unconscious

(D) spirit

(E) conscious

10. Myths are

(A) only the beliefs of primitive people

(B) untrue stories

(C) stories that help people understand their world

(D) created to fool the people

(E) not applicable to modern people

UNIT EIGHT

Feminist Analysis

The feminist movement that arose in the 1960s was preceded by a struggle for women's rights that extended throughout the previous century and a half. The resurgent movement of the 1960s built on previous accomplishments, such as obtaining the right to vote, but went further in its aspirations for economic, social, legal, and cultural equality. **Feminist analysis**, or feminist criticism, emerged from the feminist movement of the 1960s and has had a profound and lasting effect on literary criticism.

Feminist analysis studies the role of gender differences in the writing, interpreting, and analyzing of literature, both ancient and contemporary and written by both women and men. It differs from other analysis approaches previously studied in a few ways: its roots are in a social and political movement, it provides in-depth critiques of the literary analyses that preceded it, and it has encouraged related movements to formulate their own literary analyses.

Objectives

AFTER COMPLETING THIS UNIT, YOU WILL BE ABLE TO:

1. Understand the historical setting of feminism;

2. Identify the major elements of feminist analysis;

3. Distinguish between realistic and sexist literature from a feminist perspective;

4. Recognize feminist objections to other critical approaches;

5. Demonstrate critical but unbiased judgment in evaluating literature;

6. Write a feminist analysis of a literary selection.

Lesson One: **The Origins of Feminist Analysis**

L ong before the social upheavals of the 1960s and 1970s, the struggle for gender equality was evident. Influential British feminist and philosopher Mary Wollstonecraft wrote "A Vindication of the Rights of Women" in 1792 as a response to the French Revolutionary Assembly's Declaration of the Rights of Man, which likened marriage to slavery and granted men alone the rights of liberty and equality. Wollstonecraft further reveals in her essay that women are placed into subordination through flattery when they are called innocent, beautiful, or angelic. Instead of these forms of objectifying flattery, she argues, women should be thought to be as intelligent and capable as men.

Wollstonecraft wasn't the only early feminist. Sojourner Truth, an escaped slave, spoke of the injustices she experienced both as a woman and as an African American. Like Wollstonecraft, Truth questioned the idea of women's subordination as a fact of nature. In this excerpt from her speech, "Ain't I a Woman," given at the 1851 Women's Convention in Akron, Ohio, she says:

> That man over there says that women need to be helped into carriages, and lifted over ditches, and to have the best place everywhere. Nobody ever helps me into carriages, or over mud-puddles, or gives me any best place! And ain't I a woman? Look at me! Look at my arm! I have ploughed and planted, and gathered into barns, and no man could head me! And ain't I a woman? I could work as much and eat as much as a man - when I could get it - and bear the lash as well! And ain't I a woman? I have borne thirteen children, and seen most all sold off to slavery, and when I cried out with my mother's grief, none but Jesus heard me! And ain't I a woman?

The movement for women's rights and equality addresses more than legal, economic, and political issues; it also asserts that institutions, cultural values, and attitudes reflect an unfair society. In particular, feminists feel that a patriarchal, or male-dominated, society, is dehumanizing to the entire population, both male and female. Like other movements for equality, one of modern feminism's goals has been to explore the past for models and inspiration and to recover a cultural legacy. In terms of literature, two authors, Virginia Woolf and Simone de Beauvoir, were notably influential to contemporary feminism.

The writings of Virginia Woolf (1882–1941) were a precursor of feminist criticism; a successful novelist, she also wrote essays on the disadvantages of female authors in a male-dominated society and noted that her own career was obstructed by sexism. In response to the lack of freedom and space given to women working toward a profession, Woolf wrote "A Room of One's Own" (1929). The essay's famous pronouncement, "A woman must have money and a room of her own if she is to write fiction," was well understood by aspiring female writers. Woolf speculated that, had Shakespeare had a sister with equal talent, the world may never have heard of her merely because of her gender. She made a point of asking for equal opportunities for all of "Shakespeare's sisters," considering herself one of them.

While some female writers, such as Woolf herself, achieved prominence despite the male-biased world of literature in which they lived, it is important to note that other famous female authors initially wrote under male pseudonyms. In order to secure a publisher, each of the Brontë sisters initially wrote under a male pseudonym: Charlotte Brontë wrote *Jane Eyre* as Currer Bell, Anne Brontë wrote *The Tenant of Wildfell Hall* as Acton Bell, and Emily Brontë wrote *Wuthering Heights* as Ellis Bell. Mary Ann Evans, as George Eliot, wrote realist works, including *The Mill on the Floss* (1860), *Silas Marner* (1861), and *Middlemarch* (1870). Evans cited her desire to be taken seriously as one reason for using a man's name. While the **canon**, or the works of literature considered most influential, was male-biased, pseudonyms granted women access to it. These female authors' pseudonyms are a few of many examples of the reality Woolf wrote about in "A Room of One's Own."

The focus of French philosopher and feminist Simone de Beauvoir's (1908–1986) critique was somewhat different than Woolf's; de Beauvoir looked at the images of women in literature and their dehumanizing effect. In her groundbreaking book, *The Second Sex* (1949), she claimed that women are depicted as men's "Other"; their meaning can only be construed in relation to men's. In other words, men serve as the "normal" state of being, and women are a derivation of this. This theory is part of her assessment of "the great collective myth" of the portrayal of women in the works of male writers. Her influence has been far-reaching and can be seen in the goals of feminist analysis to this day.

Assertions of Feminist Analysis

Out of the struggle for women's equality arose feminist literary perspectives, which created a new school of analysis. Feminist critics assert three main points:

- In literature, a pervasively male-dominated and male-centered approach is seen from the classics of ancient Greece to present;
- The canon is biased: what has traditionally been considered great literature focuses on a male protagonist who embodies masculine interests and actions;

- It is necessary to acknowledge that race, class, nationality, historical situation, and gender each have influence in the writing and appreciation of literature.

Exercise 8.1 Devise a list of poems and novels that you consider among the Great Works or literary canon. What does this list tell you, from a feminist perspective?

Lesson Two: **Feminism and Literature**

The role that literature and its analysis may play as a force for social change is important to many social and political movements, including feminism. Feminists believe that the study of the role of gender differences in literature—from knowledge of women writers to what fictional depictions of gender may suggest—can promote awareness of discrimination, double standards, stereotypes, and oppression in people's lives, especially women. This knowledge, feminists assert, will inspire actions that will result in societal change.

Briefly, the goals of feminism, applied to literature, are:

- recovering the work of women writers to enlarge, replace, and reorder the literary canon;

- reanalyzing literature to address the male-centered approach of previous schools of criticism;

- examining the images and characters of women in literature;

- acknowledging that words like "woman" and "feminine" are **cultural constructs**, social categories that are socially defined, that have gender roles attached to them, and that may marginalize an individual's gender identity.

Reordering the Canon

History, feminist scholars suggest, is only the record of the authoritative male experience, written primarily by men, from a male perspective, for men. This results in a seriously distorted representation of the past that ignores the female experience. Likewise, those who have canonized certain Great Works, claiming that they are superior because they represent universal human truths, simply demonstrate their adherence to a male bias. Feminists, therefore, wish to engage in a reordering, rereading, and reanalyzing of the entire literary inheritance.

If literature is defined as a work of emotional or moral significance, and its creation does not rely on gender, feminists ask an obvious question: why have there been far fewer works by women than men in the canon of great literature? They answer that women are underrepresented in the canon because their work has not been brought to readers' attention, and the canon is a creation of male critics' interests. Typically, the literary canon at the time of the 1960s feminist movement included works such as *The Old Man and the Sea*, *Adventures of Huckleberry Finn*, *The Catcher in the Rye*, *1984*, *Animal Farm*, *War and Peace*, *The Invisible Man*, and *Native Son*, all of which have male authors and male protagonists.

In search of a female literary tradition, feminist scholars have noted themes, images, metaphors, and situations unique to women writers. Since the values of the male culture were different, all too many of the works by women have been overlooked. As a result, the female literary tradition is incomplete and in need of rediscovery with the kind of analysis that reflects women's experiences. Charlotte Perkins Gilman's short story "The Yellow Wallpaper" (page 278) is an example of one such previously neglected work. Other rediscovered female authors include H.D. (Hilda Doolittle), Mary Wollstonecraft, Christina Rossetti, and Elizabeth Gaskell.

Reanalyzing Literature

Many feminists argue that since previous analysis is so male dominated, previously analyzed literature must be reevaluated from a feminist perspective. Feminists are often particularly critical of the psychological theories of Sigmund Freud. Freud's theories are attacked for their general disregard for the feminine psyche, as well as for their grossly inaccurate views of women's bodies.

Moreover, such critics assert that Freud failed to consider the implications of a social environment's oppression of women and, as a result, erred in diagnosing the source of his female patients' neuroses. Worse, his critics charge, Freud generalized from his experiences with psychotics to describe the female population at large. These generalizations and errors subsequently led to simplistic theories regarding the experience of the female psyche.

Many feminists conclude that the preference for Freud among any number of practicing psychologists of his day constitutes a further extension of political oppression against women—coming as it did at the very time when women were achieving the right to vote, developing the beginnings of effective birth control, introducing the Equal Rights Amendment (1923), and, for the first time, being granted custody of their children in divorce settlements. They feel Freud's psychological views overly influenced literary analysis in ways that were, and continue to be, detrimental to the interests of women.

Feminists also often criticize theories of Carl Jung for their failure to recognize and include a feminine consciousness, and they assert that this omission has led to error-driven literary analyses. Feminists suggest that archetypal analysis fundamentally undervalues the role of women: a point that even Jung admitted late in life. This underemphasis of women may be readily observed by comparing his many archetypal male characters with his few original archetypal images of women: the *good mother*, the *terrible mother*, and the *soul mate*. Only in contemporary times have the list and roles of female archetypes been greatly expanded by Jungian theorists.

Feminists believe that any society that strives for equality must look beyond rigid, stereotypical views of gender in order to value all human beings by emphasizing their equal importance. Many feminists critics, however, employ Jung's archetypal analysis of male characters but adapt and extrapolate from his theories to provide a better understanding of female characters. This involves emphasizing women in literature as fully realized archetypes, rather than merely one-dimensional characters.

Images and Gender Roles in Literature

Feminist critics are concerned with the images of women as they have persisted in literature. Simone de Beauvoir made influential observations that are often cited in discussions of female images in literature, and gender roles in general. First, she asserted that women were portrayed either as Mary or Eve: the angelic mother or the evil seductress. *The Canterbury Tales* illustrates de Beauvoir's assertion: Chaucer's women are either associated with the church and motherhood or identified as manipulative and seductive. For example:

Mary: "The Prioress' Tale" focuses on devotion to the Virgin Mary, and the female character is portrayed as nothing more than a weeping mother.

Eve: In "The Wife of Bath," the only desire of women is to have control over their husbands and lovers. The female characters are portrayed as overbearing and manipulative.

Second, de Beauvoir said that male-dominated literature depicts women only in relationship to men, portraying them only as the "other" and not as individuals in their own right. Finally, regarding gender roles, she said, "One is not born a woman; one becomes one," meaning that the roles that men and women assume are learned and cultural, rather than biologically determined.

Exercise 8.2 Read the following poems. Compare their commentaries on gender roles. What are their social and historical contexts? Write your response in one to two paragraphs.

WOMEN'S RIGHTS

It is her right, to bind with warmest ties,
   The lordly spirit of aspiring man,
Making his home an earthly paradise,
   Rich in all joys allotted to life's span;
Twining around each fibre of his heart,
   With all the gentle influence of love's might,
Seeking no joy wherein he has no part—
   This is undoubtedly – a woman's right!
It is her right to teach the infant mind,
   Training it ever upward in its course,
To root out evil passions that would bind
   The upward current of his reason's force;
To lead the erring spirit gently back,
   When it has sunk in gloom of deepest night;
To point the shining path of virtue's track,
   And urge him forward. This is woman's right.
It is her right to soothe the couch of pain;
   There her pure mission upon earth to prove,
To calm with gentle care the frenzied brain,
   And keep her vigil there of holiest love;
To watch untiring by the lonely bed,
   Through the bright day, and in the solemn night,
'Til health ensues, or the loved form is laid
   To rest for ever. This is woman's right.
She is a flower that blossoms best, unseen,
   Sheltered within the precincts of her home;
There, should no dark'ning storm-cloud intervene,
   There, the loud-strife of worldlings never come.
Let her not scorn to act a *woman's* part,
   Nor strive to cope with manhood in its might,
But lay this maxim closely to her heart—
   That that which God ordains is surely right.

—*Rebekah Gumpert Hyneman (1812–1875)*

AUNT JENNIFER'S TIGERS

Aunt Jennifer's tigers prance across a screen,
Bright topaz denizens of a world of green.
They do not fear the men beneath the tree;
They pace in sleek chivalric certainty.

Aunt Jennifer's finger fluttering through her wool
Find even the ivory needle hard to pull.
The massive weight of Uncle's wedding band
Sits heavily upon Aunt Jennifer's hand.

When Aunt is dead, her terrified hands will lie
Still ringed with ordeals she was mastered by.
The tigers in the panel that she made
Will go on prancing, proud and unafraid.

—*Adrienne Rich (1929–2012)*

Exercise 8.3 Reread the short story "Young Goodman Brown" (page 249). What gender characterizations are present or missing? How might these biases reflect the time in which the story was written? Your response should be at least one page and include specific examples from the text.

Lesson Three: **Writing the Feminist Analysis**

The emphasis of feminist analysis differs from the previous approaches discussed in *Sequel*, but many of their techniques can be helpful in formulating ideas about the work you choose to analyze. A thorough understanding of literary elements (formalism) is vital in a constructive feminist analysis. For example, if a single male or female character is presented as one dimensional, you may wish to speculate that the author is using that character to symbolize a larger idea. Also, if you find the characterization of the protagonist reflective of the time period in which it was written (contextual), you may wish to speculate how that relates to the theme of the work. Briefly restated below are aspects of previously discussed types of literary analysis that may be helpful in writing a feminist analysis:

Reader response (page 117) postulates that it is the reader who gives meaning to the text. According to feminist analysis, the reader's response would be influenced by gender, which, in turn, is influenced by socio-economic status, ethnicity, sexual orientation, and religion.

Contextual analysis (page 113) employs knowledge of the social and historical era of the work as well as the author's biography. A feminist analysis may explore the status of women during the period in which the work was written, as well as any information about the author that contributes to his or her perspective on women.

Formalist analysis (page 135) seeks to understand the work only through the text itself, discounting the influence of any outside factors—connotation, symbols, and figurative language are paramount. For example, the connotation of words such as "women" and "men," as well as symbols and figurative language, are all useful insights in a feminist analysis.

Psychological analysis (page 153) helps to understand and interpret characters by examining their unconscious motivations and behavior. Feminist analysis is often critical of Freud; instead it examines the impact of societal forces on the psyches of women.

Archetypal analysis (page 169) looks at literature through the lens of archetypes and mythology. Jung's original three female archetypes have been greatly expanded, and these provide feminist analysis with a wider exploration of both female archetypes and archetypal situations.

The following questions should be considered in a feminist analysis:

- Were both male and female characters equally developed? If not, why not, and what effect is created in the text?
- If the author presented a stereotypical, one-dimensional, or marginalized view of women (or men), what was the impact on the work?
- What perspectives, or points of view are, or are not, seen in the work?

Exercise 8.4 Write a one-page feminist analysis of the following poem, "The New Colossus" by Emma Lazarus. Be sure to cover all the above questions for feminist analysis.

The New Colossus

Not like the brazen giant of Greek fame,
With conquering limbs astride from land to land;
Here at our sea-washed, sunset gates shall stand
A mighty woman with a torch, whose flame
Is the imprisoned lightning, and her name
Mother of Exiles. From her beacon-hand
Glows world-wide welcome; her mild eyes command
The air-bridged harbor that twin cities frame.
"Keep, ancient lands, your storied pomp!" cries she
With silent lips. "Give me your tired, your poor,
Your huddled masses yearning to breathe free,
The wretched refuse of your teeming shore.
Send these, the homeless, tempest-tost to me,
I lift my lamp beside the golden door!"

—*Emma Lazarus (1849–1887)*

Exercise 8.5 Read "The Yellow Wallpaper" (page 278). Write a feminist analysis of the story, considering the themes, metaphors, and situations as well as the context of the work. For help with planning, organizing, and writing a literary analysis, see Unit Nine, "Writing an Analysis" (page 215).

Post-Assessment:

Circle the letter of the correct answer of each question.

1. **Many feminist critics believe that the primary objective of feminist analysis should be**
   (A) political and social
   (B) social and sexual
   (C) only descriptive
   (D) only academic
   (E) psychological

2. **Previous analysis needs to be reevaluated because**
   (A) there is little new literature to analyze
   (B) it is good experience
   (C) previous analysis is male-dominated
   (D) few women can relate to male writers
   (E) it relies too little on Freud

3. **The ideal literature to feminists is**
   (A) female-dominated
   (B) when each sex is in its prescribed role
   (C) without male bias or stereotypes
   (D) androgynous
   (E) romantic

4. **Feminists feel that the archetypal analysis of Jung**
   (A) is preferable for its emphasis of the sexes
   (B) is most chauvinistic of all analytical perspectives
   (C) is without logical foundation
   (D) undervalues the role of women
   (E) neglects the contributions of the housewife

5. **Feminist critics condemn the Great Works because they**
   (A) are Freudian
   (B) were selected from Europe
   (C) combine approaches
   (D) do not represent literature equally from a female perspective
   (E) emphasize sociology

6. Feminist analysis is, in part, an outgrowth of
   (A) the antiwar movement
   (B) the women's liberation movement
   (C) the anti-nuclear movement
   (D) the movement to secure the right to vote for women
   (E) all of the above

PART THREE

Writing a Literary Analysis

UNIT NINE

Writing a Literary Analysis

Writing a literary analysis essay is an opportunity to think critically about a work's theme—its overarching idea of moral or emotional significance—and how that theme was created in the work. Often, our ideas about the meaning of a poem or work of fiction change when we read a piece for a second or third time and we become aware of how an author has constructed his or her work. We may even find multiple or even conflicting meanings.

Knowledge of both literary elements and devices, as well as critical theories, is of the utmost importance to undertaking a critical analysis. You may know from classroom discussion or your own reading that a single work of literature may be analyzed in many different ways. For instance, Charlotte Perkins Gilman's "The Yellow Wallpaper" could be analyzed from a contextual, formalist, psychological, or feminist perspective. What every successful critical analysis has in common is that its thesis, or claim, is clearly and logically supported by the literary text it examines.

Objectives

AFTER READING THIS CHAPTER YOU WILL BE ABLE TO:

1. Perform close readings and annotation of a work;

2. Select a topic for a critical analysis;

3. Narrow the topic to a working and refined thesis statement;

4. Formulate topic sentences related to the thesis;

5. Outline the essay, including introductory, body, and concluding; paragraphs

6. Draft, revise, and write a finished critical analysis essay.

Lesson One: **Annotating a Work**

There are several steps to writing a critical analysis of a literary work, whether poetry or fiction. First, readers need to be familiar with the images and events of the piece—what are the experiences or events described in the work? Second, how are those experiences or events described, and to what end? For example, does the work rely on figurative language, irony, or illusions to illustrate a theme? And finally, how might the work be interpreted using a particular style of critical analysis?

Reading and Rereading a Work

Even before annotating a literary work, you need to be very familiar with it—this may mean reading it several times before you can actually make all the notes that might occur to you. With second or third readings, new relevance and new perspectives often emerge from passages that, at first, may have seemed meaningless.

As you have seen from E. E. Cummings's poem, "in Just—" (page 40), it's a good idea to begin by asking yourself what you expect to find based on a work's title. Does the title imply an allusion or a metaphor? In Kate Chopin's "The Story of an Hour" (page 265), it seems apparent that the story will, in fact, take place in the span of an hour. This leads the reader to questions concerning the impact that an hour could potentially have on a person's life. Will it be eventful or reflective? Is the hour figurative or literal? Thinking about these questions and possibilities will prepare you for reading closely and annotating; you will know to be aware of literal and figurative connections. By being on the lookout for figurative language and literary devices, you will be better prepared to find elements of the piece that will suggest both a topic for your paper and, eventually, your thesis—the overarching statement that your paper works to prove or disprove.

Annotation

Annotation is the process of reading through a text and developing a critical commentary through notes, whether they are in the margin or on a separate piece of paper or note cards. You may want to make notes about any literary elements the author uses and possible themes of the work you come across, as well any questions that a particular critical theory may pose.

For instance, in the sample formalist analysis we will present in this chapter, identifying literary elements such as irony, diction, imagery, and foreshadowing (see Lesson Two of Formalist Analysis, page 139) will be of greatest importance. Different analytical approaches will, of course, ask different questions of a work.

Below is an example of an annotation of "The Story of an Hour." In this annotation, you will see the reader identify elements of formalism and begin to postulate ideas as to how these elements contribute to the overall meaning of the text. Keep in mind that these comments were not made on a first reading, but developed over multiple, in-depth readings.

THE STORY OF AN HOUR

1. The main character is first presented without her first name, implying that only through her marriage does she have an identity. This may imply confinement in her marriage.

2. Foreshadowing. Mrs. Mallard has heart trouble.

3. Diction. Her heart may break from this news, so it must be broken to her gently.

1-3.   Knowing that Mrs. Mallard [1] was afflicted with heart trouble, [2] great care was taken to break [3] to her as gently as possible the news of her husband's death.

4. Diction. The sentences are broken now, just like her heart should be.

5. "Sad" seems an understatement for a tragedy, implying that there may be an understated reaction in the reception of this message.

4-5.   It was her sister Josephine who told her, in broken sentences; veiled hints that revealed in half concealing. [4] Her husband's friend Richards was there, too, near her. It was he who had been in the newspaper office when intelligence of the railroad disaster was received, with Brently Mallard's name leading the list of "killed." He had only taken the time to assure himself of its truth by a second telegram, and had hastened to forestall any less careful, less tender friend in bearing the sad [5] message.

6. *Abandonment—could imply unrestrained, uninhibited, or free, as well as left alone, cast-off.*

7. *The grief spent itself—she did not spend it. This implies that she was not in control of her reaction, but it was in control of her.*

8. *This is an ironic image of comfort and happiness in a tragic circumstance.*

9. *An exhaustion from grief, but also from marriage.*

10. *Body and soul—a statement she repeats later.*

11. *An ironic image compared to the death of her husband.*

12. *The entire paragraph is an ironic setting of pleasantness, implying that the world outside of the grief-filled house is delightful—a place she would rather be. She seems to be focusing on life rather than death.*

13. *This image seems to represent hope in the blue sky, with patches of clouds representing the trauma of her husband's death. The hope shows through—still focusing on life rather than death.*

14. *Again, the grief seems to be completely physical—something she cannot control, as the sobs come up on their own, thoughtlessly.*

6-7.   She did not hear the story as many women have heard the same, with a paralyzed inability to accept its significance. She wept at once, with sudden, wild abandonment, [6] in her sister's arms. When the storm of grief had spent itself[7] she went away to her room alone. She would have no one follow her.

8-10.   There stood, facing the open window, a comfortable, roomy armchair. [8] Into this she sank, pressed down by a physical exhaustion [9] that haunted her body and seemed to reach into her soul. [10]

11-12. She could see in the open square before her house the tops of trees that were all aquiver with the new spring life. [11] The delicious breath of rain was in the air. In the street below a peddler was crying his wares. The notes of a distant song which someone was singing reached her faintly, and countless sparrows were twittering in the eaves. [12]

13.   There were patches of blue sky showing here and there through the clouds [13] that had met and piled one above the other in the west facing her window.

14.   She sat with her head thrown back upon the cushion of the chair, quite motionless, except when a sob came up into her throat and shook her, as a child who has cried itself to sleep continues to sob in its dreams. [14]

15. *A repression of the pains she felt in being tied down by marriage.*

16. *This is a loaded sentence—implying that the reaction that follows is abandoned of thought—of rationality—and instead comes from her heart and is completely natural.*

17. *Out of the image of hope.*

18. *Reaching through the ironic setting of pleasant comfort.*

19. *Heavy breathing—a physical reaction she cannot control. Foreshadowing of her heart problems.*

15-16. She was young, with a fair, calm face, whose lines bespoke repression [15] and even a certain strength. But now there was a dull stare in her eyes, whose gaze was fixed away off yonder on one of those patches of blue sky. It was not a glance of reflection, but rather indicated a suspension of intelligent thought. [16]

17-18. There was something coming to her and she was waiting for it, fearfully. What was it? She did not know; it was too subtle and elusive to name. But she felt it, creeping out of the sky, [17] reaching toward her through the sounds, the scents, the color that filled the air. [18]

19.   Now her bosom rose and fell tumultuously. She was beginning to recognize this thing that was approaching herself a little whispered word escaped her slightly parted lips. She said it over and over under her breath: "free, free, free!" The vacant stare and the look for terror that had followed it went from her eyes. They stayed keen and bright. her pulses beat fast, [19] and the coursing blood warmed and relaxed every inch of her body.

    She did not stop to ask if it were or were not a monstrous joy that held her. A clear and exalted perception enabled her to dismiss the suggestion as trivial.

20. *She would weep by reaction, not by her own consent.*

21. *Complete ownership—something her life has been void of, and something she can look forward to in her life without Brently.*

22. *This seems to be an important paragraph about the rationality of Louise's reaction. The explanation of her views on marriage illuminate the reader as to why she may not be as sad at Brently's passing as one may expect.*

23. *The confliction in her emotional attachment to Brently makes her grief conflicted, too.*

24. *Love is emotional, and she dismisses an analysis of its meaning, since she doesn't understand her emotions very well to begin with.*

25. *The only possession she seems to agree with is self-possession.*

26. *Body and soul.*

27. *The first mention of her name.*

28. *Foreshadowing.*

29. *Open to the ironic setting of pleasant comfort.*

20-21. She knew that she would weep again [20] when she saw the kind, tender hands folded in death; the face that had never looked save with love upon her, fixed and gray and dead. But she saw beyond that bitter moment a long procession of years to come that would belong to her absolutely. [21] And she opened and spread her arms out to them in welcome.

22. There would be no one to live for her during those coming years; she would live for herself. There would be no powerful will bending hers in that blind persistence with which men and women believe they have a right to impose a private will upon a fellow creature. A kind intention or a cruel intention made the act seem no less a crime as she looked upon it in that brief moment of illumination. [22]

23-25. And yet she had loved him—sometimes. Often she had not. [23] What did it matter! What could love, the unsolved mystery, [24] count for in face of this possession of self-assertion [25] which she suddenly recognized as the strongest impulse of her being!

26. "Free! Body and soul free!" [26] she kept whispering.

27-28. Josephine was kneeling before the closed door with her lips to the keyhole, imploring for admission. "Louise, [27] open the door! I beg; open the door—you will make yourself ill. [28] What are you doing, Louise? For heaven's sake, open the door."

29. "Go away, I am not making myself ill." No; she was drinking the very elixir of life through that open window. [29]

30. Looking toward the future with hope instead of the past with grief.

31. Implying illness. Foreshadowing.

32. The word "clasp" implies a traumatic grasp, as if it were difficult to walk without leaning on her sister. Foreshadowing of her illness.

33. Her husband—not dead.
34. A mundane entrance, like any other.

35. Irony—it is her husband's survival that breaks her heart.

30.   Her fancy was running riot along those days ahead of her. Spring days, summer days, and all sorts of days that would be her own. [30] She breathed a quick prayer that life might be long. It was only yesterday she had thought with a shudder that life might be long.

31-32. She arose at length and opened the door to her sister's importunities. There was a feverish [31] triumph in her eyes, and she carried herself unwittingly like a goddess of Victory. She clasped [32] her sister's waist, and together they descended the stairs. Richards stood waiting for them at the bottom.

33-34. Someone was opening the front door with a latchkey. It was Brently Mallard [33] who entered, a little travel-stained, composedly carrying his grip-sack and umbrella. [34] He had been far from the scene of accident, and did not even know there had been one. He stood amazed at Josephine's piercing cry; at Richard's quick motion to screen him from the view of his wife.

But Richards was too late.

35.   When the doctors came they said she had died of heart disease—of joy that kills. [35]

—*Kate Chopin (1851–1904)*

224

Lesson Two: **From Topic to Thesis**

L iterature is, by definition, complex and often multilayered; readers must be inquisitive and open-minded when thinking about the uses and functions of elements and devices—the possibilities are as broad as the literary evidence suggests. Remember, however, that whatever you choose to discuss in your analysis must be supported by the text. You will need to point to specific examples and quotations in the work in order to write a successful analysis.

Finding a Topic

After reading and annotating a piece, you may see a pattern emerging: a pattern of literary devices used by the author. For example, in "The Story of an Hour," foreshadowing and figurative language are often employed. If you conclude the purpose was to convey irony, was it successful? Why? You may notice a second or third literary element or device appearing frequently in a piece. An analysis can have a topic that includes more than one element or device used by the author. In this case, make sure the purpose of each is related to your thesis, the statement that will develop from your topic.

For instance, in "The Story of an Hour," what do Chopin's imagery, diction, and foreshadowing all have in common regarding their function in the piece? Do they each create a deeper understanding of Louise Mallard? Of her grief? Of her death? Do the devices work together to show a distinction between abandonment and liberation? Or is it the opposite?

When you are quite familiar with your reading selection, you can begin to identify a topic for analysis that interests you. Some formalist topics that might be considered for "The Story of an Hour" are as follows:

1. The use of figurative language to create tension and ambiguity.
2. The use of imagery to contrast freedom and restriction.
3. The use of imagery, diction, and foreshadowing to create irony.

It is important to choose a topic that is interesting enough to be worth your effort, as well as having enough material to develop a thesis and subsequent body paragraphs. Annotating a work is vital to establishing whether there is enough evidence in the text for your topic. You may also find it helpful to brainstorm with a prewriting technique like free-writing or mind mapping to make sure you have sufficient material for development.

Writing a Thesis

The process of creating a thesis from your topic is not always direct, so it is usually necessary to write a working thesis, which is developed enough to catalyze an outline or rough draft but may require more fine-tuning as you refine your paper. In this example, the reader has chosen the topic of the use of ironic imagery, diction, and foreshadowing, but there is still room to take it a step further. Here is how a thesis could develop.

> Example: "The Story of an Hour"
>
> A. The use of imagery, diction, and foreshadowing in "The Story of an Hour."
> B. The irony in Louise Mallard's reaction to the news of her husband's death.

Thesis Statements

Your thesis statement is the most important element of your paper—it is the basis of everything you will write in the subsequent paragraphs. From the attention-getting opening sentence to the concluding sentence in the final paragraph, everything must relate to the thesis. It can be difficult to write without preparation; however, if you ask yourself the correct questions before, during, and after reading a piece, then writing a thesis will come more easily.

In this example, we go back to the reader's topic of ironic imagery, diction, and foreshadowing. Here is how a thesis could develop:

> **Draft #1:** *In Kate Chopin's short work, "The Story of an Hour," Chopin creates irony through imagery, diction, and foreshadowing.*

Now ask yourself, "What is the purpose of this irony?" Is there an overarching theme created through irony?

> **Draft #2:** *In Kate Chopin's short work, "The Story of an Hour," Chopin uses imagery, diction, and foreshadowing to create irony in Louise's reaction to her husband's death.*

Still, this thesis could use a more specific aspect of the story to focus on in order to add precision to the statement. Which aspect of Louise's reaction is most ironic? Could it be that her heart breaks when her husband is alive rather than when she thinks he is dead? What does that say about the word "heartbreaking"?

Draft #3: *Throughout her story, Chopin creates irony in the word "heart-breaking" through imagery, diction, and foreshadowing in her portrayal of Louise's reaction to Brently's death.*

This thesis gives purpose to the literary devices used by Chopin: the purpose of creating irony in a common figurative expression. While this is not the only direction one could have taken this initial working thesis, it is one option in developing a thesis that will sustain an entire analysis.

Topic Sentences

A topic sentence is the sentence at the beginning of a paragraph that conveys the purpose of that paragraph, in relation to the thesis. If you list your topic sentences prior to creating an outline, you are assured that you will have identified enough material to support your thesis. Beginning with your thesis, think about the paragraph division you want in your analysis. It should be simple if your thesis is precise enough. Then, when you have carefully considered what you want to cover, write your potential topic sentences, in order, under your selected thesis. You will use these topic sentences in the outline you create. For example:

Thesis *In her short work, "The Story of an Hour," Kate Chopin creates irony in the word "heartbreaking" through imagery, foreshadowing, and diction in her portrayal of Louise's reaction to Brently's death.*

Topic Sentence #1
Chopin uses imagery throughout the piece in order to create irony in Louise's "heartbreaking" reaction to Brently's death.

Topic Sentence #2
The diction Chopin uses to show Louise's response to the loss of her husband further develops the ironic use of of the word "heartbreaking."

Topic Sentence #3
Finally, Chopin creates the ultimate irony in the word "heart-breaking" with her foreshadowing of Louise's heart disease.

Lesson Three: **The Outline**

Organizing your writing process helps to ensure that producing a literary analysis paper does not become overwhelming. Reading with enough curiosity and focus to understand the literary concepts, organize the importance of these concepts, and construct a thesis that relates these concepts to one overarching idea is not something you can easily do without preparation. Creating an outline allows you to present your thesis, topic sentences, and supporting sentences in the order in which you think they would be best presented, while allowing you to easily rearrange ideas without disassembling your paper.

Writing an outline can be very structured or quite informal. For some, it is easier to use a piece of scrap paper and jot down a few ideas haphazardly. This doesn't work for everyone; in fact, most find that it is better to be over-prepared in terms of organization. Some of the best-organized outlines consist of lettered and numbered points and sub-points that flow in a logical pattern.

For illustration purposes, a sample outline using a highly structured organization is shown. The example will take you through the process of outlining an analytical paper for Chopin's "The Story of an Hour," showing the type of information that would go in each portion of the outline.

Once you have a working thesis and possible topic sentences, you can proceed promptly to the development of your outline. In the example below, general instructions will precede specific examples for Chopin's piece in italics.

1. **Introduction**

   A. Begin with a broad attention-getting sentence. How would you best acquaint your audience with the topic you will be writing about? For example:

   The expression "heartbreaking" is one of the most common uses of figurative language.

   B. From your attention-getter, you must logically draw your reader to the thesis, which should come at the end of your introduction. Here, you lay out a few ideas relating to the content of your introduction; the goal is to draw the reader from the broad (attention-getter) to the narrow (thesis).

   "Heartbreaking" can be used to describe a variety of situations; feeling heartbreak at the loss of a loved one is one of the most common uses of the expression; feeling heartbreak at the loved one's survival is ironic.

C. Thesis

In her short work, "The Story of an Hour," Kate Chopin creates irony in the word "heartbreaking" through imagery, diction, and foreshadowing in her portrayal of Louise's reaction to Brently's death.

2. **Body Paragraph 1**—This paragraph should focus on the first point of the thesis, in this case, imagery. If there is only one point in the thesis, this paragraph should focus on one aspect of that point.

   A. Topic sentence:

   Chopin uses imagery throughout the piece in order to create irony in Louise's "heartbreaking" reaction to Brently's death.

   B. Support sentence(s). Include a direct quotation from the piece. Always support the importance of a quotation by explaining its relation to this point of your thesis in your own words:

   Louise's sorrowful response of weeping "with sudden, wild abandonment in her sister's arms" is followed by the ironic imagery of "new spring life" and a blue sky (page 265).

   C. Relate the topic of this paragraph back to the thesis in the paragraph's final sentence:

   Instead of a predominance of heartbreaking imagery, Chopin utilizes uplifting imagery in order to express the irony of Louise's reaction to Brently's death.

3. **Body Paragraph 2**—This paragraph elaborates the second point of the thesis, diction.

   A. Topic sentence:

   The diction Chopin uses to show Louise's response to the loss of her husband further develops the ironic use of the word "heartbreaking."

   B. Cite words in the text to support your topic sentence:

   "Break" the news, "broken sentences" allude to a broken heart (page 265); the meaning of "abandonment" should be loneliness, but the irony is a connotation of liberation (page 266); "free" is the word she feels in her soul— ironic in that she is expected to feel sadness instead of freedom.

C. Relate the topic of this paragraph back to the thesis in the paragraph's final sentence:

Chopin's use of diction throughout her story creates irony in Louise's reaction to Brently's demise by presenting the news as heartbreaking, but ultimately rendering it as liberating.

4. **Body Paragraph 3**—This paragraph develops the third point of the thesis, foreshadowing.

A. Topic sentence:

Finally, Chopin creates the ultimate irony in the word "heartbreaking" by foreshadowing Louise Mallard's heart disease.

B. Illustrate your topic sentence with examples:

Mrs. Mallard has heart trouble (page 265); "bosom rose and fell tumultuously" foreshadows labored breathing and being overpowered by illness (page 265); this foreshadowing of heart troubles creates irony when Louise's heart finally gives out because her husband is alive—a reader would expect the opposite, that her heart gives out from grief when she believes Brently dead.

C. Relate the topic of this paragraph back to the thesis in the paragraph's final sentence:

By employing foreshadowing to create intrigue around Louise's health, Chopin is able to create the ultimate irony in the word "heartbreaking" when Louise's heart breaks from the sudden loss of joy instead of the sudden loss of her husband.

Continue the body paragraph format for as many body paragraphs as you need—three is typical for a short paper, and works with this thesis because there are three literary devices that need to be explained and illustrated. However, you may need more to fully develop your thesis.

5. **Conclusion**

A. Begin by restating the thesis:

Whether it is through imagery, diction, or foreshadowing, Chopin employs these literary devices to convey irony in the word "heartbreaking."

B. The conclusion works like a mirror image of the introduction—after starting with the specificity of your conclusion, you need to work your way backward toward a broader sense of the topic. Where the introduction was broad-to-narrow, the conclusion needs to be narrow-to-broad:

> *It is Brently's survival that ultimately breaks Louise's heart, giving Chopin's story its ironic use of the word "heartbreaking."*

Lesson Four: **Drafting and Revising Your Analysis**

Once you have a revised thesis and have created an outline, the next step is to write the first draft of your analysis. You can check for errors or logic problems yourself, but you may wish to have another reader's input—a "fresh set of eyes." After revising for content, editing for mechanical errors, and fixing any organization or logic problems, you are ready to write your final copy.

Heartbreaking Irony:

The Ironic Composition of Kate Chopin's "The Story of an Hour"

The expression "heartbreaking" is one of the most common uses of figurative language. It can represent a person's sorrow regarding a variety of situations: a lost baseball game, a baby's cry, a couple's breakup. Seemingly, the most apt use of the word would come into play at the death of a loved one. But what if the heartbreak isn't in response to a loved one's death, but instead, survival? It is this irony that propels Kate Chopin's short story, "The Story of an Hour." When Louise hears that her husband, Brently Mallard, has been killed in a railroad disaster, she is not overwhelmed by grief, as a reader may expect, but by joy. Ultimately, her final heartbreak does not appear until her husband's death is disproved by his arrival at their front door. In "The Story of an Hour," Chopin creates irony in the word "heartbreaking" through imagery, diction, and foreshadowing in her portrayal of Louise's reaction to Brently's death.

Chopin uses imagery throughout the piece in order to create irony in Louise's "heartbreaking" reaction to Brently's death. While Chopin makes it clear that Louise did respond with sorrow at the first hearing of the news, weeping "with sudden, wild abandonment in her sister's arms," she quickly contrasts this tragic response with ironically uplifting imagery of the view from her window. Chopin writes that Louise "could see in the open square before her house the tops of trees that were all aquiver with new spring life" (page 265). The new spring life with which Louise is preoccupied is ironic, since she is surrounded by the idea of her husband's death. The irony continues when Chopin writes, "there were patches of blue sky showing here and there through the clouds that had met and piled one above the other in the west facing her window" (page 265). This first imagery of a cloudy sky seems to represent the situation in which Louise finds herself: the sky is life, while the clouds over-taking it are death's sad burden. However, this imagery becomes ironic when Louise's gaze is "fixed away off yonder on one of those patches of blue sky" (page 265). Here, Chopin expresses that Louise, who should be overwhelmed by Brently's death, is instead transfixed by the clearness with which she sees her own life in his absence: The idea of freedom "creeping out of the sky" is what engrosses her (page 265). Instead of a predominance of heartbreaking imagery, Chopin utilizes uplifting imagery in order to express the irony of Louise's reaction to Brently's death.

The diction Chopin uses to show Louise's response to the loss of her husband further develops the ironic use of the word "heartbreaking." Within the first two lines of Chopin's piece, her diction alludes to the word she is infusing with irony. First, Chopin writes, "great care was taken to break to her as gently as possible the news of her husband's death" (page 265). Here, the word "break" is used to create an image of the news as being destructive in nature, capable of breaking hearts along with happiness. Directly following, Chopin writes, "It was her sister Josephine who told her, in broken sentences" (page 265) The use of "broken" in Josephine's sentences further employs the image of the news' destructive power; it not only has the potential to break Louise's heart, but it is powerful enough to break the very sentences that hold its message. Chopin continues to give power to the news of Brently's death through diction when she describes Louise's initial reaction. Chopin writes, "She wept at once, with sudden, wild abandonment" (page 265). The word "abandonment" can mean many things, including being sadly left behind in aloneness, as well as gleeful lack of inhibition. These uses of diction to create irony continue when Chopin alerts the reader to what Louise really feels about her husband's death. The word coming to Louise, which she says "over and over under her breath," is "free" (page 265). While Chopin describes Louise's sob with the spirit of "abandonment," she creates irony in the fact that the only thing Louise can think about is her newfound "freedom"; instead of being in despair at the thought of her solitude, Louise is thrilled by the liberation that comes with it. Chopin's use of diction throughout her story creates irony in Louise's reaction to Brently's demise by presenting the news as heartbreaking, but ultimately rendering it as liberating.

Finally, Chopin creates the ultimate irony in the word "heartbreaking" with her foreshadowing of Louise's heart disease. The first mention of Louise—Mrs. Mallard—is paired with the information that she has heart trouble (page 265). From this clue, the reader is alerted to descriptions of Louise's health. Foreshadowing of her illness continues when Chopin writes, "Now her bosom rose and fell tumultuously" (page 265). On the surface, Louise's bosom rising and falling in such a chaotic manner is used to illustrate her excitement at the prospect of freedom; however, this imagery is also used to foreshadow her laborious breathing and her illness overpowering her. A similar use of foreshadowing is seen again when Chopin writes, "her pulses beat fast," (page 265) indicating simultaneous excitement and the potential for her weak heart to collapse under the pressure. Foreshadowing is used not only in imagery, but also in dialogue when Josephine cautions her sister. Josephine's warning, "you will make yourself ill," foreshadows the reality that Louise's reaction to Brently's death is overstimulating her weak heart; the irony here is that, while Josephine believes her heart is weakened by sadness, it is actually being weakened by overexcitement. Ultimately, Chopin's foreshadowing of Louise's heart problems reaches its fruition in her final irony, when Brently appears at their front door and Louise's heart breaks at his survival instead of his death. By employing foreshadowing to create intrigue in Louise's health, Chopin is able to create the ultimate irony in the word "heartbreaking" when Louise's heart breaks from the sudden loss of joy instead of the sudden loss of her husband.

Whether it is through imagery, diction, or foreshadowing, Chopin employs these literary devices to convey irony in the expression "heartbreaking." At the perceived loss of her husband, a reader can expect Louise to respond with a feeling of abandonment and sorrow. Instead, his death spurs hope for a life full of freedom and happiness. While her sister—her friend—could easily view her seclusion and tears as sorrow, the reader is aware of the ironic pleasure Louise feels at the prospect of liberation from her confining marriage. Furthermore, it isn't until Brently shows himself as alive that his continued existence pulls Louise into unendurable grief. It is Brently's survival that ultimately breaks Louise's heart, giving Chopin's story its ironic affect on the word "heartbreaking."

APPENDIX

Selected Readings of Literature for Analysis

Ulysses

It little profits that an idle king,
By this still hearth, among these barren crags,
Matched with an aged wife, I mete and dole
Unequal laws unto a savage race,
That hoard, and sleep, and feed, and know not me.
I cannot rest from travel; I will drink
Life to the lees. All times I have enjoyed
Greatly, have suffered greatly, both with those
That loved me, and alone; on shore, and when
Through scudding drifts the rainy Hyades
Vext the dim sea. I am become a name;
For always roaming with a hungry heart
Much have I seen and known, —cities of men
And manners, climates, councils, governments,
Myself not least, but honored of them all;
And drunk delight of battle with my peers,
Far on the ringing plains of windy Troy.
I am a part of all that I have met;
Yet all experience is an arch wherethrough
Gleams that untraveled world, whose margin fades
For ever and for ever when I move.
How dull it is to pause, to make an end,
To rust unburnished, not to shine in use!
As though to breathe were life! Life piled on life
Were all too little, and one to me
Little remains; but every hour is saved
From that eternal silence, something more,
A bringer of new things; and vile it were
For some three suns to store and hoard myself,
And this grey spirit yearning in desire
To follow knowledge like a sinking star,
Beyond the utmost bound of human thought.
This is my son, mine own Telemachus,
To whom I leave the scepter and the isle—
Well-loved of me, discerning to fulfil
This labor, by slow prudence to make mild
A rugged people, and through soft degrees
Subdue them to the useful and the good.
Most blameless is her, centered in the sphere
Of common duties, decent not to fail
In offices of tenderness, and pay
Meet adoration to my household gods,
When I am gone. He works his work, I mine.
There lies the port; the vessel puffs her sail:
There gloom the dark, broad seas. My mariners,

Souths that have toiled, and wrought, and thought with me—
That ever with a frolic welcome took
The thunder and the sunshine, and opposed
Free hearts, free foreheads—you and I are old;
Old age hath yet his honor and his toil.
Death closes all; but something ere the end,
Some work of noble note, may yet be done,
Not unbecoming men that strove with Gods.
The lights begin to twinkle from the rocks;
The long day wanes; the slow moon climbs; the deep
Moans round with many voices. Come, my friends,
'Tis not too late to seek a newer world.
Push off, and sitting well in order smite
The sounding furrows; for my purpose holds
To sail beyond the sunset, and the baths
Of all the western stars, until I die.
It may be that the gulfs will wash us down;
It may be we shall touch the Happy Isles,
And see the great Achilles, whom we knew.
though much is taken, much abides; and though
We are not now that strength which in old days
Moved earth and heaven, that which we are, we are:
One equal temper of heroic hearts,
Made weak by time and fate, but strong in will
To strive, to seek, to find and not to yield.

—*Alfred, Lord Tennyson (1809–1892)*

THE LOVESONG OF J. ALFRED PRUFROCK

S'io credessi che mia risposta fosse
a persona che mai tornasse al mondo,
questa fiamma staria senza piu scosse.
Ma per cio che giammai di questo fondo
non torno vivo alcun, s'i 'odo il vero,
*senza terma d'infamia ti rispondo.**

Let us go then, you and I,
When the evening is spread out against the sky
Like a patient etherised upon a table;
Let us go, through certain half-deserted streets,
The muttering retreats
Of restless nights in one-night cheap hotels
And sawdust restaurants with oyster-shells:
Streets that follow like a tedious argument
Of insidious intent

To lead you to an overwhelming question . . .
Oh, do not ask, "What is it?"
Let us go and make our visit.
In the room the women come and go
Talking of Michelangelo.
The yellow fog that rubs its back upon the window-panes,
The yellow smoke that rubs its muzzle on the window-panes,
Liked its tongue into the corners of the evening,
Lingered upon the pools that stand in drains,
Let fall upon its back the soot that falls from chimneys,
Slipped by the terrace, made a sudden leap,
And seeing that it was a soft October night,
Curled once about the house, and fell asleep.
And indeed there will be time
For the yellow smoke that slides along the street
Rubbing its back upon the window-panes;
There will be time, there will be time
To prepare a face to meet the faces that you meet;
There will be time to murder and create,
And time for all the works and days of hands
That lift and drop a question on your plate;
Time for you and time for me,
And time yet for a hundred indecisions,
and for a hundred visions and revisions,
Before the taking of a toast and tea.
In the room the women come and go
Talking of Michelangelo.
And indeed there will be time
To wonder, "Do I dare?" and, "do I dare?"
Time to turn back and descend the stair,
With a bald spot in the middle of my hair—
(They will say: "How his hair is growing thin!")
My morning coat, my collar mounting firmly to the chin,
My necktie rich and modest, but asserted by a simple pin—
(they will say: "but how his arms and legs are thing!")
Do I dare
Disturb the universe?
In a minute there is time
for decisions and revisions which a minute will reverse.
for I have known them all already, known them all—
Have known the evenings, morning, afternoons,
I have measured out my life with coffee spoons;
I know the voices dying with a dying fall
Beneath the music from a farther room.
so how should I presume?
and I have known the arms already, known them all—

Arms that are braceleted and white and bare
(But in the lamplight, downed with light brown hair!)
Is it perfume from a dress
That makes me so digress?
Arms that lie along a table, or wrap about a shawl.
And should I then presume?
And how should I begin?

. . . . .

Shall I say, I have gone at dusk through narrow streets
And watched the smoke that rises from the pipes
Of lonely men in shirt-sleeves, leaning out of windows? . . .
I should have been a pair of ragged claws
Scuttling across the floors of silent seas.

. . . . .

And the afternoon, the evening, sleeps so peacefully!
Smoothed by long fingers,
Asleep . . . tired . . . or it malingers,
Stretched on the floor, here beside you and me.
Should I, after tea and cakes and ices,
Have the strength to force the moment to its crisis?
But though I have wept and fasted, wept and prayed,
Though I have seen my head (grown slightly bald) brought in upon a platter,
I am no prophet—and here's no great matter;
I have seen the moment of my greatness flicker,
and I have seen the eternal Footman hold my coat, and snicker,
and in short, I was afraid.
And would it have been worth it, after all,
After the cups, the marmalade, the tea,
Among the porcelain, among some talk of you and me,
Would it have been worth while,
To have bitten off the matter with a smile,
To have squeezed the universe into a ball
To roll it towards some overwhelming question,
To say: "I am Lazarus, come from the dead,
come back to tell you all, I shall tell you all"—
If one, settling a pillow by her head,
should say: 'That is not what I meant at all.
That is not it, at all.'
And would it have been worth it, after all,
Would it have been worth while,
After the sunsets and the dooryards and the sprinkled streets,
After the novels, after the teacups, after the skirts that trail along
the floor—
And this, and so much more?—
It is impossible to say just what I mean!
But as if a magic lantern threw the nerves in patterns on a screen:

242

Would it have been worth while
If one, settling a pillow or throwing off a shawl,
and turning toward the window, should say:
"That is not it at all,
That is not what I meant, at all."

. . . . .

No! I am not Prince Hamlet, nor was meant to be;
Am an attendant lord, one that will do
To swell a progress, start a scene or two,
Advise the prince; no doubt, an easy tool,
Deferential, glad to be of use,
Politic, cautious, and meticulous;
Full of high sentence, but a bit obtuse;
At times, indeed, almost ridiculous—
Almost, at times, the Fool.
I grow old . . . I grow old . . .
I shall wear the bottoms of my trousers rolled.
Shall I part my hair behind? Do I dare to eat a peach?
I shall wear flannel trousers, and walk upon the beach. I have heard the mermaids
singing, each to each.
I do not think that they will sing to me.
I have seen them riding seaward on the waves
Combing the white hair of the waves blown back
When the wind blows the water white and black.
We have lingered in the chambers of the sea
By sea-girls wreathed with seaweed red and brown
'Till human voices wake us, and we drown.

—*T. S. Eliot (1888–1965)*

* "If I thought that my response would be addressed to one who might go back
alive, this flame would shake no more; but since no one ever goes back alive out of
these deeps (if what I hear to be true), without fear of infamy I answer you."

—*Dante's Inferno*

The Masque of the Red Death

The "Red Death" had long devastated the country. No pestilence had ever been so fatal, or so hideous. Blood was its Avatar and its seal—the redness and the horror of blood. There were sharp pains, and sudden dizziness, and then profuse bleeding at the pores, with dissolution. The scarlet stains upon the body and especially upon the face of the victim, were the pest ban which shut him out from the aid and from the sympathy of his fellow-men. And the whole seizure, progress, and termination of the disease, were the incidents of half an hour.

But the Prince Prospero was happy and dauntless and sagacious. When his dominions were half depopulated, he summoned to his presence a thousand hale and light-hearted friends from among the knights and dames of his court, and with these retired to the deep seclusion of one of his castellated abbeys. This was an extensive and magnificent structure, the creation of the prince's own eccentric yet august taste. A strong and lofty wall girdled it in. This wall had gates of iron. The courtiers, having entered, brought furnaces and massy hammers and welded the bolts. They resolved to leave means neither of ingress or egress to the sudden impulses of despair or of frenzy from within. The abbey was amply provisioned. With such precautions the courtiers might bid defiance to contagion. The external world could take care of itself. In the meantime it was folly to grieve, or to think. The prince had provided all the appliances of pleasure. There were buffoons, there were improvisatori, there were ballet dancers, there were musicians, there was beauty, there was wine. All these and security were within. Without was the "Red Death."

It was toward the close of the fifth or sixth month of his seclusion, and while the pestilence raged most furiously abroad, that the Prince Prospero entertained his thousand friends at a masked ball of the most unusual magnificence.

It was a voluptuous scene, that masquerade. But first let me tell of the rooms in which it was held. There were seven—an imperial suite. In many palaces, however, such suites form a long and straight vista, while the folding doors slide back nearly to the walls on either hand, so that the view of the whole extent is scarcely impeded. Here the case was very different; as might have been expected from the duke's love of the bizarre. The apartments were so irregularly disposed that the vision embraced but little more than one at a time. There was a sharp turn at every twenty or thirty yards, and at each turn a novel effect. To the right and left, in the middle of each wall, a tall and narrow Gothic window looked out upon a closed corridor which pursued the windings of the suite. These windows were of stained glass whose color varied in accordance with the prevailing hue of the decorations of the chamber into which it opened. That at the eastern extremity was hung, for example, in blue—and vividly blue were its windows. The second chamber was purple in its ornaments and tapestries, and here the panes were purple. The third was green throughout, and so were the casements. The fourth was furnished and lighted with orange—the fifth with white—the sixth with violet. The seventh apartment was closely shrouded in black velvet tapestries that hung all over the ceiling and down the walls, falling in heavy folds upon a carpet of the same material and hue. But in this chamber only, the color of the windows failed to correspond with the decorations. The panes here were scarlet—a deep blood color. Now in no one of the seven apartments was there any lamp or candelabrum, amid the profusion of golden ornaments that lay scattered to and fro or depended from the roof. There was no light of any kind emanating from lamp or candle within the suite of chambers. But in the corridors that followed the suite, there stood, opposite to each window, a heavy tripod, bearing a brazier of fire that projected its rays through the tinted glass and so glaringly illumined the room. And thus were produced a multitude of gaudy and fantastic appearances. But in the western or black chamber the effect of the firelight that streamed upon the dark hangings through the blood-tinted panes, was ghastly in the extreme, and produced so wild a look upon the countenances of those who entered, that there were few of the company bold enough to set foot within its precincts at all.

It was in this apartment, also, that there stood against the western wall, a gigantic clock of ebony. Its pendulum swung to and fro with a dull, heavy, monotonous clang; and when the minute-hand made the circuit of the face, and the hour was to be stricken, there came from the brazen lungs of the clock a sound which was clear and loud and deep and exceedingly musical, but of so peculiar a note and emphasis that, at each lapse of an hour, the musicians of the orchestra were constrained to pause, momentarily, in their performance, to hearken to the sound; and thus the waltzers perforce ceased their evolutions; and there was a brief disconcert of the whole gay company; and, while the chimes of the clock yet rang, it was observed that the giddiest grew pale, and the more aged and sedate passed their hands over their brows as if in confused reverie or meditation. But when the echoes had fully ceased, a light laughter at once pervaded the assembly; the musicians looked at each other and smiled as if at their own nervousness and folly, and made whispering vows, each to the other, that the next chiming of the clock should produce in them no similar emotion; and then, after the lapse of sixty minutes, (which embrace three thousand and six hundred seconds of the Time that flies,) there came yet another chiming of the clock, and then were the same disconcert and tremulousness and meditation as before.

But in spite of these things, it was a gay and magnificent revel. The tastes of the duke were peculiar. He had a fine eye for colors and effects. He disregarded the *decora* of mere fashion. His plans were bold and fiery, and his conceptions glowed with barbaric lustre. There are some who would have thought him mad. His followers felt that he was not. It was necessary to hear and see and touch him to be sure that he was not.

He had directed, in great part, the moveable embellishments of the seven chambers, upon occasion of this great *fête*; and it was his own guiding taste which had given character to the masqueraders. Be sure they were grotesque. There were much glare and glitter and piquancy and phantasm—much of what has been since seen in *Hernani*. There were arabesque figures with unsuited limbs and appointments. There were delirious fancies such as the madman fashions. There was much of the beautiful, much of the wanton, much of the bizarre, something of the terrible, and not a little of that which might have excited disgust. To and fro in the seven chambers there stalked, in fact, a multitude of dreams. And these—the dreams—writhed in and about, taking hue from the rooms, and causing the wild music of the orchestra to seem as the echo of their steps. And, anon, there strikes the ebony clock which stands in the hall of the velvet. And then, for a moment, all is still, and all is silent save the voice of the clock. The dreams are stiff-frozen as they stand. But the echoes of the chime die away—they have endured but an instant—and a light, half-subdued laughter floats after them as they depart. And now again the music swells, and the dreams live, and writhe to and fro more merrily than ever, taking hue from the many tinted windows through which stream the rays from the tripods. But to the chamber which lies most westwardly of the seven, there are now none of the maskers who venture; for the night is waning away; and there flows a ruddier light through the blood-colored panes; and the blackness of the sable drapery appals; and to him whose foot falls upon the sable carpet, there comes from the near clock of ebony a muffled peal more solemnly emphatic than any which reaches their ears who indulge in the more remote gaieties of the other apartments.

But these other apartments were densely crowded, and in them beat feverishly the heart of life. And the revel went whirlingly on, until at length there commenced the sounding of midnight upon the clock. And then the music ceased, as I have told; and the evolutions of the waltzers were quieted; and there was an uneasy cessation of all things as before. But now there were twelve strokes to be sounded by the bell of the clock; and thus it happened, perhaps, that more of thought crept, with more of time, into the meditations of the thoughtful among those who revelled. And thus, too, it happened, perhaps, that before the last echoes of the last chime had utterly sunk into silence, there were many individuals in the crowd who had found leisure to become aware of the presence of a masked figure which had arrested the attention of no single individual before. And the rumor of this new presence having spread itself whisperingly around, there arose at length from the whole company a buzz, or murmur, expressive of disapprobation and surprise—then, finally, of terror, of horror, and of disgust.

In an assembly of phantasms such as I have painted, it may well be supposed that no ordinary appearance could have excited such sensation. In truth the masquerade license of the night was nearly unlimited; but the figure in question had out-Heroded Herod, and gone beyond the bounds of even the prince's indefinite decorum. There are chords in the hearts of the most reckless which cannot be touched without emotion. Even with the utterly lost, to whom life and death are equally jests, there are matters of which no jest can be made. The whole company, indeed, seemed now deeply to feel that in the costume and bearing of the stranger neither wit nor propriety existed. The figure was tall and gaunt, and shrouded from head to foot in the habiliments of the grave. The mask which concealed the visage was made so nearly to resemble the countenance of a stiffened corpse that the closest scrutiny must have had difficulty in detecting the cheat. And yet all this might have been endured, if not approved, by the mad revellers around. But the mummer had gone so far as to assume the type of the Red Death. His vesture was dabbled in *blood*—and his broad brow, with all the features of the face, was besprinkled with the scarlet horror.

When the eyes of Prince Prospero fell upon this spectral image (which with a slow and solemn movement, as if more fully to sustain its rôle, stalked to and fro among the waltzers) he was seen to be convulsed in the first moment with a strong shudder either of terror or distaste; but, in the next, his brow reddened with rage.

"Who dares?" he demanded hoarsely of the courtiers who stood near him—"who dares insult us with this blasphemous mockery? Seize him and unmask him—that we may know whom we have to hang at sunrise from the battlements!"

It was in the eastern or blue chamber in which stood the Prince Prospero as he uttered these words. They rang throughout the seven rooms loudly and clearly—for the prince was a bold and robust man, and the music had become hushed at the waving of his hand.

It was in the blue room where stood the prince, with a group of pale courtiers by his side. At first, as he spoke, there was a slight rushing movement of this group in the direction of the intruder, who at the moment was also near at hand, and now, with deliberate and stately step, made closer approach to the speaker. But from a certain nameless awe with which the mad assumptions of the mummer had inspired the whole party, there were found none who put forth hand to seize him; so that, unimpeded, he passed within a yard of the prince's person; and, while the vast assembly, as if with one impulse, shrank from the centers of the rooms to the walls, he made his way uninterruptedly, but with the same solemn and measured step which had distinguished him from the first, through the blue chamber to the purple—through the purple to the green—through the green to the orange—through this again to the white—and even thence to the violet, ere a decided movement had been made to arrest him. It was then, however, that the Prince Prospero, maddening with rage and the shame of his own momentary cowardice, rushed hurriedly through the six chambers, while none followed him on account of a deadly terror that had seized upon all. He bore aloft a drawn dagger, and had approached, in rapid impetuosity, to within three or four feet of the retreating figure, when the latter, having attained the extremity of the velvet apartment, turned suddenly and confronted his pursuer. There was a sharp cry—and the dagger dropped gleaming upon the sable carpet, upon which, instantly afterwards, fell prostrate in death the Prince Prospero. Then, summoning the wild courage of despair, a throng of the revellers at once threw themselves into the black apartment, and, seizing the mummer, whose tall figure stood erect and motionless within the shadow of the ebony clock, gasped in unutterable horror at finding the grave-cerements and corpse-like mask which they handled with so violent a rudeness, untenanted by any tangible form.

And now was acknowledged the presence of the Red Death. He had come like a thief in the night. And one by one dropped the revellers in the blood-bedewed halls of their revel, and died each in the despairing posture of his fall. And the life of the ebony clock went out with that of the last of the gay. And the flames of the tripods expired. And Darkness and Decay and the Red Death held illimitable dominion over all.

—*Edgar Allan Poe (1809–1849)*

Young Goodman Brown

Young Goodman Brown came forth at sunset into the street of Salem village; but put his head back, after crossing the threshold, to exchange a parting kiss with his young wife. And Faith, as the wife was aptly named, thrust her own pretty head into the street, letting the wind play with the pink ribbons of her cap while she called to Goodman Brown.

"Dearest heart," whispered she, softly and rather sadly, when her lips were close to his ear, "prithee put off your journey until sunrise and sleep in your own bed tonight. A lone woman is troubled with dreams and such thoughts that she's afeared of herself sometimes. Pray tarry with me this night, dear husband, of all nights in the year. "

"My love and my Faith," replied young Goodman Brown, "of all nights in the year, this one night must I tarry away from thee. My journey, as thou callest it, forth and back again, must needs be done 'twixt now and sunrise. What, my sweet, pretty wife, dost thou doubt me already, and we but three months married?"

"Then God bless you!" said Faith, with the pink ribbons; "and may you find all well when you come back."

"Amen!" cried Goodman Brown. "Say thy prayers, dear Faith, and go to bed at dusk, and no harm will come to thee."

So they parted; and the young man pursued his way until, being about to turn the corner by the meeting house, he looked back and saw the head of Faith still peeping after him with a melancholy air, in spite of her pink ribbons.

"Poor little Faith!" thought he, for his heart smote him. "What a wretch am I to leave her on such an errand! She talks of dreams, too. Methought as she spoke there was trouble in her face, as if a dream had warned her what work is to be done tonight. But no, no; 'twould kill her to think it. Well, she's a blessed angel on earth; and after this one night I'll cling to her skirts and follow her to heaven."

With this excellent resolve for the future, Goodman Brown felt himself justified in making more haste on his present evil purpose. He had taken a dreary road, darkened by all the gloomiest trees of the forest, which barely stood aside to let the narrow path creep through, and closed immediately behind. It was all as lonely as could be; and there is this peculiarity in such solitude, that the traveller knows not who may be concealed by the innumerable trunks and the thick boughs overhead; so that with lonely footsteps he may yet be passing through an unseen multitude.

"There may be a devilish Indian behind every tree," said Goodman Brown to himself; and he glanced fearfully behind him as he added, "What if the devil himself should be at my very elbow!"

His head turned back, he passed a crook of the road, and, looking forward again, beheld the figure of a man, in grave and decent attire, seated at the foot of an old tree. He arose at Goodman Brown's approach and walked onward side by side with him.

"You are late, Goodman Brown, " said he. "The clock of the Old South was striking as I came through Boston; and that is full fifteen minutes agone."

"Faith kept me back a while," replied the young man, with a tremor in his voice, caused by the sudden appearance of his companion, though not wholly unexpected.

It was now deep dusk in the forest, and deepest in that part of it where these two were journeying. As nearly as could be discerned, the second traveller was about fifty years old, apparently in the same rank of life as Goodman Brown, and bearing a considerable resemblance to him, though perhaps more in expression than features. Still they might have been taken for father and son. And yet, though the elder person was as simply clad as the younger, and as simple in manner too, he had an indescribable air of one who knew the world, and who would not have felt abashed at the governor's dinner table or in King William's court, were it possible that his affairs should call him thither. But the only thing about him that could be fixed upon as remarkable was his staff, which bore the likeness of a great black snake, so curiously wrought that it might almost be seen to twist and wriggle itself like a living serpent. This, of course, must have been an ocular deception, assisted by the uncertain light.

"Come, Goodman Brown, " cried his fellow-traveller, "this is a dull pace for the beginning of a journey. Take my staff, if you are so soon weary."

"Friend," said the other, exchanging his slow pace for a full stop, "having kept covenant by meeting thee here, it is my purpose now to return whence I came. I have scruples touching the matter thou wot'st of."

"Sayest thou so?" replied he of the serpent, smiling apart. "Let us walk on, nevertheless, reasoning as we go; and if I convince thee not thou shalt turn back. We are but a little way in the forest yet."

"Too far! too far!" exclaimed the goodman, unconsciously resuming his walk. "My father never went into the woods on such an errand, nor his father before him. We have been a race of honest men and good Christians since the days of the martyrs; and shall I be the first of the name of Brown that ever took this path and kept—"

"Such company, thou wouldst say, " observed the elder person, interpreting his pause. "Well said, Goodman Brown! I have been as well acquainted with your family as with ever a one among the Puritans; and that's no trifle to say. I helped your grandfather, the constable, when he lashed the Quaker woman so smartly through the streets of Salem; and it was I that brought your father a pitch-pine knot, kindled at my own hearth, to set fire to an Indian village, in King Philip's war. They were my good friends, both; and many a pleasant walk have we had along this path, and returned merrily after midnight. I would fain be friends with you for their sake."

"If it be as thou sayest," replied Goodman Brown, "I marvel they never spoke of these matters; or, verily, I marvel not, seeing that the least rumor of the sort would have driven them from New England. We are a people of prayer, and good works to boot, and abide no such wickedness."

"Wickedness or not," said the traveller with the twisted staff, "I have a very general acquaintance here in New England. The deacons of many a church have drunk the communion wine with me; the selectmen of divers towns make me their chairman; and a majority of the Great and General Court are firm supporters of my interest. The governor and I, too—But these are state secrets."

"Can this be so?" cried Goodman Brown, with a stare of amazement at his undisturbed companion. "Howbeit, I have nothing to do with the governor and council; they have their own ways, and are no rule for a simple husbandman like me. But, were I to go on with thee, how should I meet the eye of that good old man, our minister, at Salem village? Oh, his voice would make me tremble both Sabbath day and lecture day."

Thus far the elder traveller had listened with due gravity; but now burst into a fit of irrepressible mirth, shaking himself so violently that his snake-like staff actually seemed to wriggle in sympathy.

"Ha! ha! ha!" shouted he again and again; then composing himself. "Well, go on, Goodman Brown, go on; but, prithee, don't kill me with laughing."

"Well, then, to end the matter at once," said Goodman Brown, considerably nettled, "there is my wife, Faith. It would break her dear little heart; and I'd rather break my own."

"Nay, if that be the case," answered the other, "e'en go thy ways, Goodman Brown. I would not for twenty old women like the one hobbling before us that Faith should come to any harm."

As he spoke, he pointed his staff at a female figure on the path, in whom Goodman Brown recognized a very pious and exemplary dame, who had taught him his catechism in youth, and was still his moral and spiritual adviser, jointly with the minister and Deacon Gookin.

"A marvel, truly, that Goody Cloyse should be so far in the wilderness at nightfall," said he. "But with your leave, friend, I shall take a cut through the woods until we have left this Christian woman behind. Being a stranger to you, she might ask whom I was consorting with and whither I was going."

"Be it so," said his fellow-traveller. "Betake you to the woods, and let me keep the path."

Accordingly the young man turned aside, but took care to watch his companion, who advanced softly along the road until he had come within a staff's length of the old dame. She, meanwhile, was making the best of her way, with singular speed for so aged a woman, and mumbling some indistinct words—a prayer, doubtless—as she went. The traveller put forth his staff and touched her withered neck with what seemed the serpent's tail.

"The devil!" screamed the pious old lady.

"Then Goody Cloyse knows her old friend?" observed the traveller, confronting her and leaning on his writhing stick.

"Ah, forsooth, and is it your worship indeed?" cried the good dame. "Yea, truly is it, and in the very image of my old gossip, Goodman Brown, the grandfather of the silly fellow that now is. But—would your worship believe it—my broomstick hath strangely disappeared, stolen, as I suspect, by that unhanged witch, Goody Cory, and that, too, when I was all anointed with the juice of smallage, and cinquefoil, and wolf's bane—"

"Mingled with fine wheat and the fat of a new-born babe," said the shape of old Goodman Brown.

"Ah, your worship knows the recipe," cried the old lady, cackling aloud. "So, as I was saying, being all ready for the meeting, and no horse to ride on, I made up my mind to foot it; for they tell me there is a nice young man to be taken into communion tonight. But now your good worship will lend me your arm, and we shall be there in a twinkling."

"That can hardly be," answered her friend. "I may not spare you my arm, Goody Cloyse; but here is my staff, if you will."

So saying, he threw it down at her feet, where, perhaps, it assumed life, being one of the rods which its owner had formerly lent to the Egyptian magi. Of this fact, however, Goodman Brown could not take cognizance. He had cast up his eyes in astonishment, and, looking down again, beheld neither Goody Cloyse nor the serpentine staff, but his fellow-traveller alone, who waited for him as calmly as if nothing had happened.

"That old woman taught me my catechism," said the young man; and there was a world of meaning in this simple comment.

They continued to walk onward, while the elder traveller exhorted his companion to make good speed and persevere in the path, discoursing so aptly that his arguments seemed rather to spring up in the bosom of his auditor than to be suggested by himself. As they went, he plucked a branch of maple to serve for a walking stick, and began to strip it of the twigs and little boughs, which were wet with evening dew. The moment his fingers touched them they became strangely withered and dried up as with a week's sunshine. Thus the pair proceeded, at a good free pace, until suddenly, in a gloomy hollow of the road, Goodman Brown sat himself down on the stump of a tree and refused to go any farther.

"Friend," said he, stubbornly, "my mind is made up. Not another step will I budge on this errand. What if a wretched old woman do choose to go to the devil when I thought she was going to heaven: is that any reason why I should quit my dear Faith and go after her?"

"You will think better of this by and by," said his acquaintance, composedly. "Sit here and rest yourself a while; and when you feel like moving again, there is my staff to help you along."

Without more words, he threw his companion the maple stick, and was as speedily out of sight as if he had vanished into the deepening gloom. The young man sat a few moments by the roadside, applauding himself greatly, and thinking with how clear a conscience he should meet the minister in his morning walk, nor shrink from the eye of good old Deacon Gookin. And what calm sleep would be his that very night, which was to have been spent so wickedly, but so purely and sweetly now, in the arms of Faith! Amidst these pleasant and praiseworthy meditations, Goodman Brown heard the tramp of horses along the road, and deemed it advisable to conceal himself within the verge of the forest, conscious of the guilty purpose that had brought him thither, though now so happily turned from it.

On came the hoof tramps and the voices of the riders, two grave old voices, conversing soberly as they drew near. These mingled sounds appeared to pass along the road, within a few yards of the young man's hiding place; but, owing doubtless to the depth of the gloom at that particular spot, neither the travelers nor their steeds were visible. Though their figures brushed the small boughs by the wayside, it could not be seen that they intercepted, even for a moment, the faint gleam from the strip of bright sky athwart which they must have passed. Goodman Brown alternately crouched and stood on tiptoe, pulling aside the branches and thrusting forth his head as far as he durst without discerning so much as a shadow. It vexed him the more, because he could have sworn, were such a thing possible, that he recognized the voices of the minister and Deacon Gookin, jogging along quietly, as they were wont to do, when bound to some ordination or ecclesiastical council. While yet within hearing, one of the riders stopped to pluck a switch.

"Of the two, reverend sir," said the voice like the deacon's, "I had rather miss an ordination dinner than tonight's meeting. They tell me that some of our community are to be here from Falmouth and beyond, and others from Connecticut and Rhode Island, besides several of the Indian powwows, who, after their fashion, know almost as much deviltry as the best of us. Moreover, there is a goodly young woman to be taken into communion."

"Mighty well, Deacon Gookin!" replied the solemn old tones of the minister. "Spur up, or we shall be late. Nothing can be done, you know, until I get on the ground."

The hoofs clattered again; and the voices, talking so strangely in the empty air, passed on through the forest, where no church had ever been gathered or solitary Christian prayed. Whither, then, could these holy men be journeying so deep into the heathen wilderness? Young Goodman Brown caught hold of a tree for support, being ready to sink down on the ground, faint and overburdened with the heavy sickness of his heart. He looked up to the sky, doubting whether there really was a heaven above him. Yet there was the blue arch, and the stars brightening in it.

"With heaven above and Faith below, I will yet stand firm against the devil!" cried Goodman Brown.

While he still gazed upward into the deep arch of the firmament and had lifted his hands to pray, a cloud, though no wind was stirring, hurried across the zenith and hid the brightening stars. The blue sky was still visible, except directly overhead, where this black mass of cloud was sweeping swiftly northward. Aloft in the air, as if from the depths of the cloud, came a confused and doubtful sound of voices. Once the listener fancied that he could distinguish the accents of townspeople of his own, men and women, both pious and ungodly, many of whom he had met at the communion table, and had seen others rioting at the tavern. The next moment, so indistinct were the sounds, he doubted whether he had heard aught but the murmur of the old forest, whispering without a wind. Then came a stronger swell of those familiar tones, heard daily in the sunshine at Salem village, but never until now from a cloud of night. There was one voice of a young woman, uttering lamentations, yet with an uncertain sorrow, and entreating for some favor, which, perhaps, it would grieve her to obtain; and all the unseen multitude, both saints and sinners, seemed to encourage her onward.

"Faith!" shouted Goodman Brown, in a voice of agony and desperation; and the echoes of the forest mocked him, crying, "Faith! Faith!" as if bewildered wretches were seeking her all through the wilderness.

The cry of grief, rage, and terror was yet piercing the night, when the unhappy husband held his breath for a response. There was a scream, drowned immediately in a louder murmur of voices, fading into far-off laughter, as the dark cloud swept away, leaving the clear and silent sky above Goodman Brown. But something fluttered lightly down through the air and caught on the branch of a tree. The young man seized it, and beheld a pink ribbon.

"My Faith is gone!" cried he, after one stupefied moment. "There is no good on earth; and sin is but a name. Come, devil; for to thee is this world given."

And, maddened with despair, so that he laughed loud and long, did Goodman Brown grasp his staff and set forth again, at such a rate that he seemed to fly along the forest path rather than to walk or run. The road grew wilder and drearier and more faintly traced, and vanished at length, leaving him in the heart of the dark wilderness, still rushing onward with the instinct that guides mortal man to evil. The whole forest was peopled with frightful sounds—the creaking of the trees, the howling of wild beasts, and the yell of Indians; while sometimes the wind tolled like a distant church bell, and sometimes gave a broad roar around the traveller, as if all Nature were laughing him to scorn. But he was himself the chief horror of the scene, and shrank not from its other horrors.

"Ha! ha! ha!" roared Goodman Brown when the wind laughed at him. "Let us hear which will laugh loudest. Think not to frighten me with your deviltry. Come witch, come wizard, come Indian powwow, come devil himself, and here comes Goodman Brown. You may as well fear him as he fear you."

In truth, all through the haunted forest there could be nothing more frightful than the figure of Goodman Brown. On he flew among the black pines, brandishing his staff with frenzied gestures, now giving vent to an inspiration of horrid blasphemy, and now shouting forth such laughter as set all the echoes of the forest laughing like demons around him. The fiend in his own shape is less hideous than when he rages in the breast of man. Thus sped the demoniac on his course, until, quivering among the trees, he saw a red light before him, as when the felled trunks and branches of a clearing have been set on fire, and throw up their lurid blaze against the sky, at the hour of midnight. He paused, in a lull of the tempest that had driven him onward, and heard the swell of what seemed a hymn, rolling solemnly from a distance with the weight of many voices. He knew the tune; it was a familiar one in the choir of the village meeting-house. The verse died heavily away, and was lengthened by a chorus, not of human voices, but of all the sounds of the benighted wilderness -pealing in awful harmony together. Goodman Brown cried out, and his cry was lost to his own ear by its unison with the cry of the desert.

In the interval of silence he stole forward until the light glared full upon his eyes. At one extremity of an open space, hemmed in by the dark wall of the forest, arose a rock, bearing some rude, natural resemblance either to an altar or a pulpit, and surrounded by four blazing pines, their tops aflame, their stems untouched, like candles at an evening meeting. The mass of foliage that had overgrown the summit of the rock was all on fire, blazing high into the night and fitfully illuminating the whole field. Each pendent twig and leafy festoon was in a blaze. As the red light arose and fell, a numerous congregation alternately shone forth, then disappeared in shadow, and again grew, as it were, out of the darkness, peopling the heart of the solitary woods at once.

"A grave and dark-clad company," quoth Goodman Brown.

In truth they were such. Among them, quivering to and fro between gloom and splendor, appeared faces that would be seen next day at the council board of the province, and others which, Sabbath after Sabbath, looked devoutly heavenward, and benignantly over the crowded pew, from the holiest pulpits in the land. Some affirm that the lady of the governor was there. At least there were high dames well known to her, and wives of honored husbands, and widows, a great multitude, and ancient maidens, all of excellent repute, and fair young girls, who trembled lest their mothers should espy them. Either the sudden gleams of light flashing over the obscure field bedazzled Goodman Brown, or he recognized a score of the church members of Salem village famous for their especial sanctity. Good old Deacon Gookin had arrived, and waited at the skirts of that venerable saint, his reverend pastor. But, irreverently consorting with these grave, reputable, and pious people, these elders of the church, these chaste dames and dewy virgins, there were men of dissolute lives and women of spotted fame, wretches given over to all mean and filthy vice, and suspected even of horrid crimes. It was strange to see that the good shrank not from the wicked, nor were the sinners abashed by the saints. Scattered also among their pale-faced enemies were the Indian priests, or powwows, who had often scared their native forest with more hideous incantations than any known to English witchcraft.

"But where is Faith?" thought Goodman Brown; and, as hope came into his heart, he trembled.

Another verse of the hymn arose, a slow and mournful strain, such as the pious love, but joined to words which expressed all that our nature can conceive of sin, and darkly hinted at far more. Unfathomable to mere mortals is the lore of fiends. Verse after verse was sung; and still the chorus of the desert swelled between like the deepest tone of a mighty organ; and with the final peal of that dreadful anthem there came a sound, as if the roaring wind, the rushing streams, the howling beasts, and every other voice of the unconcerted wilderness were mingling and according with the voice of guilty man in homage to the prince of all. The four blazing pines threw up a loftier flame, and obscurely discovered shapes and visages of horror on the smoke wreaths above the impious assembly. At the same moment the fire on the rock shot redly forth and formed a glowing arch above its base, where now appeared a figure. With reverence be it spoken, the figure bore no slight similitude, both in garb and manner, to some grave divine of the New England churches.

"Bring forth the converts!" cried a voice that echoed through the field and rolled into the forest.

At the word, Goodman Brown stepped forth from the shadow of the trees and approached the congregation, with whom he felt a loathful brotherhood by the sympathy of all that was wicked in his heart. He could have well-nigh sworn that the shape of his own dead father beckoned him to advance, looking downward from a smoke wreath, while a woman, with dim features of despair, threw out her hand to warn him back. Was it his mother? But he had no power to retreat one step, nor to resist, even in thought, when the minister and good old Deacon Gookin seized his arms and led him to the blazing rock. Thither came also the slender form of a veiled female, led between Goody Cloyse, that pious teacher of the catechism, and Martha Carrier, who had received the devil's promise to be queen of hell. A rampant hag was she. And there stood the proselytes beneath the canopy of fire.

"Welcome, my children," said the dark figure, "to the communion of your race. Ye have found thus young your nature and your destiny. My children, look behind you!"

They turned; and flashing forth, as it were, in a sheet of flame, the fiend worshippers were seen; the smile of welcome gleamed darkly on every visage.

"There," resumed the sable form, "are all whom ye have reverenced from youth. Ye deemed them holier than yourselves, and shrank from your own sin, contrasting it with their lives of righteousness and prayerful aspirations heavenward. Yet here are they all in my worshipping assembly. This night it shall be granted you to know their secret deeds; how hoary-bearded elders of the church have whispered wanton words to the young maids of their households; how many a woman, eager for widows' weeds, has given her husband a drink at bedtime and let him sleep his last sleep in her bosom; how beardless youths have made haste to inherit their fathers' wealth; and how fair damsels—blush not, sweet ones—have dug little graves in the garden, and bidden me, the sole guest, to an infant's funeral. By the sympathy of your human hearts for sin ye shall scent out all the places—whether in church, bed chamber, street, field, or forest—where crime has been committed, and shall exult to behold the whole earth one stain of guilt, one mighty blood spot. Far more than this. It shall be yours to penetrate, in every bosom, the deep mystery of sin, the fountain of all wicked arts, and which inexhaustibly supplies more evil impulses than human power—than my power at its utmost—can make manifest in deeds. And now, my children, look upon each other."

They did so; and, by the blaze of the hell-kindled torches, the wretched man beheld his Faith, and the wife her husband, trembling before that unhallowed altar.

"Lo, there ye stand, my children," said the figure, in a deep and solemn tone, almost sad with its despairing awfulness, as if his once angelic nature could yet mourn for our miserable race. "Depending upon one another's hearts, ye had still hoped that virtue were not all a dream. Now are ye undeceived. Evil is the nature of mankind. Evil must be your only happiness. Welcome again, my children, to the communion of your race."

"Welcome," repeated the fiend worshippers, in one cry of despair and triumph.

And there they stood, the only pair, as it seemed, who were yet hesitating on the verge of wickedness in this dark world. A basin was hollowed, naturally, in the rock. Did it contain water, reddened by the lurid light? or was it blood? or, perchance, a liquid flame? Herein did the shape of evil dip his hand and prepare to lay the mark of baptism upon their foreheads, that they might be partakers of the mystery of sin, more conscious of the secret guilt of others, both in deed and thought, than they could now be of their own. The husband cast one look at his pale wife, and Faith at him. What polluted wretches would the next glance show them to each other, shuddering alike at what they disclosed and what they saw!

"Faith! Faith!" cried the husband, "look up to heaven, and resist the wicked one."

Whether Faith obeyed he knew not. Hardly had he spoken when he found himself amid calm night and solitude, listening to a roar of the wind which died heavily away through the forest. He staggered against the rock, and felt it chill and damp; while a hanging twig, that had been all on fire, besprinkled his cheek with the coldest dew.

The next morning young Goodman Brown came slowly into the street of Salem village, staring around him like a bewildered man. The good old minister was taking a walk along the graveyard to get an appetite for breakfast and meditate his sermon, and bestowed a blessing, as he passed, on Goodman Brown. He shrank from the venerable saint as if to avoid an anathema. Old Deacon Gookin was at domestic worship, and the holy words of his prayer were heard through the open window. "What God doth the wizard pray to?" quoth Goodman Brown. Goody Cloyse, that excellent old Christian, stood in the early sunshine at her own lattice, catechizing a little girl who had brought her a pint of morning's milk. Goodman Brown snatched away the child as from the grasp of the fiend himself. Turning the corner by the meeting house, he spied the head of Faith, with the pink ribbons, gazing anxiously forth, and bursting into such joy at sight of him that she skipped along the street and almost kissed her husband before the whole village. But Goodman Brown looked sternly and sadly into her face, and passed on without a greeting.

Had Goodman Brown fallen asleep in the forest and only dreamed a wild dream of a witch-meeting?

Be it so if you will; but, alas! it was a dream of evil omen for young Goodman Brown. A stern, a sad, a darkly meditative, a distrustful, if not a desperate, man did he become from the night of that fearful dream. On the Sabbath day, when the congregation were singing a holy psalm, he could not listen because an anthem of sin rushed loudly upon his ear and drowned all the blessed strain. When the minister spoke from the pulpit with power and fervid eloquence, and, with his hand on the open Bible, of the sacred truths of our religion, and of saint-like lives and triumphant deaths, and of future bliss or misery unutterable, then did Goodman Brown turn pale, dreading lest the roof should thunder down upon the gray blasphemer and his bearers. Often, waking suddenly at midnight, he shrank from the bosom of Faith; and at morning or eventide, when the family knelt down at prayer, he scowled and muttered to himself, and gazed sternly at his wife, and turned away. And when he had lived long, and was borne to his grave a hoary corpse, followed by Faith, an aged woman, and children and grandchildren, a goodly procession, besides neighbors not a few, they carved no hopeful verse upon his tombstone, for his dying hour was gloom.

—*Nathaniel Hawthorne (1804–1864)*

A White Heron

I.

The woods were already filled with shadows one June evening, just before eight o'clock, though a bright sunset still glimmered faintly among the trunks of the trees. A little girl was driving home her cow, a plodding, dilatory, provoking creature in her behavior, but a valued companion for all that. They were going away from whatever light there was, and striking deep into the dark woods, but their feet were familiar with the path, and it was no matter whether their eyes could see it or not.

There was hardly a night the summer through when the old cow could be found waiting at the pasture bars; on the contrary, it was her greatest pleasure to hide herself away among the huckleberry bushes, and though she wore a loud bell she had made the discovery that if one stood perfectly still it would not ring. So Sylvia had to hunt for her until she found her, and call Co' ! Co' ! with never an answering Moo, until her childish patience was quite spent. If the creature had not given good milk and plenty of it, the case would have seemed very different to her owners. Besides, Sylvia had all the time there was, and very little use to make of it. Sometimes in pleasant weather it was a consolation to look upon the cow's pranks as an intelligent attempt to play hide and seek, and as the child had no playmates she lent herself to this amusement with a good deal of zest. Though this chase had been so long that the wary animal herself had given an unusual signal of her whereabouts, Sylvia had only laughed when she came upon Mistress Moolly at the swamp-side, and urged her affectionately homeward with a twig of birch leaves. The old cow was not inclined to wander farther, she even turned in the right direction for once as they left the pasture, and stepped along the road at a good pace. She was quite ready to be milked now, and seldom stopped to browse. Sylvia wondered what her grandmother would say because they were so late. It was a great while since she had left home at half-past five o'clock, but everybody knew the difficulty of making this errand a short one. Mrs. Tilley had chased the hornéd torment too many summer evenings herself to blame any one else for lingering, and was only thankful as she waited that she had Sylvia, nowadays, to give such valuable assistance. The good woman suspected that Sylvia loitered occasionally on her own account; there never was such a child for straying about out-of-doors since the world was made! Everybody said that it was a good change for a little maid who had tried to grow for eight years in a crowded manufacturing town, but, as for Sylvia herself, it seemed as if she never had been alive at all before she came to live at the farm. She thought often with wistful compassion of a wretched geranium that belonged to a town neighbor.

"'Afraid of folks,'" old Mrs. Tilley said to herself, with a smile, after she had made the unlikely choice of Sylvia from her daughter's houseful of children, and was returning to the farm. "'Afraid of folks,' they said! I guess she won't be troubled no great with 'em up to the old place!" When they reached the door of the lonely house and stopped to unlock it, and the cat came to purr loudly, and rub against them, a deserted pussy, indeed, but fat with young robins, Sylvia whispered that this was a beautiful place to live in, and she never should wish to go home.

The companions followed the shady wood-road, the cow taking slow steps and the child very fast ones. The cow stopped long at the brook to drink, as if the pasture were not half a swamp, and Sylvia stood still and waited, letting her bare feet cool themselves in the shoal water, while the great twilight moths struck softly against her. She waded on through the brook as the cow moved away, and listened to the thrushes with a heart that beat fast with pleasure. There was a stirring in the great boughs overhead. They were full of little birds and beasts that seemed to be wide awake, and going about their world, or else saying good-night to each other in sleepy twitters. Sylvia herself felt sleepy as she walked along. However, it was not much farther to the house, and the air was soft and sweet. She was not often in the woods so late as this, and it made her feel as if she were a part of the gray shadows and the moving leaves. She was just thinking how long it seemed since she first came to the farm a year ago, and wondering if everything went on in the noisy town just the same as when she was there, the thought of the great red-faced boy who used to chase and frighten her made her hurry along the path to escape from the shadow of the trees.

Suddenly this little woods-girl is horror-stricken to hear a clear whistle not very far away. Not a bird's-whistle, which would have a sort of friendliness, but a boy's whistle, determined, and somewhat aggressive. Sylvia left the cow to whatever sad fate might await her, and stepped discreetly aside into the bushes, but she was just too late. The enemy had discovered her, and called out in a very cheerful and persuasive tone,"Halloa, little girl, how far is it to the road?" and trembling Sylvia answered almost inaudibly, "A good ways."

She did not dare to look boldly at the tall young man, who carried a gun over his shoulder, but she came out of her bush and again followed the cow, while he walked alongside.

"I have been hunting for some birds," the stranger said kindly, "and I have lost my way, and need a friend very much. Don't be afraid," he added gallantly. "Speak up and tell me what your name is, and whether you think I can spend the night at your house, and go out gunning early in the morning."

Sylvia was more alarmed than before. Would not her grandmother consider her much to blame? But who could have foreseen such an accident as this? It did not seem to be her fault, and she hung her head as if the stem of it were broken, but managed to answer "Sylvy," with much effort when her companion again asked her name.

Mrs. Tilley was standing in the doorway when the trio came into view. The cow gave a loud moo by way of explanation.

"Yes, you'd better speak up for yourself, you old trial! Where'd she tucked herself away this time, Sylvy?" But Sylvia kept an awed silence; she knew by instinct that her grandmother did not comprehend the gravity of the situation. She must be mistaking the stranger for one of the farmer-lads of the region.

The young man stood his gun beside the door, and dropped a lumpy game-bag beside it; then he bade Mrs. Tilley good-evening, and repeated his wayfarer's story, and asked if he could have a night's lodging.

"Put me anywhere you like," he said. "I must be off early in the morning, before day; but I am very hungry, indeed. You can give me some milk at any rate, that's plain."

"Dear sakes, yes," responded the hostess, whose long slumbering hospitality seemed to be easily awakened. "You might fare better if you went out to the main road a mile or so, but you're welcome to what we've got. I'll milk right off, and you make yourself at home. You can sleep on husks or feathers," she proffered graciously. "I raised them all myself. There's good pasturing for geese just below here towards the ma'sh. Now step round and set a plate for the gentleman, Sylvy!" And Sylvia promptly stepped. She was glad to have something to do, and she was hungry herself.

It was a surprise to find so clean and comfortable a little dwelling in this New England wilderness. The young man had known the horrors of its most primitive house-keeping, and the dreary squalor of that level of society which does not rebel at the companionship of hens. This was the best thrift of an old-fashioned farmstead, though on such a small scale that it seemed like a hermitage. He listened eagerly to the old woman's quaint talk, he watched Sylvia's pale face and shining gray eyes with ever growing enthusiasm, and insisted that this was the best supper he had eaten for a month, and afterward the new-made friends sat down in the door-way together while the moon came up.

Soon it would be berry-time, and Sylvia was a great help at picking. The cow was a good milker, though a plaguy thing to keep track of, the hostess gossiped frankly, adding presently that she had buried four children, so Sylvia's mother, and a son (who might be dead) in California were all the children she had left. "Dan, my boy, was a great hand to go gunning," she explained sadly. "I never wanted for pa'tridges or gray squer'ls while he was to home. He's been a great wand'rer, I expect, and he's no hand to write letters. There, I don't blame him, I'd ha' seen the world myself if it had been so I could.

"Sylvy takes after him," the grandmother continued affectionately, after a minute's pause. "There ain't a foot o' ground she don't know her way over, and the wild creatur's counts her one o' themselves. Squer'ls she'll tame to come an' feed right out o' her hands, and all sorts o' birds. Last winter she got the jay-birds to bangeing here, and I believe she'd 'a' scanted herself of her own meals to have plenty to throw out amongst 'em, if I hadn't kep' watch. Anything but crows, I tell her, I'm willin' to help support,—though Dan he had an' tamed one o' them that did seem to have reason same as folks. It was round here a good spell after he went away. Dan an' his father they didn't hitch,—but he never held up his head ag'in after Dan had dared him an' gone off."

The guest did not notice this hint of family sorrows in his eager interest in something else.

"So Sylvy knows all about birds, does she?" he exclaimed, as he looked round at the little girl who sat, very demure but increasingly sleepy, in the moonlight. "I am making a collection of birds myself. I have been at it ever since I was a boy." (Mrs. Tilley smiled.) "There are two or three very rare ones I have been hunting for these five years. I mean to get them on my own ground if they can be found."

"Do you cage 'em up?" asked Mrs. Tilley doubtfully, in response to this enthusiastic announcement.

"Oh no, they're stuffed and preserved, dozens and dozens of them," said the ornithologist, "and I have shot or snared every one myself. I caught a glimpse of a white heron a few miles from here on Saturday, and I have followed it in this direction. They have never been found in this district at all. The little white heron, it is," and he turned again to look at Sylvia with the hope of discovering that the rare bird was one of her acquaintances.

But Sylvia was watching a hop-toad in the narrow footpath.

"You would know the heron if you saw it," the stranger continued eagerly. "A queer tall white bird with soft feathers and long thin legs. And it would have a nest perhaps in the top of a high tree, made of sticks, something like a hawk's nest."

Sylvia's heart gave a wild beat; she knew that strange white bird, and had once stolen softly near where it stood in some bright green swamp grass, away over at the other side of the woods. There was an open place where the sunshine always seemed strangely yellow and hot, where tall, nodding rushes grew, and her grandmother had warned her that she might sink in the soft black mud underneath and never be heard of more. Not far beyond were the salt marshes just this side the sea itself, which Sylvia wondered and dreamed much about, but never had seen, whose great voice could sometimes be heard above the noise of the woods on stormy nights.

"I can't think of anything I should like so much as to find that heron's nest," the handsome stranger was saying. "I would give ten dollars to anybody who could show it to me," he added desperately, "and I mean to spend my whole vacation hunting for it if need be. Perhaps it was only migrating, or had been chased out of its own region by some bird of prey."

Mrs. Tilley gave amazed attention to all this, but Sylvia still watched the toad, not divining, as she might have done at some calmer time, that the creature wished to get to its hole under the door-step, and was much hindered by the unusual spectators at that hour of the evening. No amount of thought, that night, could decide how many wished-for treasures the ten dollars, so lightly spoken of, would buy.

The next day the young sportsman hovered about the woods, and Sylvia kept him company, having lost her first fear of the friendly lad, who proved to be most kind and sympathetic. He told her many things about the birds and what they knew and where they lived and what they did with themselves. And he gave her a jack-knife, which she thought as great a treasure as if she were a desert-islander. All day long he did not once make her troubled or afraid except when he brought down some unsuspecting singing creature from its bough. Sylvia would have liked him vastly better without his gun; she could not understand why he killed the very birds he seemed to like so much. But as the day waned, Sylvia still watched the young man with loving admiration. She had never seen anybody so charming and delightful; the woman's heart, asleep in the child, was vaguely thrilled by a dream of love. Some premonition of that great power stirred and swayed these young creatures who traversed the solemn woodlands with soft-footed silent care. They stopped to listen to a bird's song; they pressed forward again eagerly, parting the branches,—speaking to each other rarely and in whispers; the young man going first and Sylvia following, fascinated, a few steps behind, with her gray eyes dark with excitement.

She grieved because the longed-for white heron was elusive, but she did not lead the guest, she only followed, and there was no such thing as speaking first. The sound of her own unquestioned voice would have terrified her,—it was hard enough to answer yes or no when there was need of that. At last evening began to fall, and they drove the cow home together, and Sylvia smiled with pleasure when they came to the place where she heard the whistle and was afraid only the night before.

II.

Half a mile from home, at the farther edge of the woods, where the land was highest, a great pine-tree stood, the last of its generation. Whether it was left for a boundary mark, or for what reason, no one could say; the woodchoppers who had felled its mates were dead and gone long ago, and a whole forest of sturdy trees, pines and oaks and maples, had grown again. But the stately head of this old pine towered above them all and made a landmark for sea and shore miles and miles away. Sylvia knew it well. She had always believed that whoever climbed to the top of it could see the ocean; and the little girl had often laid her hand on the great rough trunk and looked up wistfully at those dark boughs that the wind always stirred, no matter how hot and still the air might be below. Now she thought of the tree with a new excitement, for why, if one climbed it at break of day, could not one see all the world, and easily discover from whence the white heron flew, and mark the place, and find the hidden nest?

What a spirit of adventure, what wild ambition! What fancied triumph and delight and glory for the later morning when she could make known the secret! It was almost too real and too great for the childish heart to bear.

All night the door of the little house stood open and the whippoorwills came and sang upon the very step. The young sportsman and his old hostess were sound asleep, but Sylvia's great design kept her broad awake and watching. She forgot to think of sleep. The short summer night seemed as long as the winter darkness, and at last when the whippoorwills ceased, and she was afraid the morning would after all come too soon, she stole out of the house and followed the pasture path through the woods, hastening toward the open ground beyond, listening with a sense of comfort and companionship to the drowsy twitter of a half-awakened bird, whose perch she had jarred in passing. Alas, if the great wave of human interest which flooded for the first time this dull little life should sweep away the satisfactions of an existence heart to heart with nature and the dumb life of the forest!

There was the huge tree asleep yet in the paling moonlight, and small and silly Sylvia began with utmost bravery to mount to the top of it, with tingling, eager blood coursing the channels of her whole frame, with her bare feet and fingers, that pinched and held like bird's claws to the monstrous ladder reaching up, up, almost to the sky itself. First she must mount the white oak tree that grew alongside, where she was almost lost among the dark branches and the green leaves heavy and wet with dew; a bird fluttered off its nest, and a red squirrel ran to and fro and scolded pettishly at the harmless housebreaker. Sylvia felt her way easily. She had often climbed there, and knew that higher still one of the oak's upper branches chafed against the pine trunk, just where its lower boughs were set close together. There, when she made the dangerous pass from one tree to the other, the great enterprise would really begin.

She crept out along the swaying oak limb at last, and took the daring step across into the old pine-tree. The way was harder than she thought; she must reach far and hold fast, the sharp dry twigs caught and held her and scratched her like angry talons, the pitch made her thin little fingers clumsy and stiff as she went round and round the tree's great stem, higher and higher upward. The sparrows and robins in the woods below were beginning to wake and twitter to the dawn, yet it seemed much lighter there aloft in the pine-tree, and the child knew she must hurry if her project were to be of any use.

The tree seemed to lengthen itself out as she went up, and to reach farther and farther upward. It was like a great main-mast to the voyaging earth; it must truly have been amazed that morning through all its ponderous frame as it felt this determined spark of human spirit wending its way from higher branch to branch. Who knows how steadily the least twigs held themselves to advantage this light, weak creature on her way! The old pine must have loved his new dependent. More than all the hawks, and bats, and moths, and even the sweet voiced thrushes, was the brave, beating heart of the solitary gray-eyed child. And the tree stood still and frowned away the winds that June morning while the dawn grew bright in the east.

Sylvia's face was like a pale star, if one had seen it from the ground, when the last thorny bough was past, and she stood trembling and tired but wholly triumphant, high in the tree-top. Yes, there was the sea with the dawning sun making a golden dazzle over it, and toward that glorious east flew two hawks with slow-moving pinions. How low they looked in the air from that height when one had only seen them before far up, and dark against the blue sky. Their gray feathers were as soft as moths; they seemed only a little way from the tree, and Sylvia felt as if she too could go flying away among the clouds. Westward, the woodlands and farms reached miles and miles into the distance; here and there were church steeples, and white villages, truly it was a vast and awesome world

The birds sang louder and louder. At last the sun came up bewilderingly bright. Sylvia could see the white sails of ships out at sea, and the clouds that were purple and rose-colored and yellow at first began to fade away. Where was the white heron's nest in the sea of green branches, and was this wonderful sight and pageant of the world the only reward for having climbed to such a giddy height? Now look down again, Sylvia, where the green marsh is set among the shining birches and dark hemlocks; there where you saw the white heron once you will see him again; look, look! a white spot of him like a single floating feather comes up from the dead hemlock and grows larger, and rises, and comes close at last, and goes by the landmark pine with steady sweep of wing and outstretched slender neck and crested head. And wait! wait! do not move a foot or a finger, little girl, do not send an arrow of light and consciousness from your two eager eyes, for the heron has perched on a pine bough not far beyond yours, and cries back to his mate on the nest and plumes his feathers for the new day!

The child gives a long sigh a minute later when a company of shouting cat-birds comes also to the tree, and vexed by their fluttering and lawlessness the solemn heron goes away. She knows his secret now, the wild, light, slender bird that floats and wavers, and goes back like an arrow presently to his home in the green world beneath. Then Sylvia, well satisfied, makes her perilous way down again, not daring to look far below the branch she stands on, ready to cry sometimes because her fingers ache and her lamed feet slip. Wondering over and over again what the stranger would say to her, and what he would think when she told him how to find his way straight to the heron's nest.

"Sylvy, Sylvy!" called the busy old grandmother again and again, but nobody answered, and the small husk bed was empty and Sylvia had disappeared.

The guest waked from a dream, and remembering his day's pleasure hurried to dress himself that it might sooner begin. He was sure from the way the shy little girl looked once or twice yesterday that she had at least seen the white heron, and now she must really be made to tell. Here she comes now, paler than ever, and her worn old frock is torn and tattered, and smeared with pine pitch. The grandmother and the sportsman stand in the door together and question her, and the splendid moment has come to speak of the dead hemlock-tree by the green marsh.

But Sylvia does not speak after all, though the old grandmother fretfully rebukes her, and the young man's kind, appealing eyes are looking straight in her own. He can make them rich with money; he has promised it, and they are poor now. He is so well worth making happy, and he waits to hear the story she can tell.

No, she must keep silence! What is it that suddenly forbids her and makes her dumb? Has she been nine years growing and now, when the great world for the first time puts out a hand to her, must she thrust it aside for a bird's sake? The murmur of the pine's green branches is in her ears, she remembers how the white heron came flying through the golden air and how they watched the sea and the morning together, and Sylvia cannot speak; she cannot tell the heron's secret and give its life away.

Dear loyalty, that suffered a sharp pang as the guest went away disappointed later in the day, that could have served and followed him and loved him as a dog loves! Many a night Sylvia heard the echo of his whistle haunting the pasture path as she came home with the loitering cow. She forgot even her sorrow at the sharp report of his gun and the sight of thrushes and sparrows dropping silent to the ground, their songs hushed and their pretty feathers stained and wet with blood. Were the birds better friends than their hunter might have been,—who can tell? Whatever treasures were lost to her, woodlands and summer-time, remember! Bring your gifts and graces and tell your secrets to this lonely country child!

—*Sarah Orne Jewett (1849–1909)*

The Story of an Hour

Knowing that Mrs. Mallard was afflicted with a heart trouble, great care was taken to break to her as gently as possible the news of her husband's death.

It was her sister Josephine who told her, in broken sentences; veiled hints that revealed in half concealing. Her husband's friend Richards was there, too, near her. It was he who had been in the newspaper office when intelligence of the railroad disaster was received, with Brently Mallard's name leading the list of "killed." He had only taken the time to assure himself of its truth by a second telegram, and had hastened to forestall any less careful, less tender friend in bearing the sad message.

She did not hear the story as many women have heard the same, with a paralyzed inability to accept its significance. She wept at once, with sudden, wild abandonment, in her sister's arms. When the storm of grief had spent itself she went away to her room alone. She would have no one follow her.

There stood, facing the open window, a comfortable, roomy armchair. Into this she sank, pressed down by a physical exhaustion that haunted her body and seemed to reach into her soul.

She could see in the open square before her house the tops of trees that were all aquiver with the new spring life. The delicious breath of rain was in the air. In the street below a peddler was crying his wares. The notes of a distant song which someone was singing reached her faintly, and countless sparrows were twittering in the eaves.

There were patches of blue sky showing here and there through the clouds that had met and piled one above the other in the west facing her window.

She sat with her head thrown back upon the cushion of the chair, quite motionless, except when a sob came up into her throat and shook her, as a child who has cried itself to sleep continues to sob in its dreams.

She was young, with a fair, calm face, whose lines bespoke repression and even a certain strength. But now there was a dull stare in her eyes, whose gaze was fixed away off yonder on one of those patches of blue sky. It was not a glance of reflection, but rather indicated a suspension of intelligent thought.

There was something coming to her and she was waiting for it, fearfully. What was it? She did not know; it was too subtle and elusive to name. But she felt it, creeping out of the sky, reaching toward her through the sounds, the scents, the color that filled the air.

Now her bosom rose and fell tumultuously. She was beginning to recognize this thing that was approaching to possess her, and she was striving to beat it back with her will—as powerless as her two white slender hands would have been.

When she abandoned herself a little whispered word escaped her slightly parted lips. She said it over and over under her breath: "free, free, free!" The vacant stare and the look of terror that had followed it went from her eyes. They stayed keen and bright. Her pulses beat fast, and the coursing blood warmed and relaxed every inch of her body.

She did not stop to ask if it were or were not a monstrous joy that held her. A clear and exalted perception enabled her to dismiss the suggestion as trivial.

She knew that she would weep again when she saw the kind, tender hands folded in death; the face that had never looked save with love upon her, fixed and gray and dead. But she saw beyond that bitter moment a long procession of years to come that would belong to her absolutely. And she opened and spread her arms out to them in welcome.

There would be no one to live for her during those coming years; she would live for herself. There would be no powerful will bending hers in that blind persistence with which men and women believe they have a right to impose a private will upon a fellow creature. A kind intention or a cruel intention made the act seem no less a crime as she looked upon it in that brief moment of illumination.

And yet she had loved him—sometimes. Often she had not. What did it matter! What could love, the unsolved mystery, count for in face of this possession of self-assertion which she suddenly recognized as the strongest impulse of her being!

"Free! Body and soul free!" she kept whispering.

Josephine was kneeling before the closed door with her lips to the keyhole, imploring for admission. "Louise, open the door! I beg; open the door—you will make yourself ill. What are you doing, Louise? For heaven's sake open the door."

"Go away. I am not making myself ill." No; she was drinking in a very elixir of life through that open window.

Her fancy was running riot along those days ahead of her. Spring days, and summer days, and all sorts of days that would be her own. She breathed a quick prayer that life might be long. It was only yesterday she had thought with a shudder that life might be long.

She arose at length and opened the door to her sister's importunities. There was a feverish triumph in her eyes, and she carried herself unwittingly like a goddess of Victory. She clasped her sister's waist, and together they descended the stairs. Richards stood waiting for them at the bottom.

Someone was opening the front door with a latchkey. It was Brently Mallard who entered, a little travel-stained, composedly carrying his grip-sack and umbrella. He had been far from the scene of accident, and did not even know there had been one. He stood amazed at Josephine's piercing cry; at Richards' quick motion to screen him from the view of his wife.

But Richards was too late.

When the doctors came they said she had died of heart disease—of joy that kills.

—*Kate Chopin (1851–1904)*

To Build a Fire

Day had broken cold and gray, exceedingly cold and gray, when the man turned aside from the main Yukon trail and climbed the high earth-bank, where a dim and little-traveled trail led eastward through the fat spruce timberland. It was a steep bank, and he paused for breath at the top, excusing the act to himself by looking at his watch. It was nine o'clock. There was no sun nor hint of sun, though there was not a cloud in the sky. It was a clear day, and yet there seemed an intangible pall over the face of things, a subtle gloom that made the day dark, and that was due to the absence of sun. This fact did not worry the man. He was used to the lack of sun. It had been days since he had seen the sun, and he knew that a few more days must pass before that cheerful orb, due south, would just peep above the sky-line and dip immediately from view.

The man flung a look back along the way he had come. The Yukon lay a mile wide and hidden under three feet of ice. On top of this ice were as many feet of snow. It was all pure white, rolling in gentle undulations where the ice-jams of the freeze-up had formed. North and south, as far as his eye could see, it was unbroken white, save for a dark hairline that curved and twisted from around the spruce-covered island to the south, and that curved and twisted away into the north, where it disappeared behind another spruce-covered island. This dark hair-line was the trail—the main trail—that led south five hundred miles to the Chilcoot Pass, Dyea, and salt water; and that led north seventy miles to Dawson, and still on to the north a thousand miles to Nulato, and finally to St. Michael on Bering Sea, a thousand miles and half a thousand more.

But all this—the mysterious, far-reaching hair-line trail, the absence of sun from the sky, the tremendous cold, and the strangeness and weirdness of it all—made no impression on the man. It was not because he was long used to it. He was a newcomer in the land, a *chechaquo*, and this was his first winter. The trouble with him was that he was without imagination. He was quick and alert in the things of life, but only in the things, and not in the significances. Fifty degrees below zero meant eighty-odd degrees of frost. Such fact impressed him as being cold and uncomfortable, and that was all. It did not lead him to meditate upon his frailty as a creature of temperature, and upon man's frailty in general, able only to live within certain narrow limits of heat and cold; and from there on it did not lead him to the conjectural field of immortality and man's place in the universe. Fifty degrees below zero stood for a bite of frost that hurt and that must be guarded against by the use of mittens, ear-flaps, warm moccasins, and thick socks. Fifty degrees below zero was to him just precisely fifty degrees below zero. That there should be anything more to it than that was a thought that never entered his head.

As he turned to go on, he spat speculatively. There was a sharp, explosive crackle that startled him. He spat again. And again, in the air, before it could fall to the snow, the spittle crackled. He knew that at fifty below spittle crackled on the snow, but this spittle had crackled in the air. Undoubtedly it was colder than fifty below—how much colder he did not know. But the temperature did not matter. He was bound for the old claim on the left fork of Henderson Creek, where the boys were already. They had come over across the divide from the Indian Creek country, while he had come the roundabout way to take a look at the possibilities of getting out logs in the spring from the islands in the Yukon. He would be in to camp by six o'clock; a bit after dark, it was true, but the boys would be there, a fire would be going, and a hot supper would be ready. As for lunch, he pressed his hand against the protruding bundle under his jacket. It was also under his shirt, wrapped up in a handkerchief and lying against the naked skin. It was the only way to keep the biscuits from freezing. He smiled agreeably to himself as he thought of those biscuits, each cut open and sopped in bacon grease, and each enclosing a generous slice of fried bacon.

He plunged in among the big spruce trees. The trail was faint. A foot of snow had fallen since the last sled had passed over, and he was glad he was without a sled, traveling light. In fact, he carried nothing but the lunch wrapped in the handkerchief. He was surprised, however, at the cold. It certainly was cold, he concluded, as he rubbed his numb nose and cheek-bones with his mittened hand. He was a warm-whiskered man, but the hair on his face did not protect the high cheek-bones and the eager nose that thrust itself aggressively into the frosty air.

At the man's heels trotted a dog, a big native husky, the proper wolfdog, gray-coated and without any visible or temperamental difference from its brother, the wild wolf. The animal was depressed by the tremendous cold. It knew that it was no time for traveling. Its instinct told it a truer tale than was told to the man by the man's judgment. In reality, it was not merely colder than fifty below zero; it was colder than sixty below, than seventy below. It was seventy-five below zero. Since the freezing point is thirty-two above zero, it meant that one hundred and seven degrees of frost obtained. The dog did not know anything about thermometers. Possibly in its brain there was no sharp consciousness of a condition of very cold such as was in the man's brain. But the brute had its instinct. It experienced a vague but menacing apprehension that subdued it and made it slink along at the man's heels, and that made it question eagerly every unwonted movement of the man as if expecting him to go into camp or to seek shelter somewhere and build a fire. The dog had learned fire, and it wanted fire, or else to burrow under the snow and cuddle its warmth away from the air.

The frozen moisture of its breathing had settled on its fur in a fine powder of frost, and especially were its jowls, muzzle, and eyelashes whitened by its crystalled breath. The man's red beard and mustache were likewise frosted, but more solidly, the deposit taking the form of ice and increasing with every warm, moist breath he exhaled. Also, the man was chewing tobacco, and the muzzle of ice held his lips so rigidly that he was unable to clear his chin when he expelled the juice. The result was that a crystal beard of the color and solidity of amber was increasing its length on his chin. If he fell down it would shatter itself, like glass, into brittle fragments. But he did not mind the appendage. It was the penalty all tobacco chewers paid in that country, and he had been out before in two cold snaps. They had not been so cold as this, he knew, but by the spirit thermometer at Sixty Mile he knew they had been registered at fifty below and at fifty-five.

He held on through the level stretch of woods for several miles, crossed a wide flat of niggerheads, and dropped down a bank to the frozen bed of a small stream. This was Henderson Creek, and he knew he was ten miles from the forks. He looked at his watch. It was ten o'clock. He was making four miles an hour, and he calculated that he would arrive at the forks at half-past twelve. He decided to celebrate that event by eating his lunch there.

The dog dropped in again at his heels, with a tail drooping discouragement, as the man swung along the creek-bed. The furrow of the old sled-trail was plainly visible, but a dozen inches of snow covered the marks of the last runners. In a month no man had come up or down that silent creek. The man held steadily on. He was not much given to thinking, and just then particularly he had nothing to think about save that he would eat lunch at the forks and that at six o'clock he would be in camp with the boys. There was nobody to talk to; and, had there been, speech would have been impossible because of the ice-muzzle on his mouth. So he continued monotonously to chew tobacco and to increase the length of his amber beard.

Once in a while the thought reiterated itself that it was very cold and that he had never experienced such cold. As he walked along he rubbed his cheek-bones and nose with the back of his mittened hand. He did this automatically, now and again changing hands. But rub as he would, the instant he stopped his cheek-bones went numb, and the following instant the end of his nose went numb. He was sure to frost his cheeks; he knew that, and experienced a pang of regret that he had not devised a nose-strap of the sort Bud wore in cold snaps. Such a strap passed across the cheeks, as well, and saved them. But it didn't matter much, after all. What were frosted cheeks? A bit painful, that was all; they were never serious.

Empty as the man's mind was of thoughts, he was keenly observant, and he noticed the changes in the creek, the curves and bends and timber-jams, and always he sharply noted where he placed his feet. Once, coming around a bend, he shied abruptly, like a startled horse, curved away from the place where he had been walking, and retreated several paces back along the trail. The creek he knew was frozen clear to the bottom,—no creek could contain water in that arctic winter,—but he knew also that there were springs that bubbled out from the hillsides and ran along under the snow and on top the ice of the creek. He knew that the coldest snaps never froze these springs, and he knew likewise their danger. They were traps. They hid pools of water under the snow that might be three inches deep, or three feet. Sometimes a skin of ice half an inch thick covered them, and in turn was covered by the snow. Sometimes there were alternate layers of water and ice-skin, so that when one broke through he kept on breaking through for a while, sometimes wetting himself to the waist.

That was why he had shied in such panic. He had felt the give under his feet and heard the crackle of a snow-hidden ice-skin. And to get his feet wet in such a temperature meant trouble and danger. At the very least it meant delay, for he would be forced to stop and build a fire, and under its protection to bare his feet while he dried his socks and moccasins. He stood and studied the creek-bed and its banks, and decided that the flow of water came from the right. He reflected a while, rubbing his nose and cheeks, then skirted to the left, stepping gingerly and testing the footing for each step. Once clear of the danger, he took a fresh chew of tobacco and swung along at his four-mile gait.

In the course of the next two hours he came upon several similar traps. Usually the snow above the hidden pools had a sunken, candied appearance that advertised the danger. Once again, however, he had a close call; and once, suspecting danger, he compelled the dog to go on in front. The dog did not want to go. It hung back until the man shoved it forward, and then it went quickly across the white, unbroken surface. Suddenly it broke through, floundered to one side, and got away to firmer footing. It had wet its forefeet and legs, and almost immediately the water that clung to it turned to ice. It made quick efforts to lick the ice off its legs, then dropped down in the snow and began to bite out the ice that had formed between the toes. This was a matter of instinct. To permit the ice to remain would mean sore feet. It did not know this. It merely obeyed the mysterious prompting that arose from the deep crypts of its being. But the man knew, having achieved a judgment on the subject, and he removed the mitten from his right hand and helped tear out the ice-particles. He did not expose his fingers more than a minute, and was astonished at the swift numbness that smote them. It certainly was cold. He pulled on the mitten hastily, and beat the hand savagely across his chest.

At twelve o'clock the day was at its brightest. Yet the sun was too far south on its winter journey to clear the horizon. The bulge of the earth intervened between it and Henderson Creek, where the man walked under a clear sky at noon and cast no shadow. At half-past twelve, to the minute, he arrived at the forks of the creek. He was pleased at the speed he had made. If he kept it up, he would certainly be with the boys by six. He unbuttoned his jacket and shirt and drew forth his lunch. The action consumed no more than a quarter of a minute, yet in that brief moment the numbness laid hold of the exposed fingers. He did not put the mitten on, but, instead, struck the fingers a dozen sharp smashes against his leg. Then he sat down on a snow-covered log to eat. The sting that followed upon the striking of his fingers against his leg ceased so quickly that he was startled. He had had no chance to take a bite of biscuit. He struck the fingers repeatedly and returned them to the mitten, baring the other hand for the purpose of eating. He tried to take a mouthful, but the ice-muzzle prevented. He had forgotten to build a fire and thaw out. He chuckled at his foolishness, and as he chuckled he noted the numbness creeping into the exposed fingers. Also, he noted that the stinging which had first come to his toes when he sat down was already passing away. He wondered whether the toes were warm or numb. He moved them inside the moccasins and decided that they were numb.

He pulled the mitten on hurriedly and stood up. He was a bit frightened. He stamped up and down until the stinging returned into the feet. It certainly was cold, was his thought. That man from Sulphur Creek had spoken the truth when telling how cold it sometimes got in the country. And he had laughed at him at the time! That showed one must not be too sure of things. There was no mistake about it, it was cold. He strode up and down, stamping his feet and threshing his arms, until reassured by the returning warmth. Then he got out matches and proceeded to make a fire. From the undergrowth, where high water of the previous spring had lodged a supply of seasoned twigs, he got his firewood. Working carefully from a small beginning, he soon had a roaring fire, over which he thawed the ice from his face and in the protection of which he ate his biscuits. For the moment the cold of space was outwitted. The dog took satisfaction in the fire, stretching out close enough for warmth and far enough away to escape being singed.

When the man had finished, he filled his pipe and took his comfortable time over a smoke. Then he pulled on his mittens, settled the ear-flaps of his cap firmly about his ears, and took the creek trail up the left fork. The dog was disappointed and yearned back toward the fire. This man did not know cold. Possibly all the generations of his ancestry had been ignorant of cold, of real cold, of cold one hundred and seven degrees below freezing point. But the dog knew; all its ancestry knew, and it had inherited the knowledge. And it knew that it was not good to walk abroad in such fearful cold. It was the time to lie snug in a hole in the snow and wait for a curtain of cloud to be drawn across the face of outer space whence this cold came. On the other hand, there was no keen intimacy between the dog and the man. The one was the toil-slave of the other and the only caresses it had ever received were the caresses of the whip-lash and of harsh and menacing throat-sounds that threatened the whip-lash. So the dog made no effort to communicate its apprehension to the man. It was not concerned in the welfare of the man; it was for its own sake that it yearned back toward the fire. But the man whistled, and spoke to it with the sound of whip-lashes, and the dog swung in at the man's heel and followed after.

The man took a chew of tobacco and proceeded to start a new amber beard. Also, his moist breath quickly powdered with white his mustache, eyebrows, and lashes. There did not seem to be so many springs on the left fork of the Henderson, and for half an hour the man saw no signs of any. And then it happened. At a place where there were no signs, where the soft, unbroken snow seemed to advertise solidity beneath, the man broke through. It was not deep. He wet himself halfway to the knees before he floundered out to the firm crust.

He was angry, and cursed his luck aloud. He had hoped to get into camp with the boys at six o'clock, and this would delay him an hour, for he would have to build a fire and dry out his foot-gear. This was imperative at that low temperature—he knew that much; and he turned aside to the bank, which he climbed. On top, tangled in the underbrush about the trunks of several small spruce trees, was a high-water deposit of dry firewood—sticks and twigs, principally, but also larger portions of seasoned branches and fine, dry, last-year's grasses. He threw down several large pieces on top of the snow. This served for a foundation and prevented the young flame from drowning itself in the snow it otherwise would melt. The flame he got by touching a match to a small shred of birch bark that he took from his pocket. This burned even more readily than paper. Placing it on the foundation, he fed the young flame with wisps of dry grass and with the tiniest dry twigs.

He worked slowly and carefully, keenly aware of his danger. Gradually, as the flame grew stronger, he increased the size of the twigs with which he fed it. He squatted in the snow, pulling the twigs out from their entanglement in the brush and feeding directly to the flame. He knew there must be no failure. When it is seventy-five below zero, a man must not fail in his first attempt to build a fire—that is, if his feet are wet. If his feet are dry, and he fails, he can run along the trail for half a mile and restore his circulation. But the circulation of wet and freezing feet cannot be restored by running when it is seventy-five below. No matter how fast he runs, the wet feet will freeze the harder.

All this the man knew. The old-timer on Sulphur Creek had told him about it the previous fall, and now he was appreciating the advice. Already all sensation had gone out of his feet. To build the fire he had been forced to remove his mittens, and the fingers had quickly gone numb. His pace of four miles an hour had kept his heart pumping blood to the surface of his body and to all the extremities. But the instant he stopped, the action of the pump eased down. The cold of space smote the unprotected tip of the planet, and he, being on that unprotected tip, received the full force of the blow. The blood of his body recoiled before it. The blood was alive, like the dog, and like the dog it wanted to hide away and cover itself up from the fearful cold. So long as he walked four miles an hour, he pumped that blood, willy-nilly, to the surface; but now it ebbed away and sank down into the recesses of his body. The extremities were the first to feel its absence. His wet feet froze the faster, and his exposed fingers numbed the faster, though they had not yet begun to freeze. Nose and cheeks were already freezing, while the skin of all his body chilled as it lost its blood.

But he was safe. Toes and nose and cheeks would be only touched by the frost, for the fire was beginning to burn with strength. He was feeding it with twigs the size of his finger. In another minute he would be able to feed it with branches the size of his wrist, and then he could remove his wet foot-gear, and, while it dried, he could keep his naked feet warm by the fire, rubbing them at first, of course, with snow. The fire was a success. He was safe. He remembered the advice of the old-timer on Sulphur Creek, and smiled. The old-timer had been very serious in laying down the law that no man must travel alone in the Klondike after fifty below. Well, here he was; he had had the accident; he was alone; and he had saved himself. Those old-timers were rather womanish, some of them, he thought. All a man had to do was to keep his head, and he was all right. Any man who was a man could travel alone. But it was surprising, the rapidity with which his cheeks and nose were freezing. And he had not thought his fingers could go lifeless in so short a time. Lifeless they were, for he could scarcely make them move together to grip a twig, and they seemed remote from his body and from him. When he touched a twig, he had to look and see whether or not he had hold of it. The wires were pretty well down between him and his finger-ends.

All of which counted for little. There was the fire, snapping and crackling and promising life with every dancing flame. He started to untie his moccasins. They were coated with ice; the thick German socks were like sheaths of iron halfway to the knees; and the moccasin strings were like rods of steel all twisted and knotted as by some conflagration. For a moment he tugged with his numb fingers, then, realizing the folly of it, he drew his sheath-knife.

But before he could cut the strings, it happened. It was his own fault or, rather, his mistake. He should not have built the fire under the spruce tree. He should have built it in the open. But it had been easier to pull the twigs from the brush and drop them directly on the fire. Now the tree under which he had done this carried a weight of snow on its boughs. No wind had blown for weeks, and each bough was fully freighted. Each time he had pulled a twig he had communicated a slight agitation to the tree—an imperceptible agitation, so far as he was concerned, but an agitation sufficient to bring about the disaster. High up in the tree one bough capsized its load of snow. This fell on the boughs beneath, capsizing them. This process continued, spreading out and involving the whole tree. It grew like an avalanche, and it descended without warning upon the man and the fire, and the fire was blotted out! Where it had burned was a mantle of fresh and disordered snow.

The man was shocked. It was as though he had just heard his own sentence of death. For a moment he sat and stared at the spot where the fire had been. Then he grew very calm. Perhaps the old-timer on Sulphur Creek was right. If he had only had a trail-mate he would have been in no danger now. The trail-mate could have built the fire. Well, it was up to him to build the fire over again, and this second time there must be no failure. Even if he succeeded, he would most likely lose some toes. His feet must be badly frozen by now, and there would be some time before the second fire was ready.

Such were his thoughts, but he did not sit and think them. He was busy all the time they were passing through his mind. He made a new foundation for a fire, this time in the open, where no treacherous tree could blot it out. Next, he gathered dry grasses and tiny twigs from the high-water flotsam. He could not bring his fingers together to pull them out, but he was able to gather them by the handful. In this way he got many rotten twigs and bits of green moss that were undesirable, but it was the best he could do. He worked methodically, even collecting an armful of the larger branches to be used later when the fire gathered strength. And all the while the dog sat and watched him, a certain yearning wistfulness in its eyes, for it looked upon him as the fire-provider, and the fire was slow in coming.

When all was ready, the man reached in his pocket for a second piece of birch bark. He knew the bark was there, and, though he could not feel it with his fingers, he could hear its crisp rustling as he fumbled for it. Try as he would, he could not clutch hold of it. And all the time, in his consciousness, was the knowledge that each instant his feet were freezing. This thought tended to put him in a panic, but he fought against it and kept calm. He pulled on his mittens with his teeth, and threshed his arms back and forth, beating his hands with all his might against his sides. He did this sitting down, and he stood up to do it; and all the while the dog sat in the snow, its wolf-brush of a tail curled around warmly over its forefeet, its sharp wolf-ears pricked forward intently as it watched the man. And the man, as he beat and threshed with his arms and hands, felt a great surge of envy as he regarded the creature that was warm and secure in its natural covering.

After a time he was aware of the first far-away signals of sensation in his beaten fingers. The faint tingling grew stronger till it evolved into a stinging ache that was excruciating, but which the man hailed with satisfaction. He stripped the mitten from his right hand and fetched forth the birch bark. The exposed fingers were quickly going numb again. Next he brought out his bunch of sulphur matches. But the tremendous cold had already driven the life out of his fingers. In his efforts to separate one match from the others, the whole bunch fell in the snow. He tried to pick it out of the snow, but failed. The dead fingers could neither touch nor clutch. He was very careful. He drove the thought of his freezing feet, and nose, and cheeks, out of his mind, devoting his whole soul to the matches. He watched, using the sense of vision in place of that of touch, and when he saw his fingers on each side of the bunch, he closed them—that is, he willed to close them, for the wires were down, and the fingers did not obey. He pulled the mitten on the right hand, and beat it fiercely against his knee. Then, with both mittened hands, he scooped the bunch of matches, along with much snow, into his lap. Yet he was no better off.

After some manipulation he managed to get the bunch between the heels of his mittened hands. In this fashion he carried it to his mouth. The ice crackled and snapped when by a violent effort he opened his mouth. He drew the lower jaw in, curled the upper lip out of the way, and scraped the bunch with his upper teeth in order to separate a match. He succeeded in getting one, which he dropped on his lap. He was no better off. He could not pick it up. Then he devised a way. He picked it up in his teeth and scratched it on his leg. Twenty times he scratched before he succeeded in lighting it. As it flamed he held it with his teeth to the birch bark. But the burning brimstone went up his nostrils and into his lungs, causing him to cough spasmodically. The match fell into the snow and went out.

The old-timer on Sulphur Creek was right, he thought in the moment of controlled despair that ensued: after fifty below, a man should travel with a partner. He beat his hands, but failed in exciting any sensation. Suddenly he bared both hands, removing the mittens with his teeth. He caught the whole bunch between the heels of his hands. His arm muscles not being frozen enabled him to press the hand-heels tightly against the matches. Then he scratched the bunch along his leg. It flared into flame, seventy sulphur matches at once! There was no wind to blow them out. He kept his head to one side to escape the strangling fumes, and held the blazing bunch to the birch bark. As he so held it, he became aware of sensation in his hand. His flesh was burning. He could smell it. Deep down below the surface he could feel it. The sensation developed into pain that grew acute. And still he endured it, holding the flame of the matches clumsily to the bark that would not light readily because his own burning hands were in the way, absorbing most of the flame.

At last, when he could endure no more, he jerked his hands apart. The blazing matches fell sizzling into the snow, but the birch bark was alight. He began laying dry grasses and the tiniest twigs on the flame. He could not pick and choose, for he had to lift the fuel between the heels of his hands. Small pieces of rotten wood and green moss clung to the twigs, and he bit them off as well as he could with his teeth. He cherished the flame carefully and awkwardly. It meant life, and it must not perish. The withdrawal of blood from the surface of his body now made him begin to shiver, and he grew more awkward. A large piece of green moss fell squarely on the little fire. He tried to poke it out with his fingers, but his shivering frame made him poke too far, and he disrupted the nucleus of the little fire, the burning grasses and tiny twigs separating and scattering. He tried to poke them together again, but in spite of the tenseness of the effort, his shivering got away with him, and the twigs were hopelessly scattered. Each twig gushed a puff of smoke and went out. The fire provider had failed. As he looked apathetically about him, his eyes chanced on the dog, sitting across the ruins of the fire from him, in the snow, making restless, hunching movements, slightly lifting one forefoot and then the other, shifting its weight back and forth on them with wistful eagerness.

The sight of the dog put a wild idea into his head. He remembered the tale of the man, caught in a blizzard, who killed a steer and crawled inside the carcass, and so was saved. He would kill the dog and bury his hands in the warm body until the numbness went out of them. Then he could build another fire. He spoke to the dog, calling it to him; but in his voice was a strange note of fear that frightened the animal, who had never known the man to speak in such way before. Something was the matter, and its suspicious nature sensed danger—it knew not what danger, but somewhere, somehow, in its brain arose an apprehension of the man. It flattened its ears down at the sound of the man's voice, and its restless, hunching movements and the liftings and shiftings of its forefeet became more pronounced; but it would not come to the man. He got on his hands and knees and crawled toward the dog. This unusual posture again excited suspicion, and the animal sidled mincingly away.

The man sat up in the snow for a moment and struggled for calmness. Then he pulled on his mittens, by means of his teeth, and got upon his feet. He glanced down at first in order to assure himself that he was really standing up, for the absence of sensation in his feet left him unrelated to the earth. His erect position in itself started to drive the webs of suspicion from the dog's mind; and when he spoke peremptorily, with the sound of whip-lashes in his voice, the dog rendered its customary allegiance and came to him. As it came within reaching distance, the man lost his control. His arms flashed out to the dog, and he experienced genuine surprise when he discovered that his hands could not clutch, that there was neither bend nor feeling in the fingers. He had forgotten for the moment that they were frozen and that they were freezing more and more. All this happened quickly, and before the animal could get away, he encircled its body with his arms. He sat down in the snow, and in this fashion held the dog, while it snarled and whined and struggled.

But it was all he could do, hold its body encircled in his arms and sit there. He realized that he could not kill the dog. There was no way to do it. With his helpless hands he could neither draw nor hold his sheath-knife nor throttle the animal. He released it, and it plunged wildly away, with tail between its legs, and still snarling. It halted forty feet away and surveyed him curiously, with ears sharply pricked forward. The man looked down at his hands in order to locate them, and found them hanging on the ends of his arms. It struck him as curious that one should have to use his eyes in order to find out where his hands were. He began threshing his arms back and forth, beating the mittened hands against his sides. He did this for five minutes, violently, and his heart pumped enough blood up to the surface to put a stop to his shivering. But no sensation was aroused in the hands. He had an impression that they hung like weights on the ends of his arms, but when he tried to run the impression down, he could not find it.

A certain fear of death, dull and oppressive, came to him. This fear quickly became poignant as he realized that it was no longer a mere matter of freezing his fingers and toes, or of losing his hands and feet, but that it was a matter of life and death with the chances against him. This threw him into a panic, and he turned and ran up the creek-bed along the old, dim trail. The dog joined in behind and kept up with him. He ran blindly, without intention, in fear such as he had never known in his life. Slowly, as he plowed and floundered through the snow, he began to see things again,—the banks of the creek, the old timber-jams, the leafless aspens, and the sky. The running made him feel better. He did not shiver. Maybe, if he ran on, his feet would thaw out; and, anyway, if he ran far enough, he would reach camp and the boys. Without doubt he would lose some fingers and toes and some of his face; but the boys would take care of him, and save the rest of him when he got there. And at the same time there was another thought in his mind that said he would never get to the camp and the boys; that it was too many miles away, that the freezing had too great a start on him, and that he would soon be stiff and dead. This thought he kept in the background and refused to consider. Sometimes it pushed itself forward and demanded to be heard, but he thrust it back and strove to think of other things.

It struck him as curious that he could run at all on feet so frozen that he could not feel them when they struck the earth and took the weight of his body. He seemed to himself to skim along above the surface, and to have no connection with the earth. Somewhere he had once seen a winged Mercury, and he wondered if Mercury felt as he felt when skimming over the earth.

His theory of running until he reached camp and the boys had one flaw in it: he lacked the endurance. Several times he stumbled, and finally he tottered, crumpled up, and fell. When he tried to rise, he failed. He must sit and rest, he decided, and next time he would merely walk and keep on going. As he sat and regained his breath, he noted that he was feeling quite warm and comfortable. He was not shivering, and it even seemed that a warm glow had come to his chest and trunk. And yet, when he touched his nose or cheeks, there was no sensation. Running would not thaw them out. Nor would it thaw out his hands and feet. Then the thought came to him that the frozen portions of his body must be extending. He tried to keep this thought down, to forget it, to think of something else; he was aware of the panicky feeling that it caused, and he was afraid of the panic. But the thought asserted itself, and persisted, until it produced a vision of his body totally frozen. This was too much, and he made another wild run along the trail. Once he slowed down to a walk, but the thought of the freezing extending itself made him run again.

And all the time the dog ran with him, at his heels. When he fell down a second time, it curled its tail over its forefeet and sat in front of him, facing him, curiously eager and intent. The warmth and security of the animal angered him, and he cursed it till it flattened down its ears appeasingly. This time the shivering came more quickly upon the man. He was losing in his battle with the frost. It was creeping into his body from all sides. The thought of it drove him on, but he ran no more than a hundred feet, when he staggered and pitched headlong. It was his last panic. When he had recovered his breath and control, he sat up and entertained in his mind the conception of meeting death with dignity. However, the conception did not come to him in such terms. His idea of it was that he had been making a fool of himself, running around like a chicken with its head cut off—such was the simile that occurred to him. Well, he was bound to freeze anyway, and he might as well take it decently. With this new-found peace of mind came the first glimmerings of drowsiness. A good idea, he thought, to sleep off to death. It was like taking an anesthetic. Freezing was not so bad as people thought. There were lots worse ways to die.

He pictured the boys finding his body next day. Suddenly he found himself with them, coming along the trail and looking for himself. And, still with them, he came around a turn in the trail and found himself lying in the snow. He did not belong with himself anymore, for even then he was out of himself, standing with the boys and looking at himself in the snow. It certainly was cold, was his thought. When he got back to the States he could tell the folks what real cold was. He drifted on from this to a vision of the old-timer on Sulphur Creek. He could see him quite clearly, warm and comfortable, and smoking a pipe.

"You were right,—old hoss; you were right, " the man mumbled to the old-timer of Sulphur Creek.

Then the man drowsed off into what seemed to him the most comfortable and satisfying sleep he had ever known. The dog sat facing him and waiting. The brief day drew to a close in a long, slow twilight. There were no signs of a fire to be made, and, besides, never in the dog's experience had it known a man to sit like that in the snow and make no fire. As the twilight drew on, its eager yearning for the fire mastered it, and with a great lifting and shifting of forefeet, it whined softly, then flattened its ears down in anticipation of being chidden by the man. But the man remained silent. Later, the dog whined loudly. And still later it crept close to the man and caught the scent of death. This made the animal bristle and back away. A little longer it delayed, howling under the stars that leaped and danced and shone brightly in the cold sky. Then it turned and trotted up the trail in the direction of the camp it knew, where were the other food-providers and fire-providers.

—*Jack London (1876–1916)*

The Yellow Wallpaper

It is very seldom that mere ordinary people like John and myself secure ancestral halls for the summer.

A colonial mansion, a hereditary estate, I would say a haunted house, and reach the height of romantic felicity—but that would be asking too much of fate!

Still I will proudly declare that there is something queer about it.

Else, why should it be let so cheaply? And why have stood so long untenanted?

John laughs at me, of course, but one expects that in marriage.

John is practical in the extreme. He has no patience with faith, an intense horror of superstition, and he scoffs openly at any talk of things not to be felt and seen and put down in figures.

John is a physician, and *perhaps*—(I would not say it to a living soul, of course, but this is dead paper and a great relief to my mind)—*perhaps* that is one reason I do not get well faster.

You see he does not believe I am sick!

And what can one do?

If a physician of high standing, and one's own husband, assures friends and relatives that there is really nothing the matter with one but temporary nervous depression—a slight hysterical tendency—what is one to do?

My brother is also a physician, and also of high standing, and he says the same thing.

So I take phosphates or phosphites—whichever it is, and tonics, and journeys, and air, and exercise, and am absolutely forbidden to "work" until I am well again.

Personally, I disagree with their ideas.

Personally, I believe that congenial work, with excitement and change, would do me good.

But what is one to do?

I did write for a while in spite of them; but it *does* exhaust me a good deal—having to be so sly about it, or else meet with heavy opposition.

I sometimes fancy that in my condition if I had less opposition and more society and stimulus—but John says the very worst thing I can do is to think about my condition, and I confess it always makes me feel bad.

So I will let it alone and talk about the house.

The most beautiful place! It is quite alone, standing well back from the road, quite three miles from the village. It makes me think of English places that you read about, for there are hedges and walls and gates that lock, and lots of separate little houses for the gardeners and people.

There is a delicious garden! I never saw such a garden—large and shady, full of box-bordered paths, and lined with long grape-covered arbors with seats under them.

There were greenhouses, too, but they are all broken now.

There was some legal trouble, I believe, something about the heirs and coheirs; anyhow, the place has been empty for years.

That spoils my ghostliness, I am afraid, but I don't care—there is something strange about the house—I can feel it.

I even said so to John one moonlight evening, but he said what I felt was a *draught*, and shut the window.

I get unreasonably angry with John sometimes. I'm sure I never used to be so sensitive. I think it is due to this nervous condition.

But John says if I feel so, I shall neglect proper self-control; so I take pains to control myself—before him, at least, and that makes me very tired.

I don't like our room a bit. I wanted one downstairs that opened on the piazza and had roses all over the window, and such pretty old-fashioned chintz hangings! but John would not hear of it.

He said there was only one window and not room for two beds, and no near room for him if he took another.

He is very careful and loving, and hardly lets me stir without special direction.

I have a schedule prescription for each hour in the day; he takes all care from me, and so I feel basely ungrateful not to value it more.

He said we came here solely on my account, that I was to have perfect rest and all the air I could get. "Your exercise depends on your strength, my dear," said he, "and your food somewhat on your appetite; but air you can absorb all the time." So we took the nursery at the top of the house.

It is a big, airy room, the whole floor nearly, with windows that look all ways, and air and sunshine galore. It was nursery first and then playroom and gymnasium, I should judge; for the windows are barred for little children, and there are rings and things in the walls.

The paint and paper look as if a boys' school had used it. It is stripped off—the paper—in great patches all around the head of my bed, about as far as I can reach, and in a great place on the other side of the room low down. I never saw a worse paper in my life.

One of those sprawling flamboyant patterns committing every artistic sin.

It is dull enough to confuse the eye in following, pronounced enough to constantly irritate and provoke study, and when you follow the lame uncertain curves for a little distance they suddenly commit suicide—plunge off at outrageous angles, destroy themselves in unheard of contradictions.

The color is repellent, almost revolting; a smouldering unclean yellow, strangely faded by the slow-turning sunlight.

It is a dull yet lurid orange in some places, a sickly sulphur tint in others.

No wonder the children hated it! I should hate it myself if I had to live in this room long.

There comes John, and I must put this away,—he hates to have me write a word.

We have been here two weeks, and I haven't felt like writing before, since that first day.

I am sitting by the window now, up in this atrocious nursery, and there is nothing to hinder my writing as much as I please, save lack of strength.

John is away all day, and even some nights when his cases are serious.

I am glad my case is not serious!

But these nervous troubles are dreadfully depressing.

John does not know how much I really suffer. He knows there is no reason to suffer, and that satisfies him.

Of course it is only nervousness. It does weigh on me so not to do my duty in any way!

I meant to be such a help to John, such a real rest and comfort, and here I am a comparative burden already!

Nobody would believe what an effort it is to do what little I am able,—to dress and entertain, and order things.

It is fortunate Mary is so good with the baby. Such a dear baby!

And yet I *cannot* be with him, it makes me so nervous.

I suppose John never was nervous in his life. He laughs at me so about this wall-paper!

At first he meant to repaper the room, but afterwards he said that I was letting it get the better of me, and that nothing was worse for a nervous patient than to give way to such fancies.

He said that after the wallpaper was changed it would be the heavy bedstead, and then the barred windows, and then that gate at the head of the stairs, and so on.

"You know the place is doing you good," he said, "and really, dear, I don't care to renovate the house just for a three-months' rental."

"Then do let us go downstairs," I said, "there are such pretty rooms there."

Then he took me in his arms and called me a blessed little goose, and said he would go down to the cellar, if I wished, and have it whitewashed into the bargain.

But he is right enough about the beds and windows and things.

It is an airy and comfortable room as anyone need wish, and, of course, I would not be so silly as to make him uncomfortable just for a whim.

I'm really getting quite fond of the big room, all but that horrid paper.

Out of one window I can see the garden, those mysterious deepshaded arbors, the riotous old-fashioned flowers, and bushes and gnarly trees.

Out of another I get a lovely view of the bay and a little private wharf belonging to the estate. There is a beautiful shaded lane that runs down there from the house. I always fancy I see people walking in these numerous paths and arbors, but John has cautioned me not to give way to fancy in the least. He says that with my imaginative power and habit of story-making, a nervous weakness like mine is sure to lead to all manner of excited fancies, and that I ought to use my will and good sense to check the tendency. So I try.

I think sometimes that if I were only well enough to write a little it would relieve the press of ideas and rest me.

But I find I get pretty tired when I try.

It is so discouraging not to have any advice and companionship about my work. When I get really well, John says we will ask Cousin Henry and Julia down for a long visit; but he says he would as soon put fireworks in my pillow-case as to let me have those stimulating people about now.

I wish I could get well faster.

But I must not think about that. This paper looks to me as if it knew what a vicious influence it had!

There is a recurrent spot where the pattern lolls like a broken neck and two bulbous eyes stare at you upside down.

I get positively angry with the impertinence of it and the everlastingness. Up and down and sideways they crawl, and those absurd, unblinking eyes are everywhere. There is one place where two breadths didn't match, and the eyes go all up and down the line, one a little higher than the other.

I never saw so much expression in an inanimate thing before, and we all know how much expression they have! I used to lie awake as a child and get more entertainment and terror out of blank walls and plain furniture than most children could find in a toy-store.

I remember what a kindly wink the knobs of our big, old bureau used to have, and there was one chair that always seemed like a strong friend.

I used to feel that if any of the other things looked too fierce I could always hop into that chair and be safe.

The furniture in this room is no worse than inharmonious, however, for we had to bring it all from downstairs. I suppose when this was used as a playroom they had to take the nursery things out, and no wonder! I never saw such ravages as the children have made here.

The wallpaper, as I said before, is torn off in spots, and it sticketh closer than a brother—they must have had perseverance as well as hatred.

Then the floor is scratched and gouged and splintered, the plaster itself is dug out here and there, and this great heavy bed which is all we found in the room, looks as if it had been through the wars.

But I don't mind it a bit—only the paper.

There comes John's sister. Such a dear girl as she is, and so careful of me! I must not let her find me writing.

She is a perfect and enthusiastic housekeeper, and hopes for no better professions. I verily believe she thinks it is the writing which made me sick!

But I can write when she is out, and see her a long way off from these windows.

There is one that commands the road, a lovely shaded winding road, and one that just looks off over the country. A lovely country, too, full of great elms and velvet meadows.

This wallpaper has a kind of sub-pattern in a different shade, a particularly irritating one, for you can only see it in certain lights, and not clearly then.

But in the places where it isn't faded and where the sun is just so—I can see a strange, provoking, formless sort of figure, that seems to skulk about behind that silly and conspicuous front design.

There's sister on the stairs!

Well, the Fourth of July is over! The people are all gone and I am tired out. John thought it might do me good to see a little company, so we just had mother and Nellie and the children down for a week.

Of course I didn't do a thing. Jennie sees to everything now.

But it tired me all the same.

John says if I don't pick up faster he shall send me to Weir Mitchell in the fall.

But I don't want to go there at all. I had a friend who was in his hands once, and she says he is just like John and my brother, only more so!

Besides, it is such an undertaking to go so far.

I don't feel as if it was worth while to turn my hand over for anything, and I'm getting dreadfully fretful and querulous.

I cry at nothing, and cry most of the time.

Of course I don't when John is here, or anybody else, but when I am alone.

And I am alone a good deal just now. John is kept in town very often by serious cases, and Jennie is good and lets me alone when I want her to.

So I walk a little in the garden or down that lovely lane, sit on the porch under the roses, and lie down up here a good deal.

I'm getting really fond of the room in spite of the wallpaper. Perhaps because of the wallpaper.

It dwells in my mind so!

I lie here on this great immovable bed—it is nailed down, I believe—and follow that pattern about by the hour. It is as good as gymnastics, I assure you. I start, we'll say, at the bottom, down in the corner over there where it has not been touched, and I determine for the thousandth time that I will follow that pointless pattern to some sort of a conclusion.

I know a little of the principle of design, and I know this thing was not arranged on any laws of radiation, or alternation, or repetition, or symmetry, or anything else that I ever heard of.

It is repeated, of course, by the breadths, but not otherwise.

Looked at in one way each breadth stands alone, the bloated curves and flourishes—a kind of "debased Romanesque" with delirium tremens—go waddling up and down in isolated columns of fatuity.

But, on the other hand, they connect diagonally, and the sprawling outlines run off in great slanting waves of optic horror, like a lot of wallowing seaweeds in full chase.

The whole thing goes horizontally, too, at least it seems so, and I exhaust myself in trying to distinguish the order of its going in that direction.

They have used a horizontal breadth for a frieze, and that adds wonderfully to the confusion.

There is one end of the room where it is almost intact, and there, when the crosslights fade and the low sun shines directly upon it, I can almost fancy radiation after all,—the interminable grotesques seem to form around a common center and rush off in headlong plunges of equal distraction.

It makes me tired to follow it. I will take a nap I guess.

I don't know why I should write this.

I don't want to.

I don't feel able.

And I know John would think it absurd. But I must say what I feel and think in some way—it is such a relief!

But the effort is getting to be greater than the relief.

Half the time now I am awfully lazy, and lie down ever so much.

John says I mustn't lose my strength, and has me take cod liver oil and lots of tonics and things, to say nothing of ale and wine and rare meat.

Dear John! He loves me very dearly, and hates to have me sick. I tried to have a real earnest reasonable talk with him the other day, and tell him how I wish he would let me go and make a visit to Cousin Henry and Julia.

But he said I wasn't able to go, nor able to stand it after I got there; and I did not make out a very good case for myself, for I was crying before I had finished.

It is getting to be a great effort for me to think straight. Just this nervous weakness I suppose.

And dear John gathered me up in his arms, and just carried me upstairs and laid me on the bed, and sat by me and read to me till it tired my head.

He said I was his darling and his comfort and all he had, and that I must take care of myself for his sake, and keep well.

He says no one but myself can help me out of it, that I must use my will and self-control and not let any silly fancies run away with me.

There's one comfort, the baby is well and happy, and does not have to occupy this nursery with the horrid wallpaper.

If we had not used it, that blessed child would have! What a fortunate escape! Why, I wouldn't have a child of mine, an impressionable little thing, live in such a room for worlds.

I never thought of it before, but it is lucky that John kept me here after all, I can stand it so much easier than a baby, you see.

Of course I never mention it to them any more—I am too wise,—but I keep watch of it all the same.

There are things in that paper that nobody knows but me, or ever will.

Behind that outside pattern the dim shapes get clearer every day.

It is always the same shape, only very numerous.

And it is like a woman stooping down and creeping about behind that pattern. I don't like it a bit. I wonder—I begin to think—I wish John would take me away from here!

It is so hard to talk with John about my case, because he is so wise, and because he loves me so.

But I tried it last night.

It was moonlight. The moon shines in all around just as the sun does.

I hate to see it sometimes, it creeps so slowly, and always comes in by one window or another.

John was asleep and I hated to waken him, so I kept still and watched the moonlight on that undulating wallpaper till I felt creepy.

The faint figure behind seemed to shake the pattern, just as if she wanted to get out.

I got up softly and went to feel and see if the paper did move, and when I came back John was awake.

"What is it, little girl?" he said. "Don't go walking about like that—you'll get cold."

I thought it was a good time to talk, so I told him that I really was not gaining here, and that I wished he would take me away.

"Why darling!" said he, "our lease will be up in three weeks, and I can't see how to leave before.

"The repairs are not done at home, and I cannot possibly leave town just now. Of course if you were in any danger, I could and would, but you really are better, dear, whether you can see it or not. I am a doctor, dear, and I know. You are gaining flesh and color, your appetite is better, I feel really much easier about you."

"I don't weigh a bit more," said I, "nor as much; and my appetite may be better in the evening when you are here, but it is worse in the morning when you are away!"

"Bless her little heart!" said he with a big hug, "she shall be as sick as she pleases! But now let's improve the shining hours by going to sleep, and talk about it in the morning!"

"And you won't go away?" I asked gloomily.

"Why, how can I, dear? It is only three weeks more and then we will take a nice little trip of a few days while Jennie is getting the house ready. Really dear. you are better!"

"Better in body perhaps—" I began, and stopped short, for he sat up straight and looked at me with such a stern, reproachful look that I could not say another word.

"My darling," said he, "I beg of you, for my sake and for our child's sake, as well as for your own, that you will never for one instant let that idea enter your mind! There is nothing so dangerous, so fascinating, to a temperament like yours. It is a false and foolish fancy. Can you not trust me as a physician when I tell you so?"

So of course I said no more on that score, and we went to sleep before long. He thought I was asleep first, but I wasn't, and lay there for hours trying to decide whether that front pattern and the back pattern really did move together or separately.

On a pattern like this, by daylight, there is a lack of sequence, a defiance of law, that is a constant irritant to a normal mind.

The color is hideous enough, and unreliable enough, and infuriating enough, but the pattern is torturing.

You think you have mastered it, but just as you get well underway in following, it turns a back somersault and there you are. It slaps you in the face, knocks you down, and tramples upon you. It is like a bad dream.

The outside pattern is a florid arabesque, reminding one of a fungus. If you can imagine a toadstool in joints, an interminable string of toadstools, budding and sprouting in endless convolutions—why, that is something like it.

That is, sometimes!

There is one marked peculiarity about this paper, a thing nobody seems to notice but myself, and that is that it changes as the light changes.

When the sun shoots in through the east window—I always watch for that first long, straight ray—it changes so quickly that I never can quite believe it.

That is why I watch it always.

By moonlight—the moon shines in all night when there is a moon—I wouldn't know it was the same paper.

At night in any kind of light, in twilight, candlelight, lamplight, and worst of all by moonlight, it becomes bars! The outside pattern I mean. and the woman behind it is as plain as can be.

I didn't realize for a long time what the thing was that showed behind, that dim sub-pattern, but now I am quite sure it is a woman.

By daylight she is subdued, quiet. I fancy it is the pattern that keeps her so still. It is so puzzling. It keeps me quiet by the hour.

I lie down ever so much now. John says it is good for me, and to sleep all I can.

Indeed he started the habit by making me lie down for an hour after each meal.

It is a very bad habit I am convinced, for you see I don't sleep.

And that cultivates deceit, for I don't tell them I'm awake—O no!

The fact is I am getting a little afraid of John.

He seems very queer sometimes, and even Jennie has an inexplicable look.

It strikes me occasionally, just as a scientific hypothesis,—that perhaps it is the paper!

I have watched John when he did not know I was looking, and come into the room suddenly on the most innocent excuses, and I've caught him several times looking at the paper! And Jennie too. I caught Jennie with her hand on it once.

She didn't know I was in the room, and when I asked her in a quiet, a very quiet voice, with the most restrained manner possible, what she was doing with the paper—she turned around as if she had been caught stealing, and looked quite angry—asked me why I should frighten her so!

Then she said that the paper stained everything it touched, that she had found yellow smooches on all my clothes and John's, and she wished we would be more careful!

Did not that sound innocent? But I know she was studying that pattern, and I am determined that nobody shall find it out but myself!

Life is very much more exciting now than it used to be. You see I have something more to expect, to look forward to, to watch. I really do eat better, and am more quiet than I was.

John is so pleased to see me improve! He laughed a little the other day, and said I seemed to be flourishing in spite of my wallpaper.

I turned it off with a laugh. I had no intention of telling him it was because of the wallpaper—he would make fun of me. He might even want to take me away.

I don't want to leave now until I have found it out. There is a week more, and I think that will be enough.

I'm feeling ever so much better! I don't sleep much at night, for it is so interesting to watch developments; but I sleep a good deal in the daytime.

In the daytime it is tiresome and perplexing.

There are always new shoots on the fungus, and new shades of yellow all over it. I cannot keep count of them, though I have tried conscientiously.

It is the strangest yellow, that wallpaper! It makes me think of all the yellow things I ever saw—not beautiful ones like buttercups, but old foul, bad yellow things.

But there is something else about that paper—the smell! I noticed it the moment we came into the room, but with so much air and sun it was not bad. Now we have had a week of fog and rain, and whether the windows are open or not, the smell is here.

It creeps all over the house.

I find it hovering in the dining-room, skulking in the parlor, hiding in the hall, lying in wait for me on the stairs.

It gets into my hair.

Even when I go to ride, if I turn my head suddenly and surprise it—there is that smell!

Such a peculiar odor, too! I have spent hours in trying to analyze it, to find what it smelled like.

It is not bad—at first, and very gentle, but quite the subtlest, most enduring odor I ever met.

In this damp weather it is awful, I wake up in the night and find it hanging over me.

It used to disturb me at first. I thought seriously of burning the house—to reach the smell.

But now I am used to it. The only thing I can think of that it is like is the color of the paper! A yellow smell.

There is a very funny mark on this wall, low down, near the mopboard. A streak that runs round the room. It goes behind every piece of furniture, except the bed, a long, straight, even smooch, as if it had been rubbed over and over.

I wonder how it was done and who did it, and what they did it for. Round and round and round—round and round and round—it makes me dizzy!

I really have discovered something at last.

Through watching so much at night, when it changes so, I have finally found out.

The front pattern does move—and no wonder! The woman behind shakes it!

Sometimes I think there are a great many women behind, and sometimes only one, and she crawls around fast, and her crawling shakes it all over.

Then in the very bright spots she keeps still, and in the very shady spots she just takes hold of the bars and shakes them hard.

And she is all the time trying to climb through. But nobody could climb through that pattern—it strangles so; I think that is why it has so many heads.

They get through, and then the pattern strangles them off and turns them upside down, and makes their eyes white!

If those heads were covered or taken off it would not be half so bad.

I think that woman gets out in the daytime!

And I'll tell you why—privately—I've seen her!

I can see her out of every one of my windows!

It is the same woman, I know, for she is always creeping, and most women do not creep by daylight.

I see her on that long road under the trees, creeping along, and when a carriage comes she hides under the blackberry vines.

I don't blame her a bit. It must be very humiliating to be caught creeping by daylight!

I always lock the door when I creep by daylight. I can't do it at night, for I know John would suspect something at once.

And John is so queer now, that I don't want to irritate him. I wish he would take another room! Besides, I don't want anybody to get that woman out at night but myself.

I often wonder if I could see her out of all the windows at once.

But, turn as fast as I can, I can only see out of one at one time.

And though I always see her, she may be able to creep faster than I can turn!

I have watched her sometimes away off in the open country, creeping as fast as a cloud shadow in a high wind.

If only that top pattern could be gotten off from the under one! I mean to try it, little by little.

I have found out another funny thing, but I shan't tell it this time! It does not do to trust people too much.

There are only two more days to get this paper off, and I believe John is beginning to notice. I don't like the look in his eyes.

And I heard him ask Jennie a lot of professional questions about me. She had a very good report to give.

She said I slept a good deal in the daytime.

John knows I don't sleep very well at night, for all I'm so quiet!

He asked me all sorts of questions, too, and pretended to be very loving and kind.

As if I couldn't see through him!

Still, I don't wonder he acts so, sleeping under this paper for three months.

It only interests me, but I feel sure John and Jennie are secretly affected by it.

Hurrah! This is the last day, but it is enough. John is to stay in town over night, and won't be out until this evening.

Jennie wanted to sleep with me—the sly thing! but I told her I should undoubtedly rest better for a night all alone.

That was clever, for really I wasn't alone a bit! As soon as it was moonlight and that poor thing began to crawl and shake the pattern, I got up and ran to help her.

I pulled and she shook, I shook and she pulled, and before morning we had peeled off yards of that paper.

A strip about as high as my head and half around the room.

And then when the sun came and that awful pattern began to laugh at me, I declared I would finish it today!

We go away tomorrow, and they are moving all my furniture down again to leave things as they were before.

Jennie looked at the wall in amazement, but I told her merrily that I did it out of pure spite at the vicious thing.

She laughed and said she wouldn't mind doing it herself, but I must not get tired.

How she betrayed herself that time!

But I am here, and no person touches this paper but me,—not alive!

She tried to get me out of the room—it was too patent! But I said it was so quiet and empty and clean now that I believed I would lie down again and sleep all I could; and not to wake me even for dinner—I would call when I woke.

So now she is gone, and the servants are gone, and the things are gone, and there is nothing left but that great bedstead nailed down, with the canvas mattress we found on it.

We shall sleep downstairs tonight, and take the boat home tomorrow.

I quite enjoy the room, now it is bare again.

How those children did tear about here!

This bedstead is fairly gnawed!

But I must get to work.

I have locked the door and thrown the key down into the front path.

I don't want to go out, and I don't want to have anybody come in, till John comes.

I want to astonish him.

I've got a rope up here that even Jennie did not find. If that woman does get out, and tries to get away, I can tie her!

But I forgot I could not reach far without anything to stand on!

This bed will not move!

I tried to lift and push it until I was lame, and then I got so angry I bit off a little piece at one corner—but it hurt my teeth.

Then I peeled off all the paper I could reach standing on the floor. It sticks horribly and the pattern just enjoys it! All those strangled heads and bulbous eyes and waddling fungus growths just shriek with derision!

I am getting angry enough to do something desperate. To jump out of the window would be admirable exercise, but the bars are too strong even to try.

Besides I wouldn't do it. Of course not. I know well enough that a step like that is improper and might be misconstrued.

I don't like to look out of the windows even—there are so many of those creeping women, and they creep so fast.

I wonder if they all come out of that wallpaper as I did?

But I am securely fastened now by my well-hidden rope—you don't get me out in the road there!

I suppose I shall have to get back behind the pattern when it comes night, and that is hard!

It is so pleasant to be out in this great room and creep around as I please!

I don't want to go outside. I won't, even if Jennie asks me to.

For outside you have to creep on the ground, and everything is green instead of yellow.

But here I can creep smoothly on the floor, and my shoulder just fits in that long smooch around the wall, so I cannot lose my way.

Why there's John at the door!

It is no use, young man, you can't open it!

How he does call and pound!

Now he's crying for an axe.

It would be a shame to break down that beautiful door!

"John dear!" said I in the gentlest voice, "the key is down by the front steps, under a plantain leaf!"

That silenced him for a few moments.

Then he said—very quietly indeed, "Open the door, my darling!"

"I can't," said I. "The key is down by the front door under a plantain leaf!"

And then I said it again, several times, very gently and slowly, and said it so often that he had to go and see, and he got it of course, and came in. He stopped short by the door.

"What is the matter?" he cried. "For God's sake, what are you doing!"

I kept on creeping just the same, but I looked at him over my shoulder.

"I've got out at last, " said I, "in spite of you and Jane. And I've pulled off most of the paper, so you can't put me back!"

Now why should that man have fainted? But he did, and right across my path by the wall, so that I had to creep over him every time!

—*Charlotte Perkins Gilman (1860–1935)*

THE SNAKE

It was almost dark when young Dr. Phillips swung his sack to his shoulder and left the tide pool. He climbed up over the rocks and squashed along the street in his rubber boots. The street lights were on by the time he arrived at his little commercial laboratory on the cannery street of Monterey. It was a tight little building, standing partly on piers over the bay water and partly on the land. On both sides the big corrugated-iron sardine canneries crowded in on it.

Dr. Phillips climbed the wooden steps and opened the door. The white rats in their cages scampered up and down the wire, and the captive cats in their pens mewed for milk. Dr. Phillips turned on the glaring light over the dissection table and dumped his clammy sack on the floor. He walked to the glass cages by the window where the rattle-snakes lived, leaned over and looked in.

The snakes were bunched and resting in the corners of the cage, but every head was clear; the dusty eyes seemed to look at nothing, but as the young man leaned over the cage the forked tongues, black on the ends and pink behind, twittered out and waved slowly up and down. Then the snakes recognized the man and pulled in their tongues.

Dr. Phillips threw off his leather coat and built a fire in the tin stove; he set a kettle of water on the stove and dropped a can of beans into the water. Then he stood staring down at the sack on the floor. He was a slight young man with the mild, preoccupied eyes of one who looks through a microscope a great deal. He wore a short blond beard.

The draft ran breathily up the chimney and a glow of warmth came from the stove. The little waves washed quietly about the piles under the building. Arranged on shelves about the room were tier above tier of museum jars containing the mounted marine specimens the laboratory dealt in.

Dr. Phillips opened a side door and went into his bedroom, a book-lined cell containing an army cot, a reading light and an uncomfortable wooden chair. He pulled off his rubber boots and put on a pair of sheepskin slippers. When he went back to the other room the water in the kettle was already beginning to hum.

He lifted his sack to the table under the white light and emptied out two dozen common starfish. These he laid out side by side on the table. His preoccupied eyes turned to the busy rats in the wire cages. Taking grain from a paper sack, he poured it into the feeding troughs. Instantly the rats scrambled down from the wire and fell upon the food. A bottle of milk stood on a glass shelf between a small mounted octopus and a jellyfish. Dr. Phillips lifted down the milk and walked to the cat cage, but before he filled the containers he reached in the cage and gently picked out a big rangy alley tabby. He stroked her for a moment and then dropped her in a small black painted box, closed the lid and bolted it and then turned on a petcock which admitted gas into the killing chamber. While the short soft struggle went on in the black box he filled the saucers with milk. One of the cats arched against his hand and he smiled and petted her neck.

The box was quiet now. He turned off the petcock, for the airtight box would be full of gas.

On the stove the pan of water was bubbling furiously about the can of beans. Dr. Phillips lifted out the can with a big pair of forceps, opened it, and emptied the beans into a glass dish. While he ate he watched the starfish on the table. From between the rays little drops of milky fluid were exuding. He bolted his beans and when they were gone he put the dish in the sink and stepped to the equipment cupboard. From this he took a microscope and a pile of little glass dishes. He filled the dishes one by one with sea water from a tap and arranged them in a line beside the starfish. He took out his watch and laid it on the table under the pouring white light. The waves washed with little sighs against the piles under the floor. He took an eyedropper from a drawer and bent over the starfish.

At that moment there were quick soft steps on the wooden stairs and a strong knocking at the door. A slight grimace of annoyance crossed the young man's face as he went to open. A tall, lean woman stood in the doorway. She was dressed in a severe dark suit—her straight black hair, growing low on a flat forehead, was mussed as though the wind had been blowing it. Her black eyes glittered in the strong light.

She spoke in a soft throaty voice, "May I come in? I want to talk to you."

"I'm very busy just now," he said half-heartedly. "I have to do things at times." But he stood away from the door. The tall woman slipped in.

"I'll be quiet until you can talk to me."

He closed the door and brought the uncomfortable chair from the bedroom. "You see," he apologized, "the process is started and I must get to it." So many people wandered in and asked questions. He had little routines of explanations for the commoner processes. He could say them without thinking. "Sit here. In a few minutes I'll be able to listen to you."

The tall woman leaned over the table. With the eyedropper the young man gathered fluid from between the rays of the starfish and squirted it into a bowl of water, and then he drew some milky fluid and squirted it in the same bowl and stirred the water gently with the eyedropper. He began his little patter of explanation.

"When starfish are sexually mature they release sperm and ova when they are exposed at low tide. By choosing mature specimens and taking them out of the water, I give them a condition of low tide. Now I've mixed the sperm and eggs. Now I put some of the mixture in each one of these ten watch glasses. In ten minutes I will kill those in the first glass with menthol, twenty minutes later I will kill the second group and then a new group every twenty minutes. Then I will have arrested the process in stages, and I will mount the series on microscope slides for biologic study." He paused. "Would you like to look at this first group under the microscope?"

"No, thank you."

He turned quickly to her. People always wanted to look through the glass. She was not looking at the table at all, but at him. Her black eyes were on him, but they did not seem to see him. He realized why—the irises were as dark as the pupils, there was no color line between the two. Dr. Phillips was piqued at her answer. Although answering questions bored him, a lack of interest in what he was doing irritated him. A desire to arouse her grew in him.

"While I'm waiting the first ten minutes I have something to do. Some people don't like to see it. Maybe you'd better step into that room until I finish."

"No," she said in her soft flat tone. "Do what you wish. I will wait until you can talk to me." Her hands rested side by side on her lap. She was completely at rest. Her eyes were bright but the rest of her was almost in a state of suspended animation. He thought, "Low metabolic rate, almost as low as a frog's, from the looks." The desire to shock her out of her inanition possessed him again.

He brought a little wooden cradle to the table, laid out scalpels and scissors and rigged a big hollow needle to a pressure tube. Then from the killing chamber he brought the limp dead cat and laid it in the cradle and tied its legs to hooks in the sides. He glanced sidewise at the woman. She had not moved. She was still at rest.

The cat grinned up into the light, its pink tongue stuck out between its needle teeth. Dr. Phillips deftly snipped open the skin at the throat; with a scalpel he slit through and found an artery. With flawless technique he put the needle in the vessel and tied it in with gut. "Embalming fluid," he explained. "Later I'll inject yellow mass into the veinous system and red mass into the arterial system—for bloodstream dissection—biology classes."

He looked around at her again. Her dark eyes seemed veiled with dust. She looked without expression at the cat's open throat. Not a drop of blood had escaped. The incision was clean. Dr. Phillips looked at his watch. "Time for the first group." He shook a few crystals of menthol into the first watch-glass.

The woman was making him nervous. The rats climbed about on the wire of their cage again and squeaked softly. The waves under the building beat with little shocks on the piles.

The young man shivered. He put a few lumps of coal in the stove and sat down. "Now," he said. "I haven't anything to do for twenty minutes." He noticed how short her chin was between lower lip and point. She seemed to awaken slowly, to come up out of some deep pool of consciousness. Her head raised and her dark dusty eyes moved about the room and then came back to him.

"I was waiting," she said. Her hands remained side by side on her lap. "You have snakes?"

"Why, yes," he said rather loudly. "I have about two dozen rattlesnakes. I milk out the venom and send it to the anti-venom laboratories."

She continued to look at him but her eyes did not center on him, rather they covered him and seemed to see in a big circle all around him. "Have you a male snake, a male rattlesnake?"

"Well, it just happens I know I have. I came in one morning and found a big snake in—in coition with a smaller one. That's very rare in captivity. You see, I do know I have a male snake."

"Where is he?"

"Why, right in the glass cage by the window there."

Her head swung slowly around but her two quiet hands did not move. She turned back toward him. "May I see?"

He got up and walked to the case by the window. On the sand bottom the knot of rattlesnakes lay entwined, but their heads were clear. The tongues came out and flickered a moment and then waved up and down feeling the air for vibrations. Dr. Phillips nervously turned his head. The woman was standing beside him. He had not heard her get up from the chair. He had heard only the splash of water among the piles and the scampering of the rats on the wire screen.

She said softly, "Which is the male you spoke of?"

He pointed to a thick, dusty grey snake lying by itself in one corner of the cage. "That one. He's nearly five feet long. He comes from Texas. Our Pacific coast snakes are usually smaller. He's been taking all the rats, too. When I want the others to eat I have to take him out."

The woman stared down at the blunt dry head. The forked tongue slipped out and hung quivering for a long moment. "And you're sure he's a male."

"Rattlesnakes are funny," he said glibly. "Nearly every generalization proves wrong. I don't like to say anything definite about rattlesnakes, but—yes—I can assure you he's a male."

Her eyes did not move from the flat head. "Will you sell him to me?"

"Sell him?" he cried. "Sell him to you?"

"You do sell specimens, don't you?"

"Oh—yes. Of course I do. Of course I do."

"How much? Five dollars? Ten?"

"Oh! Not more than five. But—do you know anything about rattlesnakes? You might be bitten."

She looked at him for a moment. "I don't intend to take him. I want to leave him here, but—I want him to be mine. I want to come here and look at him and feed him and to know he's mine." She opened a little purse and took out a five-dollar bill. "Here! Now he is mine."

Dr. Phillips began to be afraid. "You could come to look at him without owning him."

"I want him to be mine."

"Oh, Lord!" he cried. "I've forgotten the time. He ran to the table. "Three minutes over. It won't matter much." He shook menthol crystals into the second watch-glass. And then he was drawn back to the cage where the woman still stared at the snake.

She asked, "What does he eat?"

"I feed them white rats, rats from the cage over there."

"Will you put him in the other cage? I want to feed him."

"But he doesn't need food. He's had a rat already this week. Sometimes they don't eat for three or four months. I had one that didn't eat for over a year."

In her low monotone she asked, "Will you sell me a rat?"

He shrugged his shoulders. "I see. You want to watch how rattlesnakes eat. All right. I'll show you. The rat will cost twenty-five cents. It's better than a bullfight if you look at it one way, and it's simply a snake eating his dinner if you look at it another." His tone had become acid. He hated people who made sport of natural processes. He was not a sportsman but a biologist. He could kill a thousand animals for knowledge, but not an insect for pleasure. He'd been over this in his mind before.

She turned her head slowly toward him and the beginning of a smile formed on her thin lips. "I want to feed my snake," she said. "I'll put him in the other cage." She had opened the top of the cage and dipped her hand in before he knew what she was doing. He leaped forward and pulled her back. The lid banged shut.

"Haven't you any sense?" he asked fiercely. "Maybe he wouldn't kill you, but he'd make you damned sick in spite of what I could do for you."

"You put him in the other cage, then," she said quietly.

Dr. Phillips was shaken. He found that he was avoiding the dark eyes that didn't seem to look at anything. He felt that it was profoundly wrong to put a rat into the cage, deeply sinful; and he didn't know why. Often he had put rats in the cage when someone or other had wanted to see it, but this desire tonight sickened him. He tried to explain himself out of it.

"It's a good thing to see," he said. "It shows you how a snake can work. It makes you have respect for a rattlesnake. Then, too, lots of people have dreams about the terror of snakes making the kill. I think because it is a subjective rat. The person is the rat. Once you see it the whole matter is objective. The rat is only a rat and the terror is removed."

He took a long stick equipped with a leather noose from the wall. Opening the trap he dropped the noose over the big snake's head and tightened the thong. A piercing dry rattle filled the room. The thick body writhed and slashed about the handle of the stick as he lifted the snake out and dropped it in the feeding cage. It stood ready to strike for a time, but the buzzing gradually ceased. The snake crawled into a corner, made a big figure eight with its body and lay still.

"You see," the young man explained, "these snakes are quite tame. I've had them a long time. I suppose I could handle them if I wanted to, but everyone who does handle rattlesnakes gets bitten sooner or later. I just don't want to take the chance." He glanced at the woman. He hated to put in the rat. She had moved over in front of the new cage; her black eyes were on the stony head of the snake again.

She said, "Put in a rat."

Reluctantly he went to the rat cage. For some reason he was sorry for the rat, and such a feeling had never come to him before. His eyes went over the mass of swarming white bodies climbing up the screen toward him. "Which one?" he thought. "Which one shall it be?" Suddenly he turned angrily to the woman. "Wouldn't you rather I put in a cat? Then you'd see a real fight. The cat might even win, but if it did it might kill the snake. I'll sell you a cat if you like."

She didn't look at him. "Put in a rat," she said. "I want him to eat."

He opened the rat cage and thrust his hand in. His fingers found a tail and he lifted a plump, red-eyed rat out of the cage. It struggled up to try to bite his fingers and, failing, hung spread out and motionless from its tail. He walked quickly across the room, opened the feeding cage and dropped the rat in on the sand floor. "Now, watch it," he cried.

The woman did not answer him. Her eyes were on the snake where it lay still. Its tongue, flicking in and out rapidly, tasted the air of the cage.

The rat landed on its feet, turned around and sniffed at its pink naked tail and then unconcernedly trotted across the sand, smelling as it went. The room was silent. Dr. Phillips did not know whether the water sighed among the piles or whether the woman sighed. Out of the corner of his eye he saw her body crouch and stiffen.

The snake moved out smoothly, slowly. The tongue flicked in and out. The motion was so gradual, so smooth that it didn't seem to be motion at all. In the other end of the cage the rat perked up in a sitting position and began to lick down the fine white hair on its chest. The snake moved on, keeping always a deep S curve in its neck.

The silence beat on the young man. He felt the blood drifting up in his body. He said loudly, "See! He keeps the striking curve ready. Rattlesnakes are cautious, almost cowardly animals. The mechanism is so delicate. The snake's dinner is to be got by an operation as deft as a surgeon's job. He takes no chances with his instruments."

The snake had flowed to the middle of the cage by now. The rat looked up, saw the snake and then unconcernedly went back to licking its chest.

"It's the most beautiful thing in the world," the young man said. His veins were throbbing. "It's the most terrible thing in the world."

The snake was close now. Its head lifted a few inches from the sand. The head weaved slowly back and forth, aiming, getting distance, aiming. Dr. Phillips glanced again at the woman. He turned sick. She was weaving too, not much, just a suggestion.

The rat looked up and saw the snake. It dropped to four feet and back up, and then—the stroke. It was impossible to see, simply a flash. The rat jarred as though under an invisible blow. The snake backed hurriedly into the corner from which it had come, and settled down, its tongue working constantly.

"Perfect!" Dr. Phillips cried. "Right between the shoulder blades. The fangs must almost have reached the heart."

The rat stood still, breathing like a little white bellows. Suddenly it leaped in the air and landed on its side. Its legs kicked spasmodically for a second and it was dead.

The woman relaxed, relaxed sleepily.

"Well," the young man demanded, "it was an emotional bath, wasn't it?"

She turned her misty eyes to him. "Will he eat it now?" she asked.

"Of course he'll eat it. He didn't kill it for a thrill. He killed it because he was hungry."

The corners of the woman's mouth turned up a trifle again. She looked back at the snake. "I want to see him eat it."

Now the snake came out of its corner again. There was no striking curve in its neck, but it approached the rat gingerly, ready to jump back in case it attacked. It nudged the body gently with its blunt nose, and drew away. Satisfied that it was dead, the snake touched the body all over with its chin, from head to tail. It seemed to measure the body and to kiss it. Finally it opened its mouth and unhinged its jaws at the corners.

Dr. Phillips put his will against his head to keep it from turning toward the woman. He thought, "If she's opening her mouth, I'll be sick. I'll be afraid." He succeeded in keeping his eyes away.

The snake fitted its jaws over the rat's head and then with a slow peristaltic pulsing, began to engulf the rat. The jaws gripped and the whole throat crawled up, and the jaws gripped again.

Dr. Phillips turned away and went to his work table. "You've made me miss one of the series," he said bitterly. "The set won't be complete." He put one of the watch glasses under a low-power microscope and looked at it, and then angrily he poured the contents of all the dishes into the sink. The waves had fallen so that only a wet whisper came up through the floor. The young man lifted a trapdoor at his feet and dropped the starfish down into the black water. He paused at the cat, crucified in the cradle and grinning comically into the light. Its body was puffed with embalming fluid. He shut off the pressure, withdrew the needle and tied the vein.

"Would you like some coffee?" he asked.

"No, thank you. I shall be going pretty soon."

He walked to her where she stood in front of the snake cage. The rat was swallowed, all except an inch of pink tail that stuck out of the snake's mouth like a sardonic tongue. The throat heaved again and the tail disappeared. The jaws snapped back into their sockets, and the big snake crawled heavily to the corner, made a big eight and dropped its head on the sand.

"He's asleep now," the woman said. "I'm going now. But I'll come back and feed my snake every little while. I'll pay for the rats. I want him to have plenty. And sometime— I'll take him away with me." Her eyes came out of their dusty dream for a moment. "Remember, he's mine. Don't take his poison. I want him to have it. Goodnight." She walked swiftly to the door and went out. He heard her footsteps on the stairs, but he could not hear her walk away on the pavement.

Dr. Phillips turned a chair around and sat down in front of the snake cage. He tried to comb out his thought as he looked at the torpid snake. "I've read so much about psychological sex symbols," he thought. "It doesn't seem to explain. Maybe I'm too much alone. Maybe I should kill the snake. If I knew—no, I can't pray to anything."

For weeks he expected her to return. "I will go out and leave her alone here when she comes," he decided. "I won't see the damned thing again."

She never came again. For months he looked for her when he walked about in the town. Several times he ran after some tall woman thinking it might be she. But he never saw her again—ever.

—*John Steinbeck (1902–1969)*

LAVATORY BUDDHAHOOD

One spring long, long ago in Arashiyama in Kyoto.

Ladies of the great Kyoto families, their daughters, geishas from the pleasure quarters, and prostitutes came in their spring finery to view the cherry blossoms.

"I'm so sorry to ask, but may I use your lavatory?" Women would bow, red-faced, at the gate of an unsightly farmhouse. When they went around to the back, they found the privy old and dirty with straw mats hanging around it. Every time the spring breeze blew, the Kyoto women's skin would crawl. They could hear children crying somewhere.

Seeing the distress of the Kyoto women, a peasant devised a plan. He built a tidy little privy and hung out a sign painted in black ink. "Pay toilet, three *mon*." During the flower-viewing season it was a huge success and he became a rich man.

"Lately, Hachihei has made a remarkable amount of money with his pay toilet. I think I'll build a privy next spring and knock off his business. How would that be?" one of the villagers, envious of Hachihei, said to his wife.

"That would be bad judgment on your part. You might build a privy, but Hachihei is the established business and has a clientele. You would be the newcomer. When yours didn't catch on, you'd be all the poorer."

"What you're missing is that the privy I'm thinking of wouldn't be filthy like Hachihei's. I've heard that the tea ceremony is popular in the capital, so I intend to build a privy after the style of a tearoom. First of all, for the four pillars, Yoshino logs would be dirty, so I'd use Kitayama knotwood. The ceiling would be bulrush, and I'd use a kettle chain in place of a rope. An ingenious idea, don't you think? I'd put windows in below ground level. And the planks will be of zelkova wood. The walls will be double-coated plaster, and the door will be of cypress. I'll shingle the roof with cedar and use Kurama stone for the step. Around it, I'll have a trellis with bamboo and beside the stone washbasin I'll plant a red pine. I'll build it to attract the Senke, Enshu, Uraku, Hayami, and all other schools of the tea ceremony."

The man's wife listened with a vacant air, then asked, "And how much will you charge?"

Somehow the man managed, through much tribulation, to build a splendid privy in time for the cherry blossom season. He had a priest paint the sign in showy T'ang style.

"Pay Toilet, eight *mon*."

The women of the capital merely gazed longingly at the privy, thinking it was just too beautiful to use. The man's wife pounded the floor. "Did you see that? That's why I said not to do it. You put all that money into it, and now what's going to happen?"

"There's nothing for you to get in such a huff about. Tomorrow when I go around soliciting, customers will gather like a line of ants. You get up early too, and fix me a lunch. I'll make some rounds and people will gather as though it's a village fair."

The man calmed down. But the next day he slept later than usual, waking about eight o'clock. He tucked up his kimono and hung his lunchbox around his neck. Then he looked back at his wife, grinning with sadness in his eyes.

"Well, Mother, you said this was a dream, a foolish dream. Today you'll see. Once I make my rounds they'll come in droves. If the pot gets full, put up the closed sign and have Jirohei next door dip out a couple of loads."

The man's wife thought it all terribly strange. "Make rounds," he had said. Was he planning to walk about the capital shouting, "Pay toilet! Pay toilet!"? As she was wondering, a girl soon came who tossed eight *mon* into the money box and entered the privy. After that, one after another, the customers never quit coming. The man's wife was baffled and wide-eyed as she tended the cash. Soon she put up the closed sign and there was a commotion as the pot was emptied. Before the day ended she had taken in eight *kan* and emptied the pot five times.

"My husband must be a reincarnation of the Bodhisattva Monju. It's the first time his dreams have come true."

Pleased, the man's wife bought some wine and was waiting for him when, pathetically, her husband's dead body was carried to their home.

"He died in Hachihei's pay toilet, from lumbago, it seems."

As soon as the man had left his own house that morning he had paid his three *mon*, gone into Hachihei's privy, and latched the door. Whenever anyone tried to come in, he cleared his throat. This continued until he grew hoarse and at the end of the long spring day he could not stand up.

The people of the capital heard the story.

"What a ruin for such a refined man!"

"He was an unrivaled master."

"The most stylish suicide ever in Japan."

"Lavatory Buddhahood! Hail, Amida buddha!"

There were few who did not chant these words.

—*Yasunari Kawabata (1899–1972)*

GLOSSARY OF TERMS

Allegory: A metaphoric genre (or device briefly appearing within another genre) in which abstract ideas or concepts are represented as people, objects, or situations.

Alliteration: The repetition of similar consonant sounds in the beginnings of nearby words.

Allusion: A reference to an event, a person, a place, or an object in history or previous literature or work of art.

Anima: Archetype that represents the female life force or soul within everyone, functioning to represent a person's opposite sex in the psyche.

Animus: Archetype that represents the male life force or soul within everyone, functioning to representing a person's opposite sex in the psyche.

Annotate: Reading through a text and notating important literary techniques and elements.

Antecedent Action: Events that occur prior to the opening action of a play.

Anxiety: Fear or worry, sometimes triggered by awareness of a repressed emotional state.

Apostrophe: Addressing an object as though it were living—or speaking as though an absent person were present.

Archetype: A word with Greek roots, *arche-tupos*, meaning "first type": the original pattern from which all other copies are made.

Archetypal Analysis: A method of analysis that enhances readers' critical abilities by requiring them to probe literature for symbols, imagery, and situations that suggest recurrent human circumstances.

Assonance: The repetition of internal vowel sounds. This sound device, like alliteration and consonance, helps to build rhythm and meter within a poem.

Ballad: A poem, lyrical in nature, whose written verses are sung or have been set to music and performed for audiences.

Cadence: the rhythmic sound of a poem's language.

Canon: A group of literary works generally understood as representative of the field.

Catastrophe: Point at which the protagonist, and often allies and loyal friends, dies.

Catharsis: The purgation of emotion, namely of fear and pity.

Characters: The people found within fiction—or, more simply put, the authors' cast.

Chronology: The arrangement of events in time, it is an important element for establishing a story's credibility.

Cliché: A common word or phrase that has been used repeatedly by many people, throughout history.

Climax: Where the plot's action is headed.

Close Readings: A method of reading that asks readers to explain a work's meaning by isolating its parts to see how they create the whole.

Collective Unconscious: Similarities in the unconscious shared by all humans.

Complication: The part of a story filled with rising and falling action, which builds suspense.

Concrete Poetry: Conveying the meaning of a poem through the poem's shape.

Connotation: The meaning of a word beyond its dictionary definition.

Connotative Syntax: The grammatical rules based on the language in which a work is written.

Consonance: The repetition of consonant sounds within a short area of the poem.

Contextual Analysis: A literary analysis approach that situates the text in the time and place it was created by acknowledging the author's linguistic, social and historical environment.

Core Issues: Deep issues of the human psyche, often repressed.

Defense Mechanisms: The mental processes which work to avoid conflict or anxiety.

Denial: The refusal to admit the veracity of something which is true, while avoidance is the act of keeping away from a thought process altogether.

Denotation: What a word means according to the dictionary.

Dénouement: The part of a story in which all the loose ends are neatly wrapped up.

Devil: A character who is the personification of evil. He often offers fortune, fame or power in return for a soul.

Diction: The writer's word choice.

Didactic: Written solely to teach.

Displacement: Taking one's aggression out on something or someone else, rather than the true source of conflict.

Doppelgänger: A contrasting counterpart, often an evil twin of the hero or heroine, who inspires terror on sight.

Dramatic Climax: That point at which the catastrophe becomes inevitable.

Dramatic Irony: A situation in which the reader or audience knows something a character does not.

Ego: The reality principle, which governs the id and channels the id's drives into socially acceptable outlets.

Electra Complex: A girl's unconscious rivalry with her mother for love of her father.

Epic poem: A poem narrative in style and long in length with importance to a culture or society.

Existentialism: A philosophical theory emphasizing the meaning of human existence and the emotions, responsibilities, and thoughts that contribute to the purpose of that existence.

Exposition: Necessary background information that the author provides from which the story commences.

Fall: An archetypal situation in which a hero or heroine loses power, status, or innocence.

Feminist analysis: The extension of the Feminist movement into theoretical and literary discourse, studying the role of gender differences in the writing, interpreting, and analyzing of literature, both ancient and contemporary, written by women and men.

Feminist movement: A movement which focused on the advocacy of women's rights in their political, social, and economic lives, popularized in the 1960s, but preceded by 150 years of struggle.

Figurative Language: A term that encompasses a number of literary devices, including metaphor, simile, and symbolism.

First-Person Narrator: One of the characters tells the story through his or her individualistic, subjective viewpoint.

Foil: A character intended to be contrasted either in behavior or attitudes to the main character.

Foreshadowing: Hints or clues that point the reader to what will happen later in the story.

Formalism: An approach to the interpretation of literature that asks readers to look at how a text is formed, as well as how it works to achieve its overarching effect.

Formalist Analysis: Stemming from New Criticism, a type of literary analysis that focuses on the text itself, rather than socio-historical aspects of the work or its author.

Free Verse: Popularized by Walt Whitman in the nineteenth century, a form of poetry in which the poem's rhyme scheme, syllable count, line number and arrangements adhere to no specific rules.

Freudian Slip: Unintentional expression.

Gender Roles: Socially created attributes of masculinity or femininity.

Guilt Complex: An unconscious, brooding sense of guilt.

Haiku: A Japanese unrhymed poem in seventeen syllables, usually arranged in three lines, often in a pattern of five syllables, seven syllables, and five syllables. In English, the haiku may be either rhymed or unrhymed.

Hero (Heroine): Characters noted for their noble qualities, such as courage, moral excellence, and self-sacrifice for the greater good.

Historical Analysis: The knowledge of events which occurred at or around the date of a work's creation and the intellectual and social environment out of which literature is produced.

Human Psyche: Forces in a human's mind that influence thought, personality, and behavior.

Hyperbole: Deliberate, often ironic, exaggeration.

Iambic Meter: Stressed syllable followed by unstressed syllable in a poem.

Iambic Pentameter: A meter in which a stressed syllable is followed by an unstressed syllable, repeating five times in a line.

Id: A psychic zone submerged in the unconscious to fulfill the pleasure principle.

Image: A sensory-based description within a piece of literature.

Imagery: Words that appeal to readers' senses: sight, sound, smell, touch, and taste.

Initiation: Situations usually concerned with the passage from childhood to maturity or from maturity to the wisdom of old age.

Intellectual (archetype): A person who is a mathematician, astronomer, scientist, or computer genius and exhibits one of the following behavior traits: anti-social, neutral or pro-social.

Irony: An expression in which the understood meaning is the exact opposite of its literal meaning.

Irony of Fate: The difference between what a human's hopes and expectations are and what is decreed by the gods, fate, fortune, or sheer chance.

Italian Sonnet: A 14-line poem that has a rhyme scheme of a-b-b-a a-b-b-a c-d-e-c d-e.

Linguistic Connotation: A word's meaning, beyond its dictionary definition, at the time in which it was written.

Magical Realism: A literary movement beginning in 1935 that sought to encompass both tangible and intangible human experiences in literature, in the belief that this would increase the story's authenticity and resemblance to how life is experienced.

Maiden Heroine: A heroine with the qualities of the male hero—individualism, intellect, independence—who is unhappy with the status quo, pro-active, and rejecting of the suitor.

Metaphor: A comparison of unlike things without the use of "like" or "as."

Metonymy: The use of a word in place of another word that is closely associated with it.

Modernism: A literary era between 1890-1940 in which writers were concerned with the structures existing in society and how those structures affected individuals' thoughts and actions.

Monster (archetype): A nightmarish creature that stands in the way of the hero's progress and plagues a society.

Moral: The practical lesson drawn from a story.

Motif: All the stories of a particular people's explanation of a universal question, such as creation.

Motivation: Why characters in a story behave as they do.

Myths: The enduring stories that interpret the mysteries of life and the universe for a people.

Naturalism: An extreme form of realism, popular in the late nineteenth century through the first half of the twentieth century, which takes the philosophical position that all phenomena can and should be presented as the natural result of the cause-and-effect principles of science, especially those of chemistry and physics.

Naturalistic Fiction: A story that emphasizes the clinical aspects of events.

Neurosis: A mental or emotional disorder which affects part of the personality.

New Criticism: A movement in the twentieth century that focused on a text as a stand alone work of art.

Oedipus Complex: A boy's unconscious rivalry with his father for love for his mother.

One-Dimensional Characters: Characters with superficial portrayals in literature.

Onomatopoeia: The use of words whose sound closely resembles the sound of the event or object it names.

Other: A term developed by Simone de Beauvoir to describe the depiction of women by male authors; these depictions are only in relation to men.

Outcast: a character who is condemned to wander, usually alone, after committing some crime against society.

Paradox: A contradiction that is nevertheless true.

Persona: The social personality or mask that everyone puts on to face the world.

Personification: A type of metaphor that gives human characteristics to non-human things such as abstract ideas, animals, or inanimate objects.

Plot: A sequence of actions that embody some sort of conflict, one force opposing another.

Point of View: The relationship of the story's narrator to the fictional characters and events of the story; important in establishing tone.

Preconscious: Conscious processes, which quickly become latent although they may later become conscious, or active.

Primitivism: A sub-branch of romanticism, concerned with the idea that natural or early conditions of society are the best situation for human life.

Primordial: A characteristic of archetypes, the representation of primeval original concepts.

Probability: The likelihood of a plot's events.

Projection: Ascribing one's problem to someone else and then condemning him or her for it.

Prose: Any genre of writing that is not poetry.

Prose Poetry: A type of poem in paragraph form, consisting of one or more paragraphs, often narrative in nature.

Protagonist: Main character around whom the plot revolves.

Pseudonym: A fictitious name, often employed by an author.

Psychology: The study of the human mind and its functions.

Quatrain: A four-line stanza in a poem.

Quest: An archetypal situation in which a hero or heroine must go on great search for someone or something that will bring about returned fertility to the land or a lost order to the world.

Reader Response: An approach to literary analysis that relies on readers to find meaning and understanding in a work of literature, based on their own experiences and perspectives.

Realism: The principles and characteristics of the realist movement, prominent from about 1850 to 1900. This movement was a reaction to the flights of imagination that characterized romantic writing. Realists wanted to portray an image of life as it really was.

Realist Fiction: Works that contain accurate details of everyday life, creating a sense of plausibility for the reader.

Recurrent: A characteristic of archetypes highlighting that they occur repeatedly throughout human existence for all peoples regardless of time or place.

Regression: The temporary return to a former psychology state, whether painful or pleasant, as an escape from some present difficulty.

Repression: Forcing impulses back into the unconscious.

Reversal: The dramatic turning point.

Romanticism: The principles and characteristics of the romantic movement, prominent from about 1770 to 1850, focusing on the promotion of imagination, sentiment, and individualism in artistic expression.

Romantic Fiction: Literature that emphasizes the emotional aspects of events.

Romantic Irony: Writers creating a serious mood only to make light of themselves.

Scapegoat: A person whose death in a public ritual expiates the community's sins.

Second-Person Narration: A writer's attempt to involve the reader in the story through the use of "you" throughout the narration.

Selective Memory: A complete perception of an event, but only a partial memory which involves only what a person is capable of processing.

Selective Perception: Perceiving only what one can handle, a defense mechanism which limits one's complete understanding of an event.

Semantics: The study of word meanings in language or the study of communication processes themselves.

Setting: The location where a story's events occur as well as the time or era of the action. The setting helps establish atmosphere and mood.

Shadow: The darker part of the collective unconscious.

Shakespearean sonnet (English Sonnet): A sonnet with fourteen lines, and a particular rhyme scheme (a-b-a-b-c-d-c-d-e-f-e-f-g-g).

Shakespeare's Sisters: A phrase coined by Virginia Woolf, denoting female writers struggling with male bias.

Simile: A comparison using "like" or "as."

Situational Irony: A discrepancy exists between what is expected and what actually happens.

Socratic Irony: Pretense of ignorance in a discussion to expose an opponent's fallacious logic.

Sonnet: A fourteen line verse that in Old French means "little song."

Star-Crossed Lovers: two characters whose relationship ends with the tragic death of one or both of them.

Stream of Consciousness: A narrative technique that exposes a character's unexpressed, unspoken, and unstructured thoughts.

Superego: The morality principle.

Suspense: The feeling of excitement over the uncertainty of a story's action.

Symbol: An object or image in a piece of literature with multiple meanings, often dependent on its context—whether historical, cultural, or literary—for complete understanding.

Symbolism: The use of symbols in literature to create deeper meaning.

Synecdoche: The use of a part to represent the whole.

Syntax: The order in which words appear in a small section of writing, used to alter the tone, mood, and meter of a piece of writing.

Tanka: A Japanese poem made up of five lines, the first three lines following a five, seven, five syllabic pattern, and the last two being seven syllables each.

Task: An archetypal situation in which a hero or heroine must perform some extraordinary, difficult feat in order to reassert his or her authority.

Temptress: The woman to whom the protagonist is physically attracted to and who ultimately brings about his downfall.

Theme: The overarching idea, either stated or implied, that the author wishes most to convey to the reader.

Third-Person Limited: Someone, other than a character in the story, tells the reader the tale using the pronouns "he" and "she."

Third-Person Objective: The narrator, who is outside the story, reveals the external qualities of the characters.

Third-Person Omniscient: The narrator is both all-seeing and all-knowing and chooses to tell everything to the reader.

Tone: A literary device used to express the narrator's attitude toward the subject, audience, or self, created through word choice and word order (poetry), or point of view (fiction).

Tragedy: A play involving unhappy events and often the downfall of the main character.

Trickster: An ambiguous figure that is a fool and a cheat. The trickster assumes many guises, both animal and human, to perform cruel tricks and practical jokes.

Turn: A signal of some shift in emotion relayed by a poem.

Unconscious Mind: A part of the mind wherein a person's psyche influences his or her actions in an unperceived manner.

Understatement: The opposite of hyperbole: intentional, often ironic, lack of emphasis.

Universal: A characteristic of archetypes that are unaffected by time or situation, community or culture.

Universality: A work's appeal to all peoples regardless of time or culture.

Verbal Irony: What is said by a speaker or narrator is the opposite of what is meant.

Verisimilitude: A late nineteenth century shift in the way people thought about fiction and the way writers approached it, emphasizing accuracy, especially in background information.

ACKNOWLEDGMENTS

Baker, Donald W. "Formal Application." From *Saturday Review*, included in *Formal Application: Selected Poems, 1960–1980*, Barnwood Press, 1982. Used by permission of Alison Baker.

Bishop, Elizabeth. "The Fish" from THE COMPLETE POEMS 1927–1979 by Elizabeth Bishop. Copyright © 1979, 1983 by Alice Helen Methfessel. Reprinted by permission of Farrar, Straus and Giroux, LLC.

Chula, Margaret. "hazy autumn moon" from ALWAYS FILLING, ALWAYS FULL. Copyright © Margaret Chula. Used by permission of White Pine Press.

Ciardi, John. "On Flunking a Nice Boy Out of School" from *Person to Person*. Copyright © 1964 by Rutgers, the State University. Reprinted by permission of Rutgers University Press.

Cisneros, Sandra. "Salvador Late or Early" from WOMAN HOLLERING CREEK. Copyright © 1991 by Sandra Cisneros. Published by Vintage Books, a division of Random House Inc., and originally in hardcover by Random House Inc. By permission of Susan Bergholz Literary Services, New York, NY, and Lamy, NM. All rights reserved.

Cummings, E. E. "the sky". Copyright © 1973, 1983, 1991 by the Trustees for the E. E. Cummings Trust. Copyright © 1973, 1983 by George James Firmage, "in Just—". Copyright © 1923, 1951, 1991 by the Trustees for the E. E. Cummings Trust. Copyright © 1976 by George James Firmage, "l(a". Copyright © 1958, 1986, 1991 by the Trustees for the E. E. Cummings Trust, from COMPLETE POEMS: 1904–1962 by E. E. Cummings, edited by George J. Firmage. Used by permission of Liveright Publishing Corporation.

Kawabata, Yasunari. "Lavatory Buddhahood" from PALM-OF-THE-HAND STORIES by Yasunari Kawabata, translated by Lane Dunlop and J Martin Holman. Tranlation copyright © 1988 by Lane Dunlop and J Martin Holman. Reprinted by permission of North Point Press, a division of Farrar, Straus and Giroux, LLC.

Kerouac, Jack. "In my medicine cabinet", from BOOK OF HAIKUS by Jack Kerouac, edited by Regina Weinreich, copyright © 2003 by the Estate of Stella Kerouac, John Sampas, Literary Representative. Used by permission of Penguin, a division of Penguin Group (USA) Inc.

Lee, Li-Young. "The Gift" from *Rose*. Copyright © 1986 by Li-Young Lee. Reprinted with the permission of The Permissions Company, Inc., on behalf of BOA Editions Ltd., www.boaeditions.org.

Plath, Sylvia. "Metaphors" from CROSSING THE WATER by Sylvia Plath. Copyright © by Ted Hughes. Reprinted by permission of HarperCollins Publishers.

Rich, Adrienne. "Aunt Jennifer's Tigers". Copyright © 2002, 1951 by Adrienne Rich, from THE FACT OF A DOORFRAME: SELECTED POEMS 1950-2001 by Adrienne Rich. Used by permission of W. W. Norton & Company, Inc.

Sandburg, Carl. "Fog" from CHICAGO POEMS by Carl Sandburg. Published 1992 by the University of Illinois Press.

Snyder, Gary. "Hitch Haiku" from THE BACK COUNTRY, copyright © 1968 by Gary Snyder. Reprinted by permission of New Directions Publishing Corp.

Steinbeck, John. "The Snake", from THE LONG VALLEY by John Steinbeck, copyright 1938, renewed © 1966 by John Steinbeck. Used by permission of Viking Penguin, a division of Penguin Group (USA) Inc.

Taylor, Keith. "Two days." Reprinted from IF THE WORLD BECOMES SO BRIGHT. Copyright © 2009 Wayne State University Press.

Williams, Saul. "i fear your freedom." Reprinted with the permission of Pocket Books, a Division of Simon & Schuster, Inc. From S√HE by Saul Williams. Copyright © 1999 Saul Williams.

INDEX